EGYPT UNDER EL-SISI

EGYPT UNDER EL-SISI

A Nation on the Edge

Maged Mandour

I.B. TAURIS
LONDON • NEW YORK • OXFORD • NEW DELHI • SYDNEY

I.B. TAURIS
Bloomsbury Publishing Plc
50 Bedford Square, London, WC1B 3DP, UK
1385 Broadway, New York, NY 10018, USA

BLOOMSBURY, I.B. TAURIS and the I.B. Tauris logo are trademarks of Bloomsbury Publishing Plc

First published in Great Britain 2023

Cover design: Adriana Brioso
Cover image: Rug © Andeel

A catalogue record for this book is available from the British Library.

Library of Congress Cataloging-in-Publication Data

Names: Mandour, Maged, author.
Title: Egypt under al-Sisi : a nation on the edge / Maged Mandour.
Description: London ; New York ; Oxford ; New Delhi ; Sydney : I.B Tauris. 2023. | Includes bibliographical references and index.
Identifiers: LCCN 2023020484 (print) | LCCN 2023020485 (ebook) | ISBN 9780755649136 (hardback) | ISBN 9780755649143 (pdf) | ISBN 9780755649150 (epub) | ISBN 9780755649167
Subjects: LCSH: Sīsī, ʻAbd al-Fattāḥ, 1954– | Egypt—History—2011– | Egypt—Politics and government—2011– | Egypt—Economic conditions—21st century. | Egypt—Social conditions—21st century.
Classification: LCC DT107.88 .M365 2023 (print) | LCC DT107.88 (ebook) | DDC 962.05/6—dc23/eng/20230520
LC record available at https://lccn.loc.gov/2023020484
LC ebook record available at https://lccn.loc.gov/2023020485

ISBN: HB: 978-0-7556-4913-6
ePDF: 978-0-7556-4914-3
eBook: 978-0-7556-4915-0

Typeset by RefineCatch Limited, Bungay, Suffolk
Printed and bound in Great Britain

To find out more about our authors and books visit www.bloomsbury.com and sign up for our newsletters.

CONTENTS

ACKNOWLEDGEMENTS

This book is the product of a decade of writing, and it would not have been possible without the support of the late professor George Joffe – a man who taught me the importance of bearing witness, which is what I am trying to do with this book. This book is dedicated to him. He is, indeed, sorely missed. I would also like to mention those who have helped and supported me through the years. I am indebted to Yezid Sayigh, not only for his brilliant work on the Egyptian military but also for inviting me to write for Carnegie, a turning point in my career. I would also like to thank my editor at Carnegie, Intissar Fakir, for getting the best out of me and challenging me when it counted. Finally, I would also like to thank my editors at IB Tauris, especially Sophie Rudland, for believing in the importance of this book and supporting the project.

This book is also dedicated to the women in my life. My wife has given me comfort when I doubted myself and gave me a home in exile, and my mother has borne my exile with admirable grace and fortitude. This book would not have been possible without them. As I anxiously await the arrival my unborn child, I would also like to dedicate this book to them and what they represent: a hope that the future will be better than the past and that one day, the dark days of autocracy will come to an end. Finally, this work is dedicated to the victims of autocracy in Egypt, and to those who dedicated their lives to hope. May your sacrifices not be in vain.

INTRODUCTION

'By the pricking of my thumbs,
Something wicked this way comes.'

— William Shakespeare, *Macbeth*, Act 4, Scene 1

This book is a story about a crisis, or more precisely, the morbid symptoms that came out of a crisis. On 3 July 2013, the Egyptian Defence Minister Abdel Fattah El-Sisi appeared on national television flanked by a number of prominent political figures. These included the prominent liberal Mohamed El-Baradie, Sheikh Al Azhar, the Pope of the Coptic Church and the Chairman of the Joint Chiefs of Staff, amongst others. In his address, Sisi announced the removal of Egypt's first democratically elected President, the Muslim Brotherhood's Mohamed Morsi, after mass protests calling for his ouster erupted (Sis.gov, 2013). The popularly backed military coup that ended Egypt's democratic experiment was perceived by many observers as an end to what Walter Armbrust called a state of Liminality (Armbrust, 2019, p. 207), or what Mona El-Ghobashy called Egypt's 'Revolutionary Situation' (El Ghobashy, 2021), with the core of the Mubarak regime, namely the military establishment, asserting its power and completely taking over the state apparatus, crushing the opposition in the process. Hence, even though there was a 'Revolutionary Situation', there was no 'Revolutionary Outcome' (El Ghobashy, 2021), with a swift return to the old status quo of military-backed autocracy after a brief democratic interlude. This view is also adopted by the regime as one of its main legitimizing narratives, where military intervention in 2013 was framed as an end of the state of social turmoil that the country has been experiencing since 2011: the end of the state of Liminality. Even though this narrative is very valid from a specific perspective, namely the bottom-up view of the main demands of the 2011 mass protests and the calls for democratization that sprung from it, it ignores an important aspect, specifically the top-down process of radical change driven by the military elites once they became the uncontested masters of the state. This book will map out and explore these changes and their ramifications.

The main argument presented in this book is that the Sisi regime represents a radical break in modern Egyptian history, and is significantly different than the other post-1952 regimes that preceded it. Even though there are some elements of continuity, most notably the central role that the military played in all regimes since 1952, this latest incarnation is unique in multiple ways. In this book, I will examine how the military establishment proceeded to impose deep structural changes in a manner that can be described as 'Revolutionary', indicating that Egypt's 'Revolutionary Situation' resulted in 'Revolutionary outcomes'. These 'Revolutionary' changes were made with limited popular participation, and in many ways are the antithesis of the demands of the pro-democracy movement. Indeed, once the military establishment became the uncontested master of the state, it proceeded to drastically alter not just the structure of the state, but also the ideological foundation of rule and the process of capital accumulation, giving birth to a militarized form of capitalism on a scale unseen in modern Egyptian history. These fundamental changes represent a radical break with the legacy of the Mubarak regime and its predecessors, establishing direct military rule in an unprecedent fashion. Hence, the result of the mass protest of 2011 was a radical change, but not in the form expected by its instigators. It took the form of top-down, authoritarian changes, which aimed at concentrating power in the hands of the military establishment at any cost. This laser-sharp focus on power accumulation ushered in a military dictatorship of radically new dimensions, one that has zero tolerance of dissent and which is willing to use unprecedented levels of state violence to silence it. This is a narrative that is radically different from the prevailing interpretation of the July coup and its aftermath, which views the regime as part of continuum of military-backed autocratic regimes that have ruled over Egypt since 1952. Indeed, the Sisi regime is a new phenomenon that required a fresh perspective to fully comprehend. The modus operandi of the pre-1952 regime is long gone, probably unlikely to return.

This book will attempt to chart those changes, with the rest of the Introduction dedicated to establishing an appropriate theoretical lens for understating the regime, as well as providing a brief historical overview of the role of the military in the development of the Egyptian state and its role in politics since 1952.

Gramsci and Sisi

In order to fully grasp the process of the top-down change described above, a quick detour into the realm of Marxist theory is warranted. The Italian Marxist Antonio Gramsci came up with the concept of the 'Passive Revolution' to describe the process of Italian unification under bourgeois leadership. In this conception, unlike in places like England and France that went through a complete social revolution with mass popular participation, the bourgeoisie in Italy did not go through a similar process. Simply put, they were too weak to dominate the peninsula and impose the social transformation required for complete transition to a capitalist society (Cox, 1994). In order to affect the needed changes, the northern Italian bourgeois created an alliance with the southern landlords to affect mass social change, without popular participation (Cox, 1994), in essence a revolution from above. This 'Passive Revolution' in principle is very similar to the process that the Sisi regime embarked on, but with some marked differences, which does not affect the analytical value of the concept. First, based on the Gramscian concept, a passive revolution takes places when the ruling elites are not strong enough to affect change without a broad alliance with non-ruling elites. This is not the case under Sisi. Indeed, the regime has embarked on a process of power concentration in the hands of the military establishment to an unprecedented degree, showing remarkable reluctance to have a junior civilian partner in the ruling coalition. In simpler terms, the military establishment almost rules alone, with limited civilian participation. A broad alliance with civilian elites simply does not exist. Second, we have the relationship between the regime and the masses, which is much more nuanced than one would expect. As will be shown in Chapter 1, even though the regime has eliminated all avenues for popular participation in the public sphere, it has shown a remarkable ability to summon its base when a popular show of support for its repression is required. In a way, it has used popular mobilization to silence democratic aspirations, especially during the summer of 2013, its foundational moment. Hence, there is limited and guided popular mobilization to serve clear political goals, but there is no popular participation in policy formulation or public debate, in a way where power would diffuse to the popular base of the regime. Finally, passive revolutions are theorized to occur in non-hegemonic societies, where the ruling elites are unable to garner the support of the subaltern classes: their ideas are not the dominant ideas, and they do not rule with the consent of the governed.

The case of post-coup Egypt is extremely difficult to categorize. There is a case to be made that Egypt is a non-hegemonic society, due to the considerable opposition that the regime provokes and the heavy dose of repression needed to cement its rule. However, it is also difficult to deny that the regime did, and probably still does, enjoy considerable support from large segments of society, a support that is declining but arguably remains considerable. As will be discussed in Chapter 1, the ideology of the regime and the central role that violence plays in it has also received wide popular acceptance, giving credence to the argument that its rule is indeed hegemonic. I will not attempt to give a decisive answer here, but what is important to highlight is that even if the regime is hegemonic, this does not translate into popular participation in policy formulation or an opening of the public space. On the contrary, the regime's ideological edifice is based on the supposed supremacy of the military to the detriment of all forms of civilian participation in politics. Hence, the crux of the concept remains valid, namely that the coup brought about elite-driven radical changes without popular participation.[1]

The radical changes made by the Sisi regime were not only aimed at concentrating power in the hands of the military establishment, but also at creating structural barriers to the prospect of democratization. Indeed, there is a strong argument to be made that Sisi's true and more enduring legacy are the formidable structural barriers that his regime erected in order to not just ensure that the events of 2011 were not repeated, but that if the pro-democracy movement was able to create a breach in the regime's defences, it would face considerable obstacles and resistance from within the state apparatus. Indeed, the regime's consistent policy has been the complete militarization of the state, the economy and the public space in a manner that is extremely difficult to reverse. The task in 2011 was immense; now, more than a decade after the coup, it is gargantuan. Indeed, the regime has successfully embarked on a policy that has insulated it from possible popular pressures, but this policy has also made the prospect of elite led reform extremely remote. Indeed, in its single-minded obsession of complete militarization of political life, it has created structural barriers to top-down reforms in a manner that will leave it brittle and unable to cope with social unrest. This could be the regime's Achille's heel, an argument that will be made in the rest of the book.

Before proceeding, it is worth introducing a theoretical framework of civil–military relations to better understand the different classification of military regimes, and where the Sisi regime is placed in this framework, as well as a short historical overview of the regimes that have ruled Egypt since 1952.

The man on horseback

As part of his classic study of the role of the military in politics, Samuel Finer devised a classification of the different forms of military regimes (Finer, 2002, pp. 164–204), elaborating on how the military can exert political pressure on an elected government even if they are not in control of it. Based on Finer's classification, there are three different forms of military regimes: indirect, dual and direct. The form that each regime takes depends on multiple factors, which will not be covered in detail as part of this book. My main focus is classifying the Sisi regime in one of these categories, juxtaposing it with the post-1952 regimes where the military was always central to the regime in power, whether under Nasser, Sadat or Mubarak, albeit with its influence fluctuating from one era to the other.

The first form of military rule is indirect, which is further broken down into limited or complete forms of rule. Under the indirect/limited form, the military is not in direct control of the government, but is able to exert influence or blackmail the civilian government to affect policy changes or defend its corporate interests. The case of the German and Japanese militaries in the interwar period is offered by Finer as an example, where the armed forces of both countries were able to exert considerable influence over policy without being in nominal control of the government. This influence, however, is only exerted in limited and intermittent fashion, and sometimes within the existing legal framework, whenever the interests of the military are threatened. This is contrasted with indirect/complete forms of military rule, where the military establishment exerts influence through puppet governments. Here, the military holds considerable power, but without direct control over the government and without directly populating government posts with military men. The example that Finer uses is Cuba between 1933 and 1940, until Colonel Batista was elected President. During this period, the Cuban military, under the leadership of Batista, was the real power behind the government, with the Colonel handpicking the Presidents of the Republic and removing them when he saw fit. This is what happened to President Gomez, who attempted to wrest power from Batista, only to be impeached by Parliament, which was subservient to Batista. Suffice to note that during this seven-year period, Cuba had six different presidents, until Batista successfully ran in 1940, staying in power till 1944, and again returning to power in a coup in 1952 until he was ousted by a small band of guerrilla fighters led by Castro in 1959.

Another classification of military regimes, which will be very pertinent for the classification of the Sadat and Mubarak regimes, is the dual form. In this form of military rule, the military shares power with a civilian partner in a ruling coalition. Finer uses the example of Juan Perón in Argentina as the clearest example of this type of regime, where Perón relied on the power of organized labour, as well as the military, as the foundation of his regime. Perón was able to balance these two forces against each other, and as the relative strength of each pillar fluctuated, so would its influence in the ruling coalition. For example, in his first term, Perón was able to halve the budget of the military, when civilian support for his rule was strong. The Mubarak and Sadat regimes would arguably fall in this category, as will be discussed below.

Finally, there is the classification of direct military rule, which can also be 'quasi-civilianized' based on Finer's taxonomy. In this classification the military either uses violence or fails to prevent violence against the civilian government in order to replace it and rule directly in its stead. In the case of direct military rule, the military directly controls the government, and the civilian government is removed. Here, Finer uses the case of Primo De Riveria, who took power in Spain following a coup in 1923 and installed a military junta that ruled between 1923 and 1925. There is also another, more recent, example of direct military rule, namely the coup in Myanmar in 2021, when Min Aung Hlaing, the head of the armed forces, removed the elected government and took control. He declared himself Prime Minister until elections were held, in a transitional period planned to last for two years (Mao, 2022). There is also the period after Mubarak's ouster, between 2011 and 2012, when the country was directly ruled by a military junta, the Supreme Council of the Armed Forces (SCAF), which acted as the head of the executive. There are cases, however, where a prolonged period of direct military rule raises questions about the legitimacy of the regime, and in these cases, the military hides behind a civilian cloak and becomes 'quasi-civilianized'. As Finer describes it, 'The military still rules, but they cloth themselves with the evidence of civilian support.' This is a simple question of legitimacy, as Finer argued: 'Legitimacy breeds power. Even a mock legitimacy is more compulsive to citizens than the flagrant absence of a right to rule.' The case that Finer uses to illustrate his case is none other than the Nasserist regime, which came to power in a coup in 1952. Finer argues that the Nasserist regime took its final form in 1956, with the end of the promised transitional period, when the regime created a number of weak civilian institutions, with real power emanating from the military. A new constitution was drafted with a strong presidency, a weak assembly and a single-party system, all under the control of the regime and the security services. As will be discussed below, this narrative is arguably simplistic, with later evidence appearing of a struggle between the President and the military, which Nasser lost control over early on. However, the classification remains valid, albeit with some qualifications.

These classifications will be used in the next section to take a deeper look at the role of the military in the successive regimes that ruled Egypt after 1952, placing them within this taxonomy. In doing so, the unique position of the Sisi regime will be highlighted. Before proceeding, however, it is important to mention that these classifications are malleable and the criteria is mostly subjective, hence they should be considered with caution. They should be treated as signposts to help illuminate and understand the developing complex dynamic which might not be fully apparent without using these classifications.

The military and the state

The history of the modern Egyptian military is deeply intertwined with the development of the modern state. Indeed, it is with the appointment of Mehmed Ali as the Ottoman governor of Egypt in the early nineteenth century, and his ambitions to retain the governorship on a hereditary basis, that the need to create a modern army based on universal conscription became apparent. For the first time in centuries the Arabic-speaking Egyptian peasant was forcibly taken from his land and turned into a professional soldier in the Pasha's army, a practice that bred untold social misery and entailed a gratuitous amount of political violence (Fahmy K., 1997). The peasant was not the Pasha's first choice; indeed, the Pasha only opted for mass conscription after his attempts to create a slave army from men captured in raids in Sudan failed (Fahmy K., 1997, pp. 86–9). The enslaved simply died in the long march to the army camps and they could not be moulded into a professional army. The enslavement of the Sudanese came after the Pasha's attempt to discipline the Albanian Ottoman corps (the corps that Mehmed Ali was the second in command of when he first arrived in Egypt; Fahmy K., 2018) also failed. The Albanians hatched a plan to assassinate the Vali when he tried to establish military discipline, and when their plan was discovered, they went on rampage in Cairo, not something that one would call a success in terms of instilling discipline (Fahmy K., 1997, p. 85). Only the peasant was left to act as a vehicle for the Pasha's ambition. The new army showed its discipline and effectiveness when it was successfully used against the peasants themselves. In April 1824 the peasants rebelled against the Pasha's conscription and taxation policy, with some 30,000 peasants joining the rebellion. The Pasha decided to send his new army to crush the rebellion, and apart from some minor defections, some "700 soldiers," the new army routed the rebels. There is even a story of a sergeant in the army who attacked a village only to find his father amongst the rebels. When he failed to convince his father to give up peacefully, the sergeant proceeded to kill him, earning himself a promotion to the rank of lieutenant (Fahmy K., 1997, pp. 93–7).

The process of creation of the modern Egyptian army also triggered a radical process of political transformation, which eventually led to the development of the modern Egyptian state, another passive revolution one can plausibly argue. The need to manage mass conscription, as well as feeding, clothing and arming the newly founded military, precipitated a process of state formation to serve the ambition of the Pasha. Indeed, this entailed the introduction of a national census to accurately estimate the national tax base; a modern health system to tend to the needs of the army; and even a transformation of the process of capital accumulation, with the new state holding a monopoly of the purchase of agricultural production, which it bought at low prices and later exported for much needed capital for military spending and other development projects, a process accompanied by mass state violence (Mitchell, 1991). The Pasha eventually achieved his ambition, through a series of stunning military victories against the Sultan, and was able to guarantee hereditary rule for his family, giving Egypt a semi-independent status with loose Ottoman suzerainty (Fahmy K., 1997). The final by-product of this process was the piecemeal creation of the modern Egyptian state, as the bureaucracy slowly started to develop to meet the growing needs of the Pasha and his army, and after the peace, the Khedive and his projects (Fahmy K., 2018). The Pasha and his descendants, however, could not stop the process of the economic peripheralization of the country, and by end of the century Egypt had fallen into a serious debt crisis, which led to the occupation of the country by Britain in 1882 and the end of the absolutist phase of the rule of the Mehmet Ali family (Hunter, 1984).

Even though the military and the state were born at the same time, the history of military intervention in politics started with the coup of 23 July 1952. By the eve of the coup, the semi-liberal political system that had evolved in Egypt as part of the nationalist struggle against the British occupation was on its last legs. The inability of the nationalist movement, led by the libera Wafd Party, to end the occupation, coupled with constant meddling by the King and the British in elections against the Wafd, and growing social tension over inequality and land reform, disenchanted the public (Gerges, 2018). Indeed, by the 1940s there was a rapid proliferation of paramilitary groups across the political spectrum and a growing armed resistance against the British forces stationed in the Canal zone (Gerges, 2018). This deepening social crisis allowed a small number of junior military officers to overthrow the monarchy in a bloodless coup in 1952. The leader of the group was Colonel Gamal Abdel Nasser, with General Mohamed Naguib acting as the figurehead of the movement (Gerges, 2018). I will not venture into the details of the evolution of the Nasserist regime or the struggle between Nasser and Naguib, but I will attempt to classify it based on Finer's categorization of military regimes in order to trace the evolutionary role of the military over the decades.

The first iteration of the military regimes under Nasser and the Free officers, which lasted between 1952 and 1967, can be classified as 'quasi-civilianized' direct military rule. Indeed, the Nasserist regime followed a policy of staffing the cabinet and the state bureaucracy with military personnel, a policy that was guided by two principles. First is the belief in the supremacy of the military's organizational skills over its civilian counterpart (a theme that would reappear under Sisi); second is the need to assert control over the bureaucracy. The dominance of the military is apparent when one looks at the composition of the eighteen cabinets between 1952 and 1970 (Harb, 2003). During this period, only one cabinet was headed by a civilian, while the rest were headed by military officers, with Nasser himself acting as Prime Minister eight times. Of the eighteen cabinets, only the first three were composed completely of civilians, while the rest contained a military component, accounting for an average of 36.6% of the ministerial positions. The ministerial portfolios assigned to the officers were the most influential as they included War, the Interior, War Production and National Guidance. In addition, the position of the Vice-President was always occupied by military men, highlighting the military dominance in terms of succession. The overt dominance of the military was not limited to the cabinet level, but also extended to other organs of the state and public organizations. For example, the editorial boards of national newspapers, which were nationalized in 1960, were populated by military men (Harb, 2003). This dominance even extended to the Foreign Ministry, with the seventy-two out of the top hundred positions occupied by officers in 1962, with all the ambassadors to Europe, except for three, having a military background. This dominance also extended to the regime's single party, first called the Liberation Rally, until it finally morphed into the Arab Socialist Union (ASU) in 1962. In 1962, 75% of the ASU general secretariat were military men, falling to 56.3% in 1965 (Harb, 2003). The ASU served to give the regime its 'quasi-civilianized' label.

However, it would be too simplistic to view the Nasserist regime as a monolith, with Nasser acting as a military autocrat, in sync with the interest of the military establishment. On the contrary, the regime was plagued by inter-elite rivalry between Nasser and his second-in-command and head of the armed forces, Field Marshal Abdel Hakim Amer. This rivalry split the security apparatus between the two men, with military-based security organs supporting Amer. Indeed, Amer was able to transform the military into his own fiefdom, as it continued to grow and dominate the state apparatus and policymaking, to the determinant of Nasser, leading to Nasser's loss of control over the armed forces. The creation of the ASU by Nasser was an attempt by the President to counterbalance the power of the military by revamping the political apparatus and placing it on a par with the military, as Hazem Kandil has argued. According to Sami Sharaf, the head of the Presidential Bureau of Information (PBI) and one of Nasser's closest allies, when commenting on the creation of the ASU in 1962 (Kandil, 2014, p. 57), 'We suffered an imbalance; the weight of the military was growing beyond control. Nasser created the ASU as a counter balance to the army.'

The ASU, however, failed in its task. Nasser and his associates were unable to build a genuine mass ideological party that would bind the regime base to it and act as a means to reduce the influence of the military. The ASU only acted to bind the base to the regime through the promise of material benefits, hence limiting its power (Kandil, 2014, pp. 56–76). It was only after the spectacular defeat in 1967, when the Egyptian military was crushed by Israel in six days, that Nasser could move decisively against his rival and start the long process of subduing the military. The struggle between the two men, or, more precisely, between the presidency and the military, was fraught with coup attempts, with Nasser surviving five attempted overthrows by 1970 (Bou Nassif, 2015), the most serious of which was at carried out by Amer after the defeat. Amer's defeat in the struggle with Nasser initiated the process of transforming Egypt from a military to a police state. Nasser moved decisively against the Amer loyalists after the defeat, purging more than 1,000 officers from the military and around 300 operatives from the General Intelligence Services (GIS), while charging ninety coup conspirators with treason and handing them hefty prison sentences. He also streamlined the top-heavy military command structure and reclaimed presidential control over military appointments down to the level of colonel. Nasser restructured the high command so that the heads of the different services started reporting directly to the President, which had not been the case under Amer. On 25 January 1968, Law 4, entitled 'Control of State Defence Matters and the Armed Forces', was issued, which gave the President and the War minister control over the military budget, personnel issues and procurement. Most importantly, Nasser appointed professional soldiers who resented Amer's clientelism, signalling a shift in the position of the military within the regime. The subjugation of the military was reflected in the composition of the cabinet, which saw the number of officers drop to just 21% of the total membership in 1970, as well as in the composition of the Secretariat of the ASU, which saw the percentage of military officers drop to 43%. The long march to a system of a dual military rule had begun (Kandil, 2014, pp. 91–2).

After the death of Nasser in 1970, the new President, Anwar Sadat, continued to follow a policy of reducing the power of the military establishment. He followed a policy of 'divide and rule', where he pitted individual officers against each other, while dismissing those that did not agree with his policies (Harb, 2003). More importantly, he moved to rehabilitate the ASU, in a way where it would act as a counterbalance to the military. In January 1976, after the October War in 1973 and the start of the 'infitah' policy, which refers to the policy of economic liberalization, Sadat announced the creation of the 'Manabirs' or platforms, which represented the left, centre and right of the ASU. These three platforms would later be transformed into political parties, via Law 40 of 1977, with the centrist party transforming into the ruling party, headed by the President, and eventually adopting the name of the National Democratic Party (NDP). The aim was to create a closed political system, with a hegemonic ruling party flanked by loyal opposition, a formula that would survive late into the Mubarak era. However, the stated aim of reforming the ASU was not really achieved, as its six million members simply joined the NDP; however unlike under Nasser, the membership not only included state functionary and village notables, but also extended to the new crony state-sponsored bourgeoisie, a direct result of Sadat 'infitah' policy (Kandil, 2014, p. 165). The weakened position of the military was again reflected in the composition of the cabinet, with the representation of the military establishment standing at 22.2% in 1972, while the number of governors with a military background dropping from twenty-two out of twenty-six in 1964 to just five in 1980 (Harb, 2003).

Hence, the general trend under Sadat was increased civilianization, but there are other signs that show that the military establishment continued to be an integral component of the regime, qualifying the ruling power as a dual military regime, albeit with a weakened military component. The clearest manifestation of this was the shift of the military establishment towards economic activities, under the guise of self-sufficiency. All incomes from these activities were not accounted for in the state budget, going directly into the military's own coffers with no civilian oversight. Law 32, issued in 1979, granted the military full economic independence from the government budget, while allowing it to open special commercial bank accounts (Harb, 2003). In addition, the presidency remained the exclusive domain of the military, with Sadat's Vice-President being an air force general, Hosni Mubarak, the man that would lead Egypt for thirty years (Harb, 2003). The military was also the last line of defence for the regime, which became apparent in January 1977, when riots broke out to protest against Sadat's economic policy and the lifting of some food subsidies. Similar to 2011, the police force collapsed and the military was called in to restore order.

After the assassination of Sadat in 1981, another military officer rose to the presidency, Mohamed Hosni Mubarak. The position of the military in the Mubarak regime has been subject to debate among Egypt scholars. For example, Kandil argues that by the time Mubarak came to power, the military was a waning political force and that under him its privileges were seriously curtailed, thus the military economic enterprises were aimed at alleviating the deteriorating living standards of officers in a rapidly privatizing economy (Kandil, 2014, pp. 181–93). This made it a political pigmy. This view is contrasted with the view of Mona El-Ghobashy, who characterizes the military as the core of the Mubarak regime (El Ghobashy, 2021). Indeed, there is good reason to back El-Ghobashy's view, based on Mubarak's coup-proofing strategy, which led to the growth of the power of the military, yet not its overt political role. Indeed, Mubarak based his coup-proofing strategy on two pillars: reliance on the Interior Ministry to balance the military (a policy started by Sadat), and economic incentives to keep the top brass content (Bou Nassif, 2015). In terms of expanding the power of the Interior Ministry, by the end of the Mubarak era the police had a million men in its ranks, while the Central Security Forces (CSF) had 450,000 men. This was three times the size of the military. The budget of the Interior Ministry also greatly expanded, growing from US$1.05 billion in 1990 to US$3.68 billion in 2008, increasing at three times the rate of the defence budget (Bou Nassif, 2015). This does not mean that the police could counter the military in a direct confrontation, but it remained a power that the military had to take into consideration. Indeed, the animosity between the military and the police was an open secret, with the Interior Ministry supportive of Gamal Mubarak and his apparent ambition to replace his father (Bou Nassif, 2015), a prospect that the military heavily opposed. Indeed, in 2010 the head of military intelligence and future President Abdel-Fattah El-Sisi predicted that the succession of Gamal Mubarak would trigger mass protests, advising the military command to side with the protestors against the Mubarak regime and the NDP (Kirkpatrick, 2019), showing that the military was far from subdued and apolitical.

Mubarak also continued the Sadat policy of allowing the military to expand its economic footprint, which grew at a spectacular rate under Minister of Defence Abu-Ghazalah (Abu Al Magd, 2018). Abu-Ghazalah was even widely considered a possible contender to Mubarak, since he was more popular amongst military officers and the public at large. He was removed from his post in 1989 after being implicated in a personal scandal, which was leaked to the public (Abu Al Magd, 2018). In order to pre-empt the rise of other possible contenders and to draw the military into its web of cronyism, the Mubarak regime started to staff the civilian bureaucracy with significant numbers of military officers, as Yezid Sayigh observed: 'Military retirees have come to staff all levels of local government, acting as a parallel executive and security arm ultimately reporting to the president' (Sayigh Y., 2012).

The turning point came in 1991, when Mubarak instituted a 'loyalty allowance', which was given to the officers in return for political loyalty and abstention from involvement in politics. For the vast majority this entailed appointment to the civilian bureaucracy after retirement, which allowed them to augment their military pensions but also had the effect of converting some ministries into military fiefdoms. The situation was compounded with the start of the privatization programme in the early 1990s, which opened up avenues for self-enrichment as military officers embedded themselves on the boards of directors of state companies and the civilian bureaucracy. In addition, active military officers were placed in senior positions in the Ministry of the Interior and the general intelligence services (GIS), playing a crucial role in regime maintenance and the repression of dissent. All of this was coupled with a growing economic footprint completely outside civilian oversight. Hence, even though the increased military power did not translate into an overt political role and the top brass remained loyal to Mubarak for the vast majority of his tenure, it was an integral component of the regime. Indeed, it wasn't simply a passive beneficiary of Mubarak's policies but an active participant in them. Based on this analysis, the most appropriate classification of the regime would be a dual regime, albeit with the military power substantially increasing under Mubarak compared to the Sadat years (Sayigh Y., 2012).

The position of the military at the core of the Mubarak regime meant that it was advantageously placed when the 2011 mass protests erupted. This not only placed it in a position to manage the transitional process, but enabled it to quickly dispense with the NDP and take complete control of the state after Mubarak's downfall. This also made it possible for the military to obstruct the long-awaited transition to democracy and oust Egypt's first democratically elected President in 2013, establishing direct military rule. The rest of this book is dedicated to dissecting the anatomy of the Sisi regime, but it is worth giving a short explanation for classifying the regime as direct military rule as opposed to 'quasi-civilianized'. First, as opposed to the Nasserist regime, there is no evidence of attempts by the President to create a mass civilian party that would act as a balance to the military. Indeed, even though there is a pro-Sisi civilian party controlling the Parliament, and there are Parliamentary elections regularly held, there is no evidence that this has any influence on state policy, with the Parliament simply rubber-stamping the executive decisions. In many ways, the real ruling party is now the military, which was endowed with constitutional power that supported an overt political role. Second, as will be shown below, state structures and institutions have been dramatically altered in a manner that not only eroded their independence but extended the control of the security apparatus to an unprecedent degree, significantly augmenting the power of the military. Indeed, it appears that the regime is following a deliberate policy of militarization of civilian institutions, as will be shown in the rest of the book. Finally, and arguably more profoundly, the military's economic role has grown to such an extent that it has ushered in a new phase of Egyptian capitalism, namely a militarized form of state capitalism, which has drastically altered the process of capital accumulation in the country. Hence, even though Egypt is not overtly ruled by a junta, it covertly is. Indeed, the unprecedent accumulation of political and economic power has ushered in a new form of military rule, which Egypt had not experienced before.

The road ahead

Before proceeding with the analysis, a quick note on the scope and limitation of the book is warranted, not only to set expectations but to highlight the amount of work that still needs to be done to fully understand the impact of Sisi's passive revolution. The most obvious challenge in writing about a contemporary regime is that one is chasing a moving target. Indeed, at the time of writing the regime is facing a profound economic crisis, whose full impact will only be apparent in a few years' time. In order to attempt to remedy this, the time frame of the book is set between July 2013 and September 2022, covering almost a decade of the regime's existence. I also attempted to focus on the fundamental dynamics of the regime's structure and constraints with the hope that my findings would hold for some time to come and help inform the reader on the modus operandi of the regime and its possible future trajectories. This is, of course, a hope but not a guarantee. In addition to the time frame challenge, there is another difficulty connected to scope. This book primarily takes a top-down approach, looking at the radical transformation instituted by the regime and its impact on the state and the economy, while largely disregarding the reaction of the citizenry to such policies. This might give the impression that there is no resistance to these policies, and more worryingly, the impression that Egyptian citizenry are passive inanimate objects subject to the whims of the ruler. This is not even remotely true, with active forms of resistance still persisting in spite of the regime's mass repression and the high cost incurred by those that carry on the spirit of the January Revolution. The exclusion of a bottom-up view stems from the notion that the topic is too complex and far reaching to be handled within the scope of the book. Indeed, a full study to examine the impact of the 25 January Revolution and the resistance it has bred is well worth undertaking, but is beyond the scope of this project. I do attempt to offer a quick glimpse at the end of Chapter 5 of the resistance that the regime's policies have encountered as a I try to chart the possible routes that the regime might take, but it is not sufficient to produce a full picture. Finally, there is the vantage point that I take, which is mostly looking at domestic factors and dynamics, with little focus on international trends, except for Chapter 4, where I look at the role of debt and international capital. This is not a deliberate attempt to disregard the impact of the rise of global right-wing authoritarianism on regime developments, but this merits a separate in-depth analysis, which is outside the scope of this book. Finally, the period between the mass protests of 2011 and the coup of 2013 are only briefly covered in Chapter 1 in the context of attempting to understand the regime's foundational moment. This is partly due to the limitation of this book's scope, as well as to the existence of other excellent accounts of the January Revolution and its aftermath.

In terms of the structure, the book is divided into five chapters covering different aspects of the regime evolution and policies. Chapter 1 is focused on the genesis of the regime. Anchoring the analysis in the events of the summer of 2013, I look at the role of state violence in cementing the regime's popular support, while analysing the ideological bedrock of the regime's hegemony. Chapter 2 is concerned with the radical process of transformation of the state apparatus and the extension of the military's dominance over various branches of the state. Chapter 3 examines the role of mass state violence and the modus operandi of the regime's repression. In Chapter 4 we shift gears to look at the regime's economic policy and the birth of the its version of a militarized form of state capitalism. The book concludes with Chapter 5, which looks at the possible routes that the regime's evolution can take and the resistance that its policies have provoked, attempting to chart a path into the future. At the end of each chapter, the long-term impact of the regime's policies on the prospect of democratic transition will also be discussed.

Chapter 1

GENESIS

'Do lions eat their cubs? The Egyptian Military is truly like a lion.'

— Abdel Fattah El-Sisi

The summer of 2013 witnessed one of the worst cases of state-led violence in Egyptian history. This violence ushered in a period of intense repression that is yet to abate at the time of writing. The massacres of that summer not only ended any hope of the continuation of Egypt's brief democratic experiment, but also laid down the basis for a deep social polarization, essential for the military to cement its hold on power. Indeed, without mass state violence, the military's ability to completely sideline the civilian political forces, from the Islamist to the liberal and leftist currents, would have been extremely difficult. The key to the military's success, however, lay in the solicitation of public support for the mass repression that the military unleashed, initially, against the supporters of the ousted Islamist president, later to extend to devour the secular opposition, as well as ordinary citizens that got caught in its growing tentacles. The military's ability to solicit public support for its repression stems from three, intertwined factors. First is the ability of the regime to strongly revive a deeply repressive and conservative form of Nasserism, devoid of the classical Nasserist emphasis on social justice. This form of Nasserism revived a deeply entrenched ideal in the Egyptian public psyche, namely the organic unity of the masses and their natural harmony. This allowed the new regime to frame opposition as treasonous acts, fuelled by foreign powers, aimed at disrupting this natural harmony, allowing the regime to garner popular support for its repression. The second and third factors behind the military's ability to foster public support for its repression are very closely connected. During its year in power, the Muslim Brotherhood's attempts at monopolizing power, and its reported courting of the security services, alienated other civilian forces, except for some Islamists groups. This was combined with the fear of the secular forces, and among large segments of the urban classes of the domination of the Brotherhood and the establishment of religious rule, which allowed the military to easily co-opt a large number of secular figures, whose support was essential for the early success of the coup. Indeed, on the eve of the mass protest of 30 June 2013, the military was able to exploit an already deepening political crisis, which could have been averted if the Brotherhood had understood the magnitude of the impending calamity and that a minimum level of accommodation with other political forces was necessary to avert the danger of a military takeover. In the end, the stubbornness of the Brotherhood and the gullibility, as well as an outright authoritarian streak, of the secular opposition allowed the military to sideline both factions, using a popularly backed tidal wave of repression to do so.

The first wave of repression, and the popular support on which it was based, not only paved the way for the Sisi presidency, but also allowed the military to completely take over the state apparatus and use its new-found supremacy to reshape the state and the economy in its own image. In essence, it laid the foundation for Sisi's passive revolution, which was carried out with considerable levels of violence. As Walter Armbrust has noted, 'The violence of 2013 has . . . become a part of the new political system. The system cannot exist without it' (Armbrust, 2019, p. 207).

Indeed, an analysis of events of the second half of 2013 is critical for understanding the foundation of the regime and how the military came to be the predominant power in the land. Such an analysis is also of critical importance for understanding the future trajectory of the regime, as well as the prospect of democratic transition in the country. Indeed, the deep social wounds of that summer need to be reckoned with in order for any prospect of peaceful coexistence to be realized. The poisonous ideological legacy of these events is its most dangerous, and arguably most durable, consequence. These acts of mass state violence required the support of large segments of the population, which entailed an indoctrination in an ideology that is deeply authoritarian and chauvinistic, with fascist undertones. This is a massive hurdle to overcome. It is very hard to argue that the military takeover of 2013, and the repression that followed it, was not immensely popular among large segments of society. Indeed, one can even plausibly argue that these acts of violence were performed with a certain level of popular participation, a fact that Sisi likes to remind his audience of whenever the regime is threatened.

This popular participation, which I will call 'societal repression', not only refers to direct acts of physical repression but also to the social ostracization of members of the opposition, both Islamist and secular, as well as enthusiastic support for the regime's repression. This process, which was primarily fuelled by the regime's propaganda, had a number of significant consequences. First, it allowed the regime not only to consolidate its base but also to create a strong psychological bond with large segments of the population, who saw themselves as partners in the regime campaign to rid the country of traitors, to protect the state from imminent collapse and to preserve traditional values. The fear of social chaos, however, not only stems from the fear of political upheaval or an Islamist takeover but also from the challenge posed to the conservative, heteronormative values that have been dominant in Egyptian society for decades. Indeed, as Armbrust has argued, using the concept of liminality developed by anthropologist Victor Turner, the mass protest of 2011 created a condition of transition between two normative social states, where everything seemed possible (Armbrust, 2019). This condition enabled the questioning of existing social norms in a way that caused deep angst for a large conservative audience, who saw the military as a the means to end the prevailing condition of social flux. This challenge, which emerged from the mass protest of 2011, has elicited a ferocious response from the regime and its support base and has been one of the main arenas of struggle between the regime and various segments of the opposition. The second, no less significant, consequence of 'societal repression' is that participation in the regime's repression required a belief in a number of fantastical conspiracy theories, bordering on the absurd. This belief was necessary for the regime not only to indoctrinate its followers in its version of Nasserism, but to instil an authoritarian, unquestioning mindset amongst its base, a real-life example of Orwellian 'Double Think', where regime propaganda is taken as an absolute truth, even when it is blatantly contradictory to facts on the ground (Orwelll, 1949).

The summer of 2013 was the regime's moment of hegemony, as defined by the Italian Marxist Antonio Gramsci, in which the ruling classes lead by the consent of the governed, and their ideas seep into the rest of society, becoming dominant amongst the masses (Gramsci, 1996). This does not mean that there was no opposition to the regime and its extremely repressive policies, but it means that the ascendancy of Sisi and the military to the pinnacle of power enjoyed wide popular support. This support was only forthcoming due to the regime's promise to protect the state from collapse and to end what was marketed as social chaos, by any means necessary. The regime's violence became the root of its popularity, as its moment of hegemony was rooted in the severe repression of the opposition. This highlights the dichotomy of

Sisi's passive revolution. Even though it was carried out from above, it did enjoy mass popular support and, as will be discussed below, popular mobilization was used to stifle popular participation in politics. This moment of hegemony paved the way for the establishment of direct military rule, but like any moment, it is fleeting, and the question of what come next might be the most important question that Egyptians have to answer in their lifetime.

This chapter starts with a brief[1] overview of the events that led to the July coup and what I consider to be the regime's foundational moment, namely the massacres of the summer of 2013. Using this vantage point, the rest of the chapter will examine the regime's ideological construct and how a repressive version of Nasserism with Islamist undertones was revived with the aim of soliciting popular participation in the state's campaign of mass violence. The chapter ends with an overview of the long-term consequences of these developments and their possible impact on democratization.

A summer of massacres

On 14 August 2013 the worst massacre of protestors in Egyptian history took place, when Egyptian security forces dispersed the sit-in of President Morsi's supporters in Raba square. The estimated death toll was at least 817 victims . Even though the exact number is not known, however, the premeditated nature of the massacre is. Indeed, based on the Human Right Watch report, the killing of protesters in the summer of 2013 by Egyptian security forces was, likely, a crime against humanity, deliberately planned by the highest echelons of the security apparatus. The Raba massacre was preceded and accompanied by a number of comparatively smaller massacres, which claimed the lives of hundreds of Brotherhood supporters as they attempted to resist the military coup that ousted Egypt's first democratically elected President. This included, for example, the Republican Guard massacre, when the security forces opened fire on a peaceful sit-in in front of the Republican Guard headquarters, killing sixty-one people, and the Manassa Memorial massacre, when security forces opened fire on a peaceful demonstration of Muslim Brotherhood supporters protesting against the coup, killing ninety-five people. The total estimated death toll of this mass bloodletting stands at 1,150, which is most likely an underestimation (HRW, 2014).

The road to the Raba massacre and the ability of the security forces to commit such atrocities with no accountability can only be understood if we look at the political context surrounding these acts of killing, namely, the Brotherhood's year in power and the deep polarization that it produced.

President Morsi was elected in a very tight race, running against Mubarak's last Prime Minister and former Air Force general Ahmed Shafiq. Morsi was only able to win the election after an important swing vote within the revolutionary camp backed him in order to prevent the apparent candidate of the old regime from winning the presidency. Morsi won the election with 51.7% of the vote, a razor thin margin (Guardian, 2012). The Brotherhood had already alienated the revolutionary and secular forces during the transitional period by allying itself with the military (Jabra, 2014), which proceeded to suppress popular demands for more radical reforms. This does not mean that there was no tension between the two forces, as the Brotherhood attempted to deliberately marginalize other civilian forces and to limit the push for more radical change, seeing the electoral process rather than protest and strikes as the best way to affect change and manage the military (El Ghobashy, 2021). This played directly into the hands of the military. Indeed, when Morsi came to power, the political landscape was already extremely polarized, with revolutionary forces, as well as the old regime and the security establishment, lined up against the Brotherhood, all for their own reasons. As Ewan Stein has argued, even though it won every election after Mubarak's ouster, the Brotherhood was not in control of the state, as it faced significant resistance from parts of the bureaucracy and the security establishment (Stein, 2015).

In many ways, the Brotherhood continued to act as a loyal opposition rather than as a party in power. In essence, instead of attempting to create a broad coalition of civilian forces to counter the old regime, and the security establishment, including the military, Morsi and the Brotherhood used clumsy tactics of attempting to consolidate power in their own hands, while appeasing the security establishment. For example, there were no serious attempts carried out by the new administration to reform the security apparatus. On the contrary, police repression continued unabated. For example, in the first ten months of the Morsi presidency, 3,460 cases of arbitrary arrests by the security forces were recorded, including 500 children (Hosni, 2012). Morsi also attempted to publicly appease the security forces and to whitewash their image. For example, in March 2013, he praised the police in a bizarre statement in which he highlighted the positive role the police played in the mass protest of 2011 that ousted Mubarak. Morsi's statement garnered much ridicule and public anger at the time, since the initial call for demonstrations in 2011 was issued under the guise of protesting against police brutality, which was rampant under Mubarak (Abdel Hafiz, 2013). More significant were the choices that Morsi made when forming his first government, which was sworn in on 2 August 2012. Morsi opted for bureaucratic insiders, with nine ministers being retained, including those of the so-called sovereign ministries, namely the ministries of the Interior, Defence, Foreign Affairs and Finance. For the Ministry of the Interior, Morsi retained the Mubarak regime stalwart Ahamed Gamal El-Din, who was a police chief in Aysuit during the 2011 mass protests, where he was notorious for his dispersal of the protests on the second day of the uprising (El Ghobashy, 2021, p. 176). This government not only failed to fulfil the electoral promise to form a national unity government, but signalled Morsi's reconciliatory approach to the police, which only acted to enrage the opposition and public opinion. Adding insult to injury, when there was a limited government reshuffle on 6 January, the Interior Minister was replaced with another Mubarak regime insider, Mohamed Ibrahim, who would later be one of the men responsible for the bloodletting in Raba. If Morsi's intention was to appease the coercive apparatus of the state, then the policy failed miserably, with the police and military police refraining from repressing anti-Morsi protests or protecting the Muslim Brotherhood offices, which were attacked and burned repeatedly during Morsi's tenure (El Ghobashy, 2021, p. 191). Morsi even chose to shelve a report, which he had commissioned, that detailed the police and military's responsibility for the mass killing of protestors in the period between 25 January 2011 and his swearing-in on 30 June 2012. The report not only implicated the police, but also documented the role of the armed forces in the killings and torture of protesters (El Ghobashy, 2021, p. 192). This not only left the President open to accusations of complicity in the state killing of protestors by human rights activists and the families of the victims, but also deprived him of a potent weapon for mobilizing public opinion for police reform and weakening the military's popular base.

Ultimately, these actions were not enough to protect Morsi or the Brotherhood when the inevitable clash with the military took place just a year after he had come to power. As the level of polarization increased and the Brotherhood felt more and more isolated, it committed another dramatic blunder, which only acted to heighten the polarization. This was the decision to ally with more conservative Islamist factions, specifically the Salafist and ex-jihadists who renounced violence, yet kept their conservative outlook. These factions included men like Assem Abdel Maged (Fahmy I., 2013), a leading member of Gama Isalmiya, an insurgent group that had waged a deadly campaign against the security forces and civilians in the 1980 and 1990s (Ashour, 2013), and Tarek El Zomor, one of the main conspirators in the assassination of Sadat, who became the Secretary General of the Salafist Building and Development Party after 2011 and a close ally of the Brotherhood (Egypt Today, 2017). The right-wing turn by the Brotherhood only acted to foment the fear of religious rule in the country, an abhorrent thought for a large number of Egyptians. It is important to note that competition between the Salafis and the Brotherhood was widespread and that relations between the two were not always cordial. However, during the Morsi presidency, as the Islamist–secular divide became more prominent, relations with some of the Salafi factions became more enmeshed as the Brotherhood attempted to muster as much support as possible. This support, however, was not uniform and across the Salafi spectrum, with the Nur Party, the largest Salafi party, throwing its support behind the military coup in 2013.

These clumsy policies were also combined with attempts at amassing power at the expense of other political forces, which led to the immediate eruption of popular protest and continuous clashes between opponents of the Brotherhood and its supporters, as the Brotherhood attempted to exert control over the public space. The clearest example of this was the constitutional declaration of November 2012, which gave Morsi dictatorial powers (Sabry B., 2012). The declaration was part of an ongoing struggle with the judiciary, as Morsi attempted to shield the Constituent Assembly, responsible for drafting the constitution, from possible dissolution by the courts, which had already dissolved Egypt's first democratically elected Parliament since the 1950s (El Ghobashy, 2021, p. 184). This led to the eruption of mass protests, which saw Morsi's declaration – which placed his decisions above judicial review – as a naked power grab rather than an attempt to protect the democratic process. The Brotherhood attempted to repress the protests by mobilizing its own supporters, which was another colossal mistake. This led to violent clashes between the two camps (Retuers, 2012), claiming the lives of ten protestors. The declaration was promptly cancelled on 9 December, bowing to popular pressure (France 24, 2012), but not without heavily damaging the credibility of the President. These low-intensity clashes became a permanent feature of the increasingly polarized political system, sowing a sense of chaos and lawlessness. After only a year in power, the road was paved for a military coup that would oust Morsi, establish direct military rule and open up the flood gates of mass state violence.

On 30 June, organized mass protests against the rule of the Brotherhood erupted, which provided the popular cover for a coup that promptly followed on 3 July. The protests were called for by the youth movement 'Tamaroud', with some evidence later appearing of apparent coordination between this movement and the military, also involving financial support from the United Arab Emirates (Al Araby, 2015). The mass protests that erupted on 30 June provided the necessary cover for the military to remove Morsi after the latter refused to make any substantial concessions or to call for early presidential elections, the original demand of the protestors. The removal of Morsi, however, does not explain the ability of the military to establish direct military rule, ending Egypt's democratic experiment, but the state of political polarization does help explain this development. Indeed, after only a year in power, the Brotherhood's attempt at power monopolization, combined with the fear of religious rule, the Brotherhood's general political incompetence, deep-state machinations and a very hostile media landscape, produced an extreme state of polarization, which was exploited by the military. After Morsi's removal, the military exploited the situation to establish direct military rule, under a civilian cloak, which was popularly backed. This wide popular support stemmed from a simple yet powerful promise, namely, the removal of the Brotherhood from the political scene, the restoration of order and an end to social unrest. Hence, once Morsi was removed, an orchestrated propaganda campaign started to emerge, eliciting public support for the massacre and, more importantly, for the elimination of the Brotherhood as a legitimate political actor and, implicitly, the repression of all forms of protests. The propaganda campaign anchored itself in the fear of violence from the Brotherhood and its supporters. For example, before the dispersal of the sit-in, the government claimed that Raba was an armed sit-in, which provided a platform for sectarian rhetoric, incited acts of terror and disrupted the lives of local residents (HRW, 2014). There were even claims that protestors had been able to procure chemical and heavy weapons from Syria, which was presented as a factor in delaying the dispersal of the sit-in (El Rashidi, 2015). In a memorable television segment, Ahmed Musa, a pro-military talk-show host known for his emotional outbursts, played a video claiming to show a mortar or a similar weapon wrapped in the Egyptian flag in the Raba sit-in. The video shown by Musa simply featured a rectangular object wrapped in the flag; it was impossible to discern the nature of the object in question. After the dispersal, no heavy weapons were found in the sit-in area (Armbrust, 2019). When violence against the Brotherhood by the security forces started to escalate, an absurd theory began to appear in the media, namely that Brotherhood members were provoking the security forces or killing themselves to garner Western sympathy. One of the proponents of this theory was Lamis El Hadidi, another prominent talk-show host. After the Republican guard massacre, Hadidi insisted that members of the Brotherhood had killed one another to gain sympathy: 'They found themselves being killed by their own friends – some of them, and the investigation will show that' (Kirkpatrick, 2019, p. 258). No investigation has ever confirmed anything to that effect, while numerous eyewitness accounts claim that the Brotherhood protestors were killed by members of the security forces (Kirkpatrick, 2019, p. 255).

The genius tactic, however, that would be the anchor not only of the massacre but also the mass repression by the regime, was a call made by Sisi, the then Defence Minister, three weeks before the massacre, for a mass demonstration to grant him and the military a 'mandate to combat terrorism' (Karam, 2014). In essence, in the polarized context of the time and with the continuous hints of a government plan to violently disperse the sit-in, this was a call for popular participation in a mass act of repression– a call that was heeded by thousands the following Friday. Sisi had cleverly inverted the equation, using the power of popular mobilization to repress it, laying down the foundation for widespread state violence with mass social participation. The reaction of the Brotherhood to the brewing storm was abysmal, as it turned inwards in an attempt to maintain the cohesion of its base. Calls for violence bellowed from the loudspeakers in the sit-in, sometimes with a strong sectarian overtone (Kandil, 2014). These calls only served to stoke up fear amongst opponents of the Brotherhood, as well as apolitical Egyptians, who naturally found themselves siding with the military as the best guarantor for stability and physical safety. The situation was compounded by reports of abductions and torture carried out by Brotherhood supporters of suspected inflators, which, based on a fact-finding report issued by the National Human Rights Council (NHCR), a government body, led to eleven deaths (NHRC, 2014). It is difficult to verify these reports, but what matters is that they were widely believed, which only helped to swell support for dispersal of the sit-in.[2]

The stage was now set for the worst massacre of protesters in Egyptian history, with what appears to have been deliberate and lethal intent. For example, based on both the HRW and the NCHR reports, the security forces used mass indiscriminate fire against the protestors leading to large number of unnecessary casualties. Adding insult to injury, the assumption that the sit-in was armed proved to be false, with only fifteen firearms recovered from the sit-in site, which had contained an estimated 85,000 protesters (HRW, 2014). This is hardly sufficient to justify such a mass use of deadly force, which left at least hundreds dead. The low number of casualties within the ranks of the security forces also attest to minimal threat posed by the sit-in, with just eight members of the security forces killed in clashes with the protestors. The NCHR report also states that the protestors were only given 25 minutes to evacuate, which was not deemed sufficient time for thousands of protesters to leave the camp site. In addition, the evacuation call was made when the security forces were already positioned on the line of confrontation, with skirmishes erupting between the two sides. The HRW report also states that the calls were not heard by the vast majority of the demonstrators and that the use of live ammo started almost immediately. The most damning part of both reports, however, is the documentation of the failure of the security forces to provide safe passage to those that wished to leave, turning the protest site into a mass killing field. Indeed, based on the NCHR report, locals assisted in arresting those that attempted to leave the sit-in through the designated safe passages, and handed them over to security forces. The scale of the expected casualties was well known to the security services, as evidenced at a meeting with human rights organizations, before the dispersal, in which an Interior Ministry official stated that he expected casualties to reach 3,500, an astronomical figure. The HRW report recommended that key members of the security establishment should be investigated for their role in the massacre, including the Interior Minister Mohamed Ibrahim, the Defence Minister Abdel Fattah al-Sisi, Special Forces head and commander of the Raba operation Medhat Menshawy and the head of the General Intelligence Services, Mohamed Farid Tohamy (HRW, 2014).

The violent dispersal of the sit-in begat more violence by the security forces, as well by supporters of the ousted President. For example, on the day of the dispersal, forty-two churches were attacked and burned across the country, most likely by supporters of the ousted President, leading to four deaths (HRW, 2013). The sectarian rhetoric emerging from the sit-in can be plausibly identified as one the main causes for the nationwide attacks. Another prominent example of the unrest was the Kerdasa massacre, when the Kerdasa police stations was attacked by fifty militants, leading to the death of eleven members of the security forces (Abdel Latif, 2013). On the other hand, the security forces continued to use mass, deadly repression against the supporters of the Brotherhood. For example, on 16 August, the security forces opened fire on hundreds of protesters in front of Azbakiya police station in the Abbasiyya, in central Cairo, killing one hundred and twenty (HRW, 2014). As a result of the summer of mass violence, by the end of the year the Brotherhood had been designated as a terror group by the new regime, ending its brief tenure as a legitimate actor on the Egyptian political scene and branding all the members of the mass organization as terrorists (Guardian, 2013).

It is important to note, however, that even though there were acts of violence committed by members of the Brotherhood or its supporters, the organization itself did not shift to a systematic policy of violent confrontation with the new regime. On the contrary, the Brotherhood appeared committed to the path of civil resistance, despite the massive pressure it endured and the radicalizing effects of years of state violence, with violence committed by its members being limited to small cohorts with no official endorsement by the organization (Ardovini E., 2022). Indeed, it was the regime that was the largest perpetrator of mass violence, which was essential for it to cement its base and to build a hegemonic ideological construct.

The ascendance of the military and the completion of the coup would not have been possible without the active support of a large array of secular political figures, either connected to the revolutionary camp or the old regime. This includes names like Amr Moussa, Mohamed El-Baradie and Hamdeen Sabahi, spanning the old regime, the liberals and the left (Carnegie Endowment, 2013). The complicitly of the opposition in the coup was revealed in an interview with Amr Hamzawy, the prominent academic and liberal opposition figure, who was a member of the Salvation Front, a loose coalition of opposition forces during Morsi's tenure. In this interview, Hamzawy stated that dominant thinking amongst the opposition at the time was to trigger a military coup, using mass protests, to oust Morsi, rather than force the President to call for an early election (Podcast 11, 2021). Indeed, El-Baradie is reported to have told the group that 'without the military we have no chance', a clear reference to his strategy of triggering a military intervention (Kirkpatrick, 2019, p. 216). After the coup, prominent liberal figures like Mohamed El-Baradie (France 24, 2013) and leftist figures like Kamal Abou Eitta (Al Ahram, 2013) served in the military-controlled civilian government, helping to legitimatize the coup. For example, El-Baradie, the previous head of the Atomic Energy Agency and a Noble laureate, took the post of Vice President of Foreign Affairs and made a number of appearances in Western media outlets pleading the case of the military, arguing that the military's intervention was not a coup and that it is was necessary to avoid a slide into civil war and fascism (Al Arabiya, 2013). El-Baradie would later resign in protest after the violent dispersal of the Brotherhood sit-in (Reuters, 2013). On the other hand, leftist politicians like Kamal Abou Eitta continued to serve in the government, even after the massacres occurred, in effect providing legitimacy for the mass repression that the new regime was unleashing. Ezz El Din Shokry Fisher, a liberal politician, academic, novelist and advisor to El-Baradie, provided a damning indictment of the transitional government, painting a picture of an ineffectual government, dominated by the military establishment, with extremely repressive tendencies (Podcast 11, 2021). This manifested itself when the transitional government issued the draconian Protest Law, to be discussed in detail in the next chapter, which was essential for closing the public space and giving the security apparatus free reign to supress protest at will. The victims of the law were not only members of the Brotherhood but also secular and youth democracy activists, who became the targets of the security forces as they attempted to reverse the gains made after the mass protest of 2011. Indeed, to a large extent the secular members of the government collaborated with the military to repress their own base.

There is also circumstantial evidence that the intelligence services were working closely with the National Salvation Front to bring down Morsi. This became apparent in a leaked phone call between El-Sayyid El Badawi, the then head of the Wafd Party, and an unnamed member of the intelligence services. In the call, which took place in early 2012, Badawi floated the idea that he would solicit the backing of the Brotherhood for a proposed presidential run. The response of the unnamed officer was chilling:

> Oh, Sayyid, the upcoming period will be a dark one for the Brotherhood ... Armed militias will slaughter them in their own houses. Egypt will be full of orchestrated 'terrorism' to retaliate against the Brotherhood and seek revenge for the revolution that brought down the security apparatus.
>
> Kirkpatrick, 2019, p. 198

The headquarters of the Wafd Party was the meeting point for of the Salvation Front, and by early 2013 it had become apparent to members of the Front that the intelligence services were working to oust Morsi, with Badawi declaring in a meeting that 'The State institutions were with us' (Kirkpatrick, 2019, p. 199). Even though the evidence is circumstantial, there is clear complicity in terms of legitimizing the coup and directly supporting the new regime's repressive policy in the early stages. The Salvation Front also attempted to justify the escalating violence against the Brotherhood in the immediate aftermath of the coup, paving the way for the Raba massacre. For example, after the Republican Guard massacre, the Salvation Front called a press conference and held up a banner that read 'Muslim Brotherhood–American Conspiracy Against the Revolution'. The spokesperson for the Front declared in the press conference that 'We expect violent acts from the side of the Muslim Brotherhood' (Kirkpatrick, 2019, p. 255). This facilitated the de-humanization of the Brotherhood, intensifying the polarization and paving the way for the Raba massacre.

The road to the coup and the repression that followed was paved by a dangerous mix of opportunism, incompetence and an autocratic mindset across the political divide. Indeed, the policies of the Brotherhood helped create a polarized political system, which allowed the military to intervene. The opportunism of the secular opposition and the authoritarian streak of some of its members provided the coup with legitimacy and allowed the military to consolidate its position, as the undisputed master in Egyptian politics. The blame for the end of Egypt's short democratic experiment lay with all sides

The Sisification of Nasserism

Even though the Sisi regime is not overtly ideological compared to the communist or Nazi regimes of the twentieth century, it has nonetheless constructed a robust ideological edifice, with strong roots in one of Egypt's most powerful ideological currents, namely Nasserism. Indeed, even though Nasserism suffered a spectacular blow in 1967, with Egypt's devastating defeat in the Six-Day War, exacerbated by the death of its founder in 1970 and its official dismantling at the hands of Sadat in the 1970s, some of its most regressive aspects continued to be deeply rooted in the Egyptian public psyche, across the political divide (Gerges, 2018). These aspects were revived by the nascent military regime leading up to and after the coup of 2013, constructing a new variant of Nasserism, which is devoid of the classical Nasserist emphasis on social justice, anti-imperialism and glorification of the masses, while rejuvenating its most totalitarian aspects. These aspects include a view of the nation as an organic whole, in natural harmony, rather than a collection of different social groups with conflicting interests that need to be managed through a democratic political system. This view has two important consequences. First, it allows the regime to brand any form of opposition as something alien to the 'nation', and hence something that can be repressed with as much violence as needed. Differences are seen as a threat to the 'nation's' perennial harmony and organic unity. The second consequence is a clear disdain for parliamentary democracy, due to the fact that it is a political system based on the aforementioned assumption namely that the existence of different social groups with different interests can only be expressed through a democratic and pluralistic political system.

These views were expressed by Nasser himself in an article that he penned in 1955, which will be quoted at length since it is very illustrative of Nasser's ideology. For example, when considering parliamentary democracy and elaborating on the aims of his nascent military dictatorship, he argued that:

> These, then, are the aims of the revolution: to end the exploitation of people, to realize national aspirations and to develop the mature political consciousness that is an indispensable preliminary for a sound democracy. The revolution seeks to bridge the gulf between social classes and to foster the spirit of altruism which marks a cultivated individual and a cohesive group. Our ultimate aim is to provide Egypt with a truly democratic and representative government, not the type of parliamentary dictatorship which the Palace and a corrupt 'pasha' class imposed on the people. In the past, parliament was a body for blocking social improvement.
>
> Nasser, 1955

Nasser also expressed his views on the opposition, namely the Muslim Brotherhood and the communist movement, the two political forces that could plausibly challenge his rule at the time:

> As we plan for the future, we have also had to clean out the corrupt past, especially the subversive or reactionary groups which have spread their tentacles wide in the land. The greatest internal enemies of the people are the Communists who serve foreign rulers, the Moslem Brotherhood which still seeks rule by assassination in an era that has outlived such practices, and the old-time politicians who would like to re-establish exploitation.
>
> Nasser, 1955

In terms of actual policies, Nasser was true to his word, presiding over the systematic dismantling of the pre-1952 state institutions, banning political parties and violently repressing the opposition, while allowing the military to accumulate enough political power to dominate the state. In the end he was to lose control of the military establishment, with disastrous consequences (Gerges, 2018), including ending any form of pluralism and allowing the regime to completely dominate the public space. The Nasserist regime's relationship with the labour movement is another hallmark of the Nasserist period, in that even though the working class benefited from increased material benefits and an improved social standing, any attempts at developing an independent labour movement were mercilessly crushed. As Joel Benin argued, the new leadership of the Nasser regime, the Revolutionary Command Council (RCC), explicitly rejected the concept of class struggle, adopting the view that the working class is part of a broad coalition of popular forces led by the army, echoing the aforementioned view of the organic unity of the nation (Benin, 1989). This led to the nationalization of the labour movement and the end of its independence. The clash with labour came early on, when a strike and riot broke out in the Misr Fine Spinning and Weaving Co. in Kafr al-Dawwar on 12 August 1952. Even though the workers demonstrated in favour of the new regime, expecting it to respond to their demands, the military quickly clashed with the striking workers. In a hastily convened military trial, two workers, Mustafa Khamis and Muhammad al-Baqri, were sentenced to death – a draconian punishment aimed at instilling the nascent regime's dominance over the labour movement (Benin, 1989). Interestingly, very similar to 2011, the Muslim Brotherhood allied itself with the nascent Nasserist regime, as it broadly supported the abrogation of democracy and the repression of the opposition (Gerges, 2018).

The 'sameness' of the Egyptian nation, however, is a construct that predates Nasser and one that is deeply entrenched in Egyptian nationalism. Nasser, like Sisi, simply tapped into a pre-existing ideological construct. As Fawaz Gerges has astutely argued, Egyptian nationalism developed in response to British colonization of Egypt, hence a concept of 'sameness' in opposition to the 'other' became prevalent. This conception allowed political forces like the secular nationalist movement, represented by the Free Officers, and the Muslim Brotherhood to claim a hegemonic position within the nationalist movement as the true representatives of the 'nation'. This claim also caused these movements to develop extremely anti-democratic tendencies, as they cast their opponents as traitors to the 'nation' and hence not real Egyptians (Gerges, 2018). Thus, the development of an extreme form of chauvinistic nationalism is deeply embedded in the Egyptian public psyche, which was taken to new heights by Sisi and his regime. This was echoed by Khaled Fahmy, the prominent historian, who argued that the traditional nationalist conception of Egyptian national identity sees Egypt as an already existing social entity from time immemorial, extending all the way back to Pharaonic times. Echoing Gerges, Fahmy also argued that this conception views the Egyptian nation as organically and racially homogeneous, with Egyptianess trumping other historic identities like Ottoman or Muslim (Fahmy K., 1997). In this romantic discourse the military plays a prominent role, as it is the establishment of the modern, conscription-based Egyptian army in the first half of the nineteenth century that allowed the Egyptian peasants to rediscover their national identity, while serving in Mehmed Ali's wars. This discourse omits the significant resistance that the Egyptian rural population put up against conscription, as well as the level of social deprivation, violence and misery inflicted on the mass of the population by Mehmed Ali (Fahmy K., 1997). The conception of the organic unity of the nation also plays a role in dampening social conflict, since, simply put, any form of struggle over the distribution of wealth or political and economic rights can be interpreted as sabotage of this perceived 'unity'. Indeed, as Louis Althusser argued, nationalism only acts to submerge class consciousness and stifle social strife (Carnoy, 1983), a role that Nasserism plays extremely well.

Another aspect of the Nasserist ideological construct is the position of the military as the spearhead of nationalist development and the struggle against imperialism, which Nasser made clear in his 1955 article:

> Revolution was the only way out. And it came in 1952, led by the army and backed by the nation. In the pre-revolutionary period the army was an instrument in the hand of despotic rulers who used it against the nationalist movements. Now it understood its position and joined the ranks of the people to head the movement for national liberation.
>
> Nasser, 1955

Hence, it was the army that was at the spearhead of the anti-imperialist struggle, as Benin argued, the head of a popular coalition of forces in the fight against colonialism and national development (Benin, 1989). This was reflected in the position of the military in the new regime, as Nasser presided over the construction of a military dictatorship, where the military grew so powerful that Nasser had to contend with sharing power with his nominal second-in-command, and the head of the armed forces, Field Marshal Ammer. It took the defeat of 1967 for the balance of power to tilt against the overt dominance of the military establishment (Kandil, 2014). This ideological construct laid the ground for, not just the popular acceptance of the overt dominance of the military in political life, but also the propagation of conspiracy theories to demonize the opposition, a practice that both Nasser and Sisi perfected. The central role of the military also implied that mass social change would come from the top down, with minimal popular participation. Indeed, Nasser presided over the establishment of a political system with little or no checks and balances, where power was concentrated in the executive branch and the military establishment, enabling the regime to initiate top-down wide-scale social changes. Therefore, the state became central in the Nasserist development project, which also made it central to the popular Egyptian conception of politics, stability and social development.

Based on this development, a simple yet effective formula was created, which allowed Sisi to initiate a powerful message, with strong ideological appeal, anchored in Nasserism. Starting from the premise of the organic unity of the nation, the opposition can be painted as social groups outside the 'nation', since, simply put, they threaten the nation's natural harmony. However, this conception is only plausible if the regime, or, more precisely, the military, is able to portray itself as a representative of the nation and the guardian of the state, which it has been very successful in doing. Hence, opposition to the military regime is equated with treason to the nation, and thus should be repressed by any means necessary. The narrative used to solicit popular support involved the propagation of numerous conspiracy theories, including the claim that the events of 2011, the groups that participated in it and those who support it are part of a systemic effort to destroy the Egyptian state, which was only thwarted by the military's intervention in 2013.

Before proceeding with the analysis of Sisi's appropriation of Nasserism, two qualifying points need to be made. First, even though the narrative of the unity of the nation is pervasive, it is far from being the only narrative. Indeed, one of the enduring outcomes of the 2011 mass protests, and the fleeting opening of the public space that followed, is the appearance of new narratives that implicitly challenge the national conception of 'sameness'. This would partially explain the extreme popular reaction from the regime base to these contending narratives, and the groups that support them, since they contest deeply held nationalist beliefs.[3] The second qualifying point is that the prevalence of these previously highlighted elements of Nasserism has ebbed and flowed, and so has its appeal. Indeed, during the Mubarak year, when the regime was labelled a 'Liberal Autocracy' (Anani, 2008), the ideological appeal of some aspects of Nasserism had fallen to a low point. The most prominent example is the dominant position of the military, which by then had lost a significant amount of political power and social prestige compared to the days of Nasser, a process that had already started under

Sadat (Kandil, 2014). Hence, Sisi did not accelerate a rising trend but tapped into an already existing ideological legacy and recast it to suit the purpose of the regime, laying down a strong ideological foundation for a new form of military dictatorship.

Indeed, once the military took over, regime officials and regime-controlled media outlets orchestrated a propaganda campaign aimed at creating a foundational myth. The fundamental element of this myth is the casting of the events of 2011 as part of an ongoing conspiracy by foreign powers aimed at destroying the state. This plot was, allegedly, pursued by fifth columnists, consisting of the pro-democracy activists and the Muslim Brotherhood, and was only averted by the intervention of the military in 2013 to remove Morsi. This myth places the military as the guardian of the state, a literal embodiment of the nation and a protector of national unity. It is based on the assumption of the supremacy of the military as an institution, as well as an Orientalist view of the citizenry as weak, inept, child-like and lazy (Kirkpatrick, 2019, p. 305), since they were so easily duped by the conspiracy. The cherry on top of the cake is the casting of Sisi as an embodiment of the myth, a man who saved the state as the head of the armed forces on the eve of the coup of 2013, and the massacres that followed. It is important to note that the foundation of this narrative was already in place, as Walter Armbrust showed in his study of the role of Trickster in the post-revolutionary period of 2011–13 (Armbrust, 2019). In his study, Armbrust focused on Tawifk Ukasha, a media personality who developed a cult-like following amongst supporters of the military establishment and the Mubarak regime, with rural lower and lower-middle-class backgrounds. After the fall of Mubarak in 2011, Ukasha used his talk show to propagate a number of fantastical conspiracy theories about the foreign origins of the mass protests that led to the downfall of Mubarak. In this narrative, Ukasha connected a number of foreign powers with the pro-democracy protest movement and the Muslim Brotherhood in their joint bid to destroy the state, and by extension the country (Armbrust, 2019). Ukasha was not the only one propagating these theories, but he was the most prominent voice in an orchestrated campaign aimed at defaming the insurrection. Hence, by the time of the 2013 coup, the groundwork was already laid; all that was needed now was its expansion, which is exactly what Sisi did.

The regime's foundational myth was systematically built up over the years through various statements made by Sisi himself and other regime officials, on talk shows and even television series. The examples are too many to list in total, but a few should suffice to illustrate the pattern. For example, in October 2014 Sisi warned of a 'major conspiracy threatening the existence of Egypt, and aimed at breaking the will of its people and its military' (BBC, 2014). The details of said conspiracy were never spelled out. The theme of conspiracies against the state remained a staple in Sisi speeches across the years. For example, in April 2016, Sisi warned of fourth- and fifth-generation wars, aimed at spreading disinformation amongst the public, alluding to the existence of a conspiracy to spread disinformation in the country, using electronic battalions (Al Shorouk, 2016). The concept of fourth-generation wars is closely connected to American neo-conservative William Lind, with the phrase first appearing in the late 1980s. Lind was obsessed with the infiltration of those he called 'Cultural Marxists', and their impact on American culture and society. Under the pen name Thomas Hobbes, Lind published a novel called *Victoria*, in which he predicted the break-up of the United States due to overt 'political correctness', with a Christian state developing in New England, allying itself with a reconstituted Czarist Russia (Armbrust, 2019, p. 232). The concept of fourth-generation wars simply refers to the use of disinformation, funding subversive NGOs and spreading rumours as a method of warfare, broadening the concept of war to include non-military action. This endlessly elastic concept is a godsend for conspiracy theorists and provides endless justification for state repression. Ukasha, the pro-regime talk-show host, was the first to introduce the term in Egyptian political discourse. Sisi would later pick it up as part of the official narrative of the regime, and up the ante by coining the term fifth-generation wars. The official use of the term came as early as February 2015, when Sisi attempted to use the concept to discredit a leaked audio recording in which he used derogatory language in referring to his Gulf patrons, and how the military was extracting rent from them for its own ends. In his speech, Sisi tried to cast doubt on the authenticity of the leak, arguing that it was part of the 'fourth generation war' (Armbrust, 2019, p. 233), in essence claiming that the recording was faked. The affinity between American neo-conservative conspiracy theories and Sisi's official discourse is striking, but it also provides an insight into the close connection between Sisi and Trump and why Trump referred to Sisi as his favourite dictator.

This theme would continue; for example, in September 2019 a workshop was held in a state-sponsored youth conference entitled 'The effects of disinformation on the State, in the context of fourth generation wars' (El Gali, 2019), another example of blatant regime propaganda. Sisi has also portrayed the mass protests of 2011 as at worst a conspiracy, or at best an ill-advised attempt at change. In November 2018, Sisi warned of 'national suicide' that might result from 'poorly thought out attempts at change', alluding to the mass protest of 2011. He continued to state that Egypt could have become a victim of civil strife, with children growing up in refugee camps. The implication was that without the coup of 2013, Egypt would have followed a similar path to Syria, Iraq and Libya (RT, 2018). In September 2019, Sisi took a much harsher tone, with the regime facing the prospect of possible protests as a result of leaks by Mohamed Ali, a contractor connected to the regime, revealing high levels of systemic graft. Sisi described the 2011 mass protests as a conspiracy against Egypt, which targeted the military and the Interior Ministry, stating that a prerequisite for the success of the conspiracy was a weakening of the military, implicitly placing the military as the guardian of the nation, with its opponents cast outside the nation (Arabic Post, 2019). All these statements have a common thread, namely the casting of the opposition as an existential threat to the state and the unity of the nation, thereby establishing justification for mass state violence against the threat.

Public statements by Sisi about the conspiracy against the state were supplemented by statements from public figures and other politicians praising the coup, as well as the role of the military in defending the state. For example, in June 2022, Mostafa Barky, the Nasserist journalist and parliamentarian, stated that Sisi and the military saved the country from a civil war in 2013, arguing that the 'terrorist' Muslim Brotherhood was trying to erase Egypt's national identity (Al Akhbar, 2022). Barky also accused the Brotherhood of sabotaging the Egyptian economy by spreading rumours about poor economic performance (Al Akhbar, 2022). This sentiment was seconded by another Nasserist writer, Abdel Halim Qandeel, who was a staunch opponent of the Mubarak regime. Qandeel stated in June 2022 that Egypt was 'ill for 40 years before the 30th of June', implying that it was the coup of 2013 that rejuvenated the nation (Al Akhbar, 2022).

This view of the military as a supreme political force and a guardian of the state was not confined to rhetoric, but was also a matter of state policy. This was reflected in the constitutional amendment of 2019, which established the military as the guardian of the secular nature of the state and the protector of democratic rights, thus providing a legal foundation for repeated military intervention in politics. The belief in the organic unity of the nation was also manifested in the way that parliamentary elections were carried out under Sisi, which witnessed not just extensive intervention by the security apparatus but also saw a drive to create a unified list, containing not only regime-affiliated parties but members of the domesticated opposition. The details of these policies will be covered in the following chapter, but it is important to highlight the notion that this ideological construct was essential for the process of state restructuring that the regime embarked on, and the direct military rule that emerged. As highlighted by Finer, belief in the military's supremacy is an essential prerequisite for military intervention in politics and, in the case of Egypt, the establishment of direct military rule.

The regime propaganda campaign, however, sometimes took bizarre turns, with cases of extreme hyperbole. The most notable example was the saga of General Ibrahim Abdulatty, popularly known as General Abdulatty Kofta (Al Araby, 2021). In February 2014, the general announced that the military had invented a device that could cure both hepatitis C and HIV. The proposed cure was a medical device that could detect and destroy the virus, almost instantly. General Abdulatty stated that he would extract the virus from the patient, and give it back to him as a piece of Kofta, which the patient could eat. Even though there was no scientific evidence to support these claims, the pro-regime media pushed the narrative to new heights (El Dahshan, 2014), even after the scientific advisor to the interim President Adly Mansour, Essam Hegy, was extremely critical of the announcement due to its lack of scientific merit (Abdelaziz and Abedine, 2014). The military even announced that the miracle cure would be available in military hospitals and clinics starting from July 2014, only to backtrack a month before that date (Loveluck, 2014). It was later established that General Abdulatty was not a medical professional nor a scientist, and that he was previously sentenced to one month in jail in 2007 for impersonating a doctor and practising without a license (Al Araby, 2021). His connection to the military was also questionable. Abdulatty was granted the rank of honorary general after the head of the engineering authority became attracted to the general's ideas, in spite of having no formal affiliation with the military establishment (Armbrust, 2019, p. 229). How Abdulatty was able to convince the military brass to support his bizarre claim to have found a miracle cure remains a mystery, but it is indicative of the level of prevalent polarisation that a charlatan was able to spin such a ridiculous state-sponsored lie that a large number of Egyptians believed.

When describing the opposition, remaining true to the regime narrative, Sisi coined a new term: 'The people of evil' (BBC, 2016). The term started to gain currency in 2016, when popular opposition to the transfer of the two islands in the Red Sea, Tiran and Sanafir, from Egyptian to Saudi sovereignty became apparent. However, it first made an appearance during Sisi's speech inaugurating the new Suez Canal in

2015 (Armbrust, 2019, p. 223). Even though it was never explicitly defined, it became clear that Sisi used it to describe the opposition in general, with specific mention of those who doubted and criticized the regime's 'achievements' (RT, 2019). Sisi used a rhetoric that not only framed the opposition as evil but also framed the regime as good, and the conflict between them as an existential struggle between good and evil: a biblical image par excellence. The framing of the opposition as evil and treasonous was not only a rhetorical device but also laid down the foundation of mass repression. Indeed, the leadership of the Brotherhood, including the ousted President, were accused of collaborating with foreign powers, including Qatar and Hamas, with the ousted President standing trial on charges of treason and conspiring with foreign powers (BBC, 2018). On the other hand, members of the secular opposition were often charged with joining a terrorist organization and spreading false news, all consistent with the above-mentioned statements and rhetoric.

This ideological construct was not only confined to statements made by Sisi and regime officials, but was also popularized in a three-part TV series called *The Choice*, which chronicled the deeds of the military in combating the 'people of evil'. The series included a dramatization of the massacres of the summer of 2013, the events of coup of 2013 and the insurgency in Sinai from the perspective of the military establishment. Indeed, the military regime, building on the polarization of 2013 and the massacres that followed, has built an enduring ideological edifice, anchored in state violence, with a mass following – a legacy that will prove durable and toxic for decades to come.

Societal repression

In order to entrench this form of neo-Nasserism, and to tether its base to it, the regime sought to implicate large segments of the population in its repression, either by calling for them to support it or to actively participate in it. The most notable example of this strategy was Sisi's call for mass demonstrations in July 2013 to authorize him to combat 'terrorism', in essence, seeking a popular mandate for the massacre of Brotherhood supporters. This mandate implicated large segments of the population in the massacres that followed, creating an organic bond between the regime and its base, while making its narrative more appealing and convincing. Support for the regime's repression was not confined to the moral level, as there is some evidence of direct participation in repression.

For example, there are reports that during the Raba massacre the protestors who tried to leave the campsite were arrested by locals and handed over to the security forces, this denial of safe passage was regarded as one of the reasons for the dramatically increased death toll (NHRC, 2014). This was followed by a number of reports of locals directly participating in the physical dispersal of marches by Brotherhood supporters. For example, in October 2013 in the village of Kafr Magar, located in the Delta, there were reports of attacks by locals on a march by Brotherhood supporters, once the latter started to chant against the military and the then Defence Minister Sisi (Abou El Eineen, 2013). Similar scenes occurred in late 2013 and early 2014 in the provinces of Shariqya (Bahrawy, 2014), Damietta (El Khodary, 2013), Fayoum (Fargaly, 2014) and Gharbiay (Shebl, 2014), mostly in smaller villages. This is not to argue that this was a major trend, but it is nonetheless indicative of the level of polarization and the ability of the regime to mobilize popular support for its repression. The regime would reinforce that trend with the introduction of a hotline to the Interior Ministry, in November 2013, enabling citizens to call in to report on suspected Brotherhood members (El Deeb, 2014). After a car bomb attack in December 2013, targeting the Security Headquarters in the Delta city of Mansoura, left fifteen dead and one hundred injured, the calls to the hotline tripled. At the funeral of one of the victims, the crowds chanted 'The people want the execution of the Brotherhood' and then commenced to set fire to the car of a man who flashed a pro-Morsi symbol, while other attacks targeted the houses of leading members of the Brotherhood (BBC, 2013). The use of the citizen informant tactic was not restricted to the Brotherhood, as it was reused in March 2018 (Egyptain Streets, 2018). This time a new hotline was set up for citizens to report on false news and rumours that could compromise national security – code for reports against fellow citizens who held views opposed to the regime.

This popular participation had a number of significant consequences. First, it allowed the regime to widen its net of repression, such that minor acts of defiance could lead to severe consequences. Second, it allowed the regime to legitimatize its repression, since, according to its narrative, this repression had a popular mandate and was an expression of the organic will of the 'people'. Finally, and most importantly, it entrenched the regime's ideological edifice in the public discourse, while allowing the regime to cement its support base, paving the way for subsequent waves of repression along with the proliferation of conspiracy theories and chauvinistic nationalism to justify it. Indeed, popular participation in the regime's repression has made it an enduring feature and an ideological necessity for the military regime to continue to claim a right to rule, making repression a goal rather than an end.

Sisi the Islamist

Sisi's version of Nasserism is accompanied by another potent ideological force, namely a state-sponsored form of Islamism that uses religious images and rhetoric to justify its repression of the Brotherhood. In a way, this is an attempt to beat the Brotherhood at its own game, by claiming the mantle of piousness and social conservativism from the grasp of the Islamist group. This is coupled with an attempt to claim the mantel of 'religious modernizer', as the regime tries to appeal to its heterogenous base, in a complex and delicate balancing act. This tendency, however, is not limited to the realm of rhetoric, as it is also accompanied by a policy of extending regime control over independent religious institutions, namely Al-Azhar, by playing the modernization card. This is part of the regime's drive to concentrate power in its own hands, as well as part of an attempt to create a top-down state-sponsored version of Islam that the regime can use to discredit its opponents.

In terms of rhetoric and the justification of repression, the regime has been unsparing in its use of religious imagery in portraying the Brotherhood as an extremist sect that is worthy of repression. For example, in February 2019, Dar El Ifta, the national religious institution responsible for issuing religious opinions, tweeted that the Muslim Brotherhood was the Khawarij[4] of this age and that fighting them was the highest form of jihad (BBC, 2019). This effectively lent credence to the terrorist label attached to the group, by evoking a piece of Islamic history to justify its repression, while giving religious legitimacy to the regime's violence against the group. This was not the only statement that justified mass state violence, with Ali Goma, the ex-Mufti who became a member of the 2021 Parliament, making a number of similar pronouncements (Al Badawi, 2021). For example, in January 2015, Goma stated that the Brotherhood was '[t]he most evil of God's creation' and that those that 'kill them or are killed by them are blessed' (Al Anba, 2015) – a clear demonization of the Brotherhood, not only justifying their repression but their physical liquidation as well. Similar statements would continue to be made by Goma in the succeeding years, such as in September 2020, when he declared that '[s]haring' the fake news disseminated by the Brotherhood should be considered a cardinal sin (Ezzeldin, 2020), a pronouncement clearly aimed at discouraging citizens from sharing social media posts critical of the regime.

The use of religious rhetoric not only aimed at justifying repression, but was also used to create a legitimizing narrative for the regime as one that was authentic to 'Islamic' values, in its effort to outbid its Islamist rival. For example, in March 2015, Goma stated that contrary to what some claimed, the regime was implementing Sharia, calling for those that disagreed to move to Saudi Arabia (CNN, 2015). Sisi himself would continuously use religious imagery in his speeches, claiming divinely inspired talents and a connection to godly powers. For example, in June 2015, during a meeting with the Egyptian diaspora in Germany, Sisi claimed that 'God created me a doctor, able to identify alignments, which is a blessing from God' (Al Watan, 2015). Besides the clear megalomania of the statement, Sisi was implicitly claiming divine providence for his actions. This would later be repeated in October 2021, when he claimed that all the regime's achievements were accomplished due to 'Divine support' (Abdel Alim, 2021). In this statement the divine sanction moves from Sisi himself to the entire regime, as one supported directly by God. In another statement made in the same month, Sisi claimed that he would 'argue' against those who claimed that the regime was corrupt in front of God on judgement day, once again claiming divine approval for the regime's policies (Abdel Azzem, 2020).

This rhetoric, however, was also accompanied by a litany of repressive policies aimed at brandishing not only the regime's Islamist credentials but also its conservative and patriarchal credentials, in an attempt to appeal to its conservative base. This manifested itself in the regime's policy towards minorities, women and the LGBTQ+ community. For example, in 2014 (Farid, 2014), 2015 (Al Ahram, 2015) and 2018 (Egypt Today, 2018), Egyptian security forces raided cafes and arrested people that were openly breaking the fast in Ramadan, even though it was not illegal to do so. This was an obvious effort to polish the regime's Islamist credentials. This was not only a discriminatory act against secular-minded Egyptians but also against the country's large Christian minority, as the regime tried to control and Isalmize the public space in its attempt to outbid its Islamist rivals. In terms of dealing with Egypt's Christian minority, the regime failed to pass the Unified House of Worship law, a long-standing demand, which would have equalized the legal requirements for building churches, mosques and any other type of house of worship. Instead, in August 2016, Parliament approved a law dedicated to regulating the building of churches, which continued to impose heavy restrictions on the process, while allowing local governors to deny building permits without a clear reason. In essence, this continued a policy of systematic discrimination against Egypt's Christian minority (Roddy, 2016). This attitude was also manifested in the regime's patriarchal treatment of women. The most infamous example of this is the case of Tik Tok girls, which took place in 2020. The case revolved around the arrest of a number of female content creators for the social media app Tik Tok, who were charged with 'Inciting debauchery, and offending Egyptian Family Values' (Egyptian Front, 2020). Six of the women arrested were sentenced to two or three years in prison. Two women, Haneen Hossam and Mawada al-Adham, were acquitted on appeal in July 2021, only to be retried under the more serious charge of Human Trafficking. Both received draconian custodial sentences, with Hossam sentenced to ten years and Al-Adahm to six years, all for dancing in Tik Tok videos (BBC, 2022) in a manner that would be considered provocative by a conservative audience. This was not the only case involving women, with multiple female content creators arrested, tried and sentenced to either heavy fines a prison sentences – or both (Begum, 2021).

The repression of women went hand in hand with the repression of the LGBTQ+ community, with at least seventy-five people arrested in October 2017 as part of a crackdown triggered by the raising of the Rainbow flag in a music concert in Cairo (EIPR, 2018). The activist Sarah Hegazy was amongst those arrested, and reported being abused by her cellmates, who were encouraged to do so by the security personnel during her detention (Aboulenein, Reuters, 2017). Hegzay would later leave Egypt and commit suicide in June 2020, as a result of her ordeal (Younes, 2020). The crackdown was accompanied by an anti-queer media campaign, which accused homosexuals of receiving funding from abroad as part of a foreign plot to destroy Egyptian society. The Public Prosecutor even ordered the state security prosecutor, whose remit covers terrorism cases, to investigate the Rainbow incident, illustrating the regime's intent to deal with the incident at the highest level. Of the seventy-five arrested, all except two were charged with the 'habitual practice of debauchery'. The remaining two were charged with joining a banned group, a veiled reference to the Brotherhood. This mass wave of arrests, however, was part of an escalating pattern of repression. For example, the average number of arrests made for 'habitual debauchery' between the last quarter of 2013 and late 2017 showed a fivefold increase on the figures for the 2000–2013 period, the military coup clearly marking the beginning of a surge in repression of the LGBTQ+ community (EIPR, 2017). This conservative outlook was even enshrined in the post-coup constitution, in Article 10, which highlighted the family as the cornerstone of society. The family, in turn, was anchored in religion and national morals, with the state designated as responsible for safeguarding the family unit (Manshurat, 2019). This allowed the security apparatus to repress women and other minorities, and impose a patriarchal worldview, under the guise of protecting family values, which appeals to the regime's deeply conservative base while allowing it to compete with the Islamists on their own turf.

The regime's base, however, is heterogeneous, and an important segment of it is the secular urban middle and upper classes, who saw the military coup as the only way to circumvent religious rule. As such, the regime has followed a complex policy of appealing to its conservative base while also attempting to claim the mantel of 'religious modernizer' and 'protector of minorities', a delicate balancing act that it has been fairly successful in pursuing. The regime also weaponized this modernization rhetoric in its attempts to impose control over one of the few remaining national institutions that had escaped its mastery, namely Al-Azhar, one of the most important centres of Islamic learning and theology in the Muslim world, while also repressing independent religious reformers who escaped the regime's direct control.

In its attempt to claim the mantle of 'religious modernizer' and advocate of women's and minority rights, the regime achieved a number of historic firsts. For example, in June 2014, in a decree issued by interim President Adly Mansour, sexual harassment was deemed a criminal offence, punishable by up to five years in prison (BBC, 2014). In 2021, the law was amended, redefining sexual harassment as a felony rather than a misdemeanour, and increasing the penalties for it (Abdelaal, 2021). This was in response to the rampant rise of sexual harassment in the country; a UN survey, conducted in 2013, showed that 99.3% of Egyptian women were subject to some form of sexual harassment, ranking Egypt as the worst Arab country on this issue (El-Rifae, 2014). In addition, the regime's policy of appointing women ministers was a clear attempt to visibly show its support for female empowerment. For example, in January 2018 the regime appointed six female ministers in a historic first, representing 17.6% of the total number of ministers in the cabinet (Egypt Independent, 2018), with the number increasing to eight in the cabinet reshuffle in June of the same year (Shalaby, 2018). In a similar move, in March 2022, Judge Radwa Helmy was appointed to sit on the State Council, the first female judge to do so (Arab News, 2022). Her appointment came after the independence of the judiciary had been severely curtailed as a result of the constitutional amendment of 2019, which will be covered in the next chapter. Helmy's appointment was a politically calculated move by the regime, a top-down decision rather than a reflection of grassroot, democratic changes in the position of women in the judiciary. The regime followed a similar policy in terms of dealing with the Christian community, namely making high-profile appointments to give the appearance of equality. For example, in February 2022, Sisi appointed Judge Bolous Fahmy, a Coptic Christian, as the head of the Constitutional Court, yet another historic first (Mohammad, 2022). This was preceded by the appointment of Manal Awad Mikhail, a Coptic woman, as the Governor of Damietta, also the first appointment of its kind (Al Arabiya, 2018). Sisi has also made a habit of attending Christmas Mass in a token show of support for the Christian community. So, even though the regime has implemented a policy that is mostly conservative, repressive and deeply patriarchal, it has also attempted to give the appearance of secularism and equality by making high-profile appointments of minorities and women to public positions, while repressing the vast majority of the minorities in question. This is a vivid example of tokenism and a top-down approach to civil liberties, where the regime decides who, in each vulnerable social group, is worthy of receiving rights and who is not.

The regime has also embarked on a (mostly rhetorical) campaign of religious reform, intermingled with legal endeavours aimed at curtailing Al-Azhar's independence. For example, in September 2019, as part of a habitual call for religious renewal, Sisi stated that the interpretation of some religious texts was outdated by 800 years, linking the outdated interpretation to the rise of religious extremism (Badawi, 2019). The call for religious renewal had become habitual by the time of that speech, with Sisi repeating the same call no fewer than sixteen times between July 2014 and January 2020 (Nassar, 2020). Arguably the most controversial of these statement was that of February 2017, when he called for law prohibiting oral divorce, a long-standing Islamic tradition (El Shalakany, 2017). This statement was so controversial that the High Ulama Council in Al-Azhar issued a statement openly opposing the President, arguing that oral divorce had been part of Islamic tradition since the time of the Prophet (France 24, 2017). The open clash between Al-Azhar and the regime took another public turn in January 2020, when Shiekh Al Azhar, Ahmed Al Tayeb, openly clashed with the head of Cairo University, Mohamed Othman, after the latter called for a renewal of the Islamic tradition, echoing a number of calls made by Sisi (BBC, 2020). In an indirect rebuff to Sisi, through a response to Othman, El-Taybe stated that religious reforms should not alter Islamic heritage. The clashes between the regime and Al-Azhar were part of an ongoing struggle, as Al-Azhar tried to maintain its independence against the centralizing tendencies of the regime, an independence guaranteed in Article 7 of the post-coup constitution. The struggle with Al-Azhar appeared shortly after the coup, when Al-Tayeb made a statement immediately after the start of the massacre in Raba, criticizing the violent dispersal of the sit-in (YouTube, 2013) – it was the only national institution to do so, in a rare case of public dissent.

This defiance galvanized the regime, not only to engage in verbal sparring with Al-Azhar but to attempt to legally circumvent its independence. This became apparent in August 2020 when Sisi issued a decree designating Dar El-Ifta, the religious institution responsible for issuing religious rulings and under the nominal control of Al-Azhar, as a civil institution of a special character (RT, 2021). This legal manoeuvre allowed Sisi to extend the tenure of Shawky Alam as the Grand Mufti for one year, even though he had reached retirement age (Al Masry Al Youm, 2021). This extension was seen as a clear imposition on the authority of Al-Azhar, which usually selects the Mufti from members of the High Ulama Council. The appointment of Alam was preceded by another legislative manoeuvre, in July 2020, when Parliament started to discuss a law to designate Dar-El Ifta as an independent institution, in effect creating a parallel religious authority to the unruly Al-Azhar, but one under the control of the regime (BBC, 2020). The law aroused so much opposition from Al-Azhar (Abdel Monem, 2020) that, in a rare backdown, the regime was forced to postpone voting on the bill (Al Jazzera, 2020). The regime's claim to be a 'religious modernizer' should be seen as part of its power struggle with Al-Azhar and its desire create a state-sponsored version of Islam, rather than as a real ideological conviction.

The duplicity of the regime was apparent in the repressive policy it followed when dealing with religious reformers that were not under its direct control. For example, in August 2020, security forces arrested Reda Abdel Rahman, a prominent Quranic thinker, on charges of terrorism. Abdel Rahman was accused of joining the Islamic State, even though Quranism is enough to brand him as an apostate, which is the official position of Al-Azhar, let alone the Islamic State (EIPR, 2021). There is also the case of Islam El-Behairy, the prominent religious thinker and reformer, who was sentenced to one year in prison, in July 2016, for 'contempt of religion' (Abdel Hameed, 2016), a charge used to repress religious heterogeneity. These reformers could have been natural allies for the regime, if indeed religious renewal had really been on the agenda, but they might have also challenged the regime's conservative policy, hence their repression was inevitable. Another motive for their repression was, once again, to brandish the regime's conservative credentials as a protector of traditional social values and religious uniformity.

The regime has therefore followed a delicate balancing act of appealing to different constituencies, branding itself as deeply conservative, while attempting to appear as a bulwark against religious extremism and a promoter of religious reform. This policy has been mostly effective in garnering public support, allowing each constituency to interpret the regime's policies from its own vantage point, while the historic repression of minorities in Egypt has continued.

The end game

The regime's moment of hegemony is anchored in a state of polarization and mass state violence. This ideological construct has proven to be extremely appealing, and far more enduring than one would have expected in the summer of 2013. The secret of this appeal lies in the ability of the regime to perpetuate a state of political and social polarization, as well as cultivating the deep historical roots of the regime's revamped version of Nasserism. Indeed, the regime's ability to appeal to its base is anchored in mass state violence that needs to continue in order to justify direct military rule. In simpler terms, the regime needs permanent internal enemies, traitors, terrorists and social deviants to repress in order for its narrative to continue to appeal to its base. This has a number of intended and unintended consequences that will have long-terms effects on Egypt's prospects for democratic transition. The clearest intended consequence is the indoctrination of a large segment of society in the regime's anti-demodectic ethos, which is anchored in notions of national unity, sameness and a conception of Egyptian national identity as ethereal. This indoctrination acts as a strong barrier against the development of a democratic and civic ethos, which is necessary for democratic practice to flourish. The indoctrination is necessary not only for the military to remain in power but to justify the military's monopoly of political power and its restructuring of the state and the economy in a manner that has not been seen since 1952, all in the name of a Sisified version of Nasserism. Indeed, it provided the ideological base for Sisi's passive revolution and its moment of hegemony.

The intended consequences, however, are also accompanied by unintended repercussions, which will severely restrict the regime's policy options. For example, the regime's ideological construct, which relies heavily on the vilification of the opposition and the insistence on the necessity of repression, will act as an ideological straitjacket stifling elite-led reform. In other words, the regime requires a state of perpetual crisis in order to remain in power – if the crisis is resolved, then the ideological appeal of the regime fades away. This leaves the regime with limited policy options, besides repression, in dealing with the opposition. Hence, the prospect of national reconciliation or the easing of repression becomes an unlikely prospect, since repression is now an ideological necessity that the regime cannot escape. This leaves the regime ill-equipped to deal with social unrest, since rather than absorb social protest through accommodation, it is more likely to call on mass repression as its preferred policy response, severely curtailing the ability of the regime to absorb popular anger through concessions. If it does otherwise, the regime would be subjected to immense pressure, not only from its popular base but also from within the security apparatus which have been deeply indoctrinated in this ideology. Sisi and his regime have not only taken a large segment of the population hostage, but have inadvertently taken themselves and their supporters along with them.

Chapter 2

THE NEW LEVIATHAN

'Egypt is a Semi-State.'

— Abdel Fattah El-Sisi

The concentration of political power in the hands of the military establishment following the coup of 2013 required radical changes in the state structure. This not only refers to legal and constitutional changes that vested the military with vast powers, but also the nature of the political system and the role of civilians in it. Indeed, there has been a thorough militarization of the state apparatus, with the dominance of the security services extending to the legislatives and judicial branches of government, beyond anything that the security services under the Mubarak regime were capable of. Even though there is a certain level of continuity between Mubarak and Sisi, most notably the dominance of the security apparatus in unelected local government, there are radical differences between the two autocrats – differences that characterize the shift from a system of dual military rule to direct military rule and the rise of the military as the uncontested master of the state.

The significance of this development should not be underestimated. Indeed, the Egyptian state has undergone a process of structural regression, in which the classic separation of powers between the executive, judicial and legislative branches has been almost completely eroded. Furthermore, as will be discussed in detail below, the military has now been placed in a dominant position vis-à-vis the presidency as a result of the latest constitutional amendments, a precaution in case the post slips out of the hands of the generals. The consequences of this process are legion and deeply troubling for the prospect of democratic transition. First, the entrenchment of the military establishment as the master of the state apparatus creates an institutional interest in maintaining the status quo. Hence, the struggle for democratic rights becomes a struggle against the military establishment, going beyond Sisi. Second, the process of state restructuring not only concentrates power in the hands of the military but also reduces the capacity of other organs of the state to provide public goods, as will be illustrated in the regime's response to the Covid-19 pandemic, considered below. Finally, any attempts at a democratic transition, even limited liberal reform, would require the complete overhaul of the state apparatus, not only at the constitutional and national levels but also at the level of local government, a herculean task to say the least. These hurdles are immense and will ensure that democratic transition is delayed by years, if not decades.

The dominance of the military over the state apparatus, however, was not straightforward or without difficulties. Indeed, there was some significant resistance to this hard-line approach, most notably within the judiciary, which manifested itself during the transfer of the two Red Sea islands, Tiran and Sanafir, from Egyptian to Saudi sovereignty. There was also some resistance to the consolidation of power under Sisi within the ranks of the top brass, which came to the fore during the presidential election of 2018. However, the notion that resistance to Sisi's re-election can be equated with resistance to the consolidation of power under the military needs to be treated with caution and methodically analysed, as the two are not naturally synonymous. This will be done at the end of this chapter.

The expansion of the power of the military establishment, however, was not only confined to the apparatus of the state. On the contrary, through the control of the state, the military was able to assemble a myriad of repressive laws that ensured the closure of the public space, providing a legal framework for its repression. Indeed, the military's dominance over the state precipitated a process of 'depoliticization' of the public space, which ensured the military's dominance over the everyday lives of ordinary Egyptians, in a truly Orwellian fashion. The power of the state, and the military, now penetrates the minds and consciousness of millions of Egyptians, in a truly unprecedent scale. Indeed, dominance over the state apparatus was an essential prerequisite for the success of Sisi's passive revolution and the far-reaching social changes that the regime initiated.

Before proceeding with a detailed analysis, it is worth elaborating on what I mean by the word 'state' within the context of this book. Gramsci presented a number of definitions for the term in his *Prison Notebooks*, written while imprisoned by the Fascist regime in Italy.[1] The one that I find most relevant to the case of Egypt under direct military rule is a definition that views the state as merger between the concepts of civil and political society. In simpler terms, the state as a social formation contains both: the public apparatus of the state (political society), such as the judicial system, and the private apparatus (civil society), like the media, education system and so on (Carnoy, 1983). Accordingly, the state is everywhere and is the tool used by the ruling classes to project their power over society, which is very germane to the Egyptian case. Indeed, the ultimate goal of the Egyptian military establishment is not only dominance over the public state apparatus, but the use of its position to accumulate social power, extending the boundaries of the state so that it swallows up the private sphere – establishing total dominance over society and transforming the public space into a militarized space. This metaphor has been used by Zineb Abu-El Magd in her detailed study of the military's economic empire (Abu Al Magd, 2018), albeit through a Foucaultian theoretical lens. Abu-El Magd has argued that the military's economic dominance allowed it to penetrate the lives of ordinary Egyptians, transforming the country into a military camp. In this chapter, however, I intend to use the metaphor to examine the military's dominance over the state and its ability to use the state apparatus to transform the public space, in a manner that is unique to Sisi and his regime.

The ideological bedrock of this process can be traced back to the Sissified version of Nasserism that the regime adopted after the coup, with the superiority of the military establishment being its most salient aspect. Indeed, without the wide popular acceptance of this ideological construct the regime would not have been able to implement such radical changes without a significant popular backlash. The massacres of the summer of 2013 and the popular support that the regime enjoyed were a critical turning point and essential for empowering the military to radically alter the state in its own image.

This chapter starts with an examination of the constitutional and legal framework that paved the way for the military's dominance of the state apparatus, as well as the myriad of repressive laws used to penetrate the public space. This is followed by an examination of the impact of this militarization on the regime response to the Covid-19 pandemic, which illustrates the consequence of this relentless militarization in what should have been a technocratic response to a public health crisis. Finally, the chapter closes with an examination of dissent in the ranks of the elites against this trend, and the responses of the regime to this resistance, as well as the impact of this militarization on the prospect of democratic transition.

A militarized constitution

On 23 April 2019, the National Election Authority announced the results of a referendum on constitutional amendments proposed to the 2014 constitution. The results, to no one's surprise, was a resounding win for the 'Yes' vote, with 88% of voters approving the proposed amendments. The amendment that received the most attention was the change in Article 140, which extended the presidential term of office from four to six years. Article 241 was also added to allow Sisi to run two additional six-year terms, starting in 2024. This opens the way for Sisi to stay in power till 2036. At the time, the specious argument was made that Sisi should be allowed to run again for two additional terms since he will be sworn on the basis of a new constitution, even though the two-terms limit remained in place. Besides the extension of the Sisi presidency, there are other, arguably much more important, amendments that drastically extend the powers of the military, well beyond the rights granted in the 2014 constitution, which was already extremely favourable to the military establishment. The military's power grab has, effectively, undermined the structure of the modern Egyptian state, establishing it as the guardian of the constitutional order, while severely encroaching on the concept of the separation of powers (Egypt Information Portal, 2019).

The most notable amendment is the alteration to Article 200, which describes the constitutional role of the military. This amendment extends the military's duties to include the 'protection of the constitution, democracy, the state and its secular nature, and personal freedoms'. This phrase has radical implications, the most notable of which is that it paves the way for continued military intervention in politics, if and when it deems that the secular nature of the state, democracy or personal freedoms are threatened by an elected, civilian government. This is very cynical, considering that the military autocracy has been the main violator of the freedoms mentioned in the amendment. In fact, this is the military's option of last resort, in the event that popular pressure forces a free election and that a civilian government is elected. This is a very similar argument to the one made by the Algerian military on the eve of the coup in 1992, when elections won by FIS were voided, triggering a bloody civil war that lasted the better part of a decade (Evans and John, 2007). Hidden in the language of the amendment is a very dangerous ideological imperative, which identifies the military with the 'state' rather than with the elected government of the day. It assumes that since the military is serving the 'state', then the military –

and only the military – is able to defend the 'state' against the incompetence of civilians. In other words, the amendment assumes that the military's supremacy over civilians is the natural order of things. This assumption is deeply rooted in the regime's ideological construct, where the 'state' is imagined as an almost mythical entity that has to be protected against the folly of civilian politicians and the demands for democratization. In essence, the amendment turns the concept of popular sovereignty on its head, with the source of sovereignty transferred from the popular will to the military, as the ultimate guardian of the 'state'. This entrenches a paternalistic attitude towards the citizenry, as incompetent simpletons who, in a moment of folly, might elect a government that could destroy the 'state'. Finer identifies acceptance of civilian supremacy as one of the pre-conditions for restraining a military's interventionist appetite (Finer, 2002). This is clearly not the case in Egypt, where prospective future coups now have a solid constitutional basis.

This is not the only amendment that enhanced the constitutional position of the military. For example, in the 2014 constitution, Article 234 stipulated that the selection of the Minister of Defence required the approval of the Supreme Council of the Armed Forces (SCAF). This article was due to expire on the conclusion of the first two presidential terms after the constitution was ratified. In 2019, this term limit was removed, meaning that the President requires the approval of SCAF to appoint the Minister of Defence, in effect ensuring that the top brass have a veto over the position. This, in essence, allows the military to select its own head, and strengthens its position in relation to the President. This is yet another insurance policy in case a candidate not in sync with the top brass is ever nominated for the post. Furthermore, Article 201 stipulates that the Minister of Defence has to be a military officer, ensuring that no civilian can holds the position. This, in essence, transforms the military into a fiefdom, completely beyond civilian control.

In addition to increasing the power of the military within the political system, the 2019 amendments increased the military's direct reach into the public space. This comes in the form of Article 204, which pertains to the jurisdiction of the military's judicial system. This article stipulates that military courts have jurisdiction in any case that involves military buildings, bases, equipment, public finances, military factories and any public building that is officially protected by the military. In the 2014 constitution the phrase 'direct transgression' was used in the article, slightly restricting the military courts' jurisdiction, but in the 2019 version the word 'direct' was removed. This dramatically increased the reach of military courts, enabling them to target dissent and further extend their authority into civilian life. Prior to this, on 27 October 2014, Sisi had issued a presidential decree, the 'Law for Protection of Public and Vital Entities', in which the military was tasked with the protection of public buildings and infrastructure, directly extending the jurisdiction of military courts, since any interference with those buildings now fell within their remit (Kingsley, 2014). Public buildings and infrastructure are therefore considered to be under military protection, even if domestic security forces are the ones actually tasked with safeguarding the buildings. This decree was intended to last for two years; however, it was made permanent in October 2021 (Ali, 2021). The consequences of this law and the aforementioned constitutional amendment are legion. For example, military courts can be used to repress labour dissent, if an industrial action is organized in one of the military's factories or commercial enterprises, which, considering the military's growing economic footprint, is a gloomy prospect for labour rights.[2] In addition, public protests would also fall under the jurisdiction of military courts if public buildings were involved in such protests. Thus, the buildings in question no longer need to be directly affected by protests, hence all forms of protest can theoretically fall under the jurisdiction of military courts. As a consequence, some 7,420 civilians have been tried by military courts between 2014 and 2016. Most defendants were sentenced after mass trials that failed to apply due process, but instead reached verdicts based on confessions extracted under torture (HRW, 2016).

The expansion of the power of the military within the constitutional order was accompanied by a deliberate reduction in the independence of the judiciary. This can be seen as a response to the struggle with some senior judges over the transfer over the two islands in the Red Sea from Egyptian to Saudi sovereignty. The most relevant of the constitutional amendments is the alteration made to Article 185, which gave the President the power to appoint the head of judicial authorities from a pool of seven candidates, determined by seniority. The article also provides for the creation of a High Council for Judicial Authorities, headed by the President, which is responsible for the appointment, promotion and disciplining of members of the various judicial bodies. The encroachment on the independence of the judiciary also extends to the Supreme Constitutional Court (SCC), which, theoretically, could act as a bulwark against the regime's policies. Article 193 was amended to give the President the power to select the head of the court from a pool of the five most senior vice presidents of the court. Previously, the President only issued the appointment decree, but did not make the selection himself. The President was also granted the authority to select these vice presidents from a pool of two candidates, one nominated by the head of the SCC and the other by its General Assembly. The amendments also give the President the power to appoint the head and members of the SCC's Commissioners Committee – a panel of experts that provides non-binding legal opinions – from among nominees provided by the SCC president

The curtailing of the power of the judiciary also extended to the State Council, a system of courts which adjudicates disputes between different public administrative bodies and between the state and the populace. In other words, it is the place where cases of state corruption or abuse could be raised. In the 2019 amendments, the role of the State Council was dramatically reduced. Most notably, the review of contracts in which the state is a party is no longer automatic; cases now need to be referred to the court. The cases referred to the State Council are those stipulated by law, which is issued by the military-controlled Parliament. This reduces the supervisory role of the State Council, opening up the opportunity for more graft and making it more difficult for the judiciary to challenge the executive. No judicial body was named to replace the State Council in the performance of an automatic review of state contracts.

The final nail in the coffin of judicial independence is the process for the selection of the Attorney General. The amendment to Article 189 gives the President the power to select and appoint the Attorney General from a pool of three candidates nominated by the High Judicial Council. Before the amendment, the power to appoint the Attorney General was in the hands of the High Judicial Council alone, with the President simply responsible for issuing the final decree that confirmed the appointment.

The curtailing of the power of the State Council and the judiciary came in response to the dispute over the transfer of the two Red Sea islands, Tiran and Sanafir, from Egyptian to Saudi sovereignty, which will be covered later in this chapter. However, it is important to consider the history of the State Council during the Mubarak era to fully appreciate the significance of the changes that have been made. By the early 1990s the administrative courts, which are part of the State Council, started to emerge as an area of contention between the opposition and the Mubarak regime. The opposition started to file lawsuits against the regime to reverse certain policies, using the State

Council as a tool for agitation and the mobilization of public opinion against the regime. For example, in 1996 the leaders of a number of opposition parties and a number of prominent case lawyers filed a law suit against the second round of the ongoing public sector privatization programmes. The government lawyer pointed out, not inaccurately, that a case like this should be resolved in the Parliament and not in court, but the main goal was to stir public opinion, and in that the opposition was successful. The court heard, and gave its opinion on, topics ranging from the privatization of refuse collection in the cities (which was struck down by the court) to the controversial gas deal with Israel and the right of the Mubarak regime to have civilians tried in military courts. In some cases the court overturned government policy, while in others it ruled against the plaintiff. This growing contestation in the court system coincided with a growing movement for judicial independence in the country, which directly challenged the Mubarak regime (El Ghobashy, 2021, pp. 68–75). Hence, the constitutional amendment introduced by Sisi had a clear and primary goal, namely to ensure that it would no longer be possible for opponents of the regime to use the courts to further their cause.

The constitutional framework described above reflects the nature of governance in Egypt, that is, the reality of direct military rule. Indeed, the military has tailored a constitution that not only ensures an uncontested position of legal supremacy, but also erodes the basis of the modern Egyptian state by undermining the independence of the judiciary – a policy that has dramatic consequences. The legal position of the military means that any attempts at democratization would first require a reform of the Egyptian constitutional order that would place the military in a subordinate position to the elected government and restore judicial independence. This is a daunting challenge, since it would require a fundamental ideological shift within the military establishment towards acceptance of civilian supremacy, and an identification with the government of the day rather than with the abstract 'state'. This is a hurdle that will require strong popular pressure to overcome.

The military's legal immunity

The dominant constitutional position that the military enjoys is augmented by a number of laws that provide its members with legal immunity against possible prosecution for acts of political violence and fiscal misconduct. In July 2018, the Egyptian Parliament approved a new law entitled 'The Law for Treatment of Senior officers of the Armed Forces' (Reuters, 2018). This law has a number of important elements, which frees the military from any restraints when repressing dissenting (Manshurat, 2018). It also increases Sisi's control over the top brass and ensures its unity, in essence preventing any senior generals from challenging Sisi in a future election. Article 1 of the law gives the President the power to recall any senior officer out of retirement to serve in the Armed Forces for life. The ranks that qualify as 'senior' are not specified in the law, giving the President the flexibility to select any officer he sees fit. This provision acts to quell the presidential ambitions of the top brass, since Egyptian law prohibits active members of the Armed Forces from running for public office (Gad, 2018). It is notable that this law was issued after the ex-Chief of Staff Sami Annan attempted to run for President in 2018, in a case of rare dissent against Sisi (the details of this will be covered below). This prohibition, which is the 'stick' part of the equation, is also accompanied by a 'carrot', namely Article 2, which gives the recalled senior officer the rank of minister. This is also coupled with Articles 3 and 4, which give the President the right to grant unspecified privileges to the recalled officers, as well as the power to grant them any military decorations that he sees fit. These decorations and ranks have a direct impact on the level of financial compensation that the officer in question receives. Hence, senior officers are compensated financially in lieu of pursuing any political ambitions, strengthening Sisi's control over the top generals.

The law also grants immunity to senior members of the Armed Forces for any acts they may have committed in their official capacity, covering the period from 3 July 2013 to 10 January 2016. This was the period that witnessed the worst massacres of protestors in modern Egyptian history, where hundreds were killed by the security forces, including the Raba and Republican Guard massacres.[3] The immunity granted also includes diplomatic immunity, which applies in the case of an officer who travels abroad. In essence, the regime is acting to protect the top brass from possible legal prosecution, both domestically and internationally,[4] bearing in mind that there is mounting and tangible evidence of crimes against humanity committed by the regime (HRW, 2014). It is also worth noting that Egypt is not a member of the International Criminal Court (ICC), and hence human rights abuses in the country can only be referred to the court by the Security Council, an unlikely prospect considering the regime's position as a Western ally (ICC, 2011).

The immunity of the military is further augmented by other laws and constitutional articles, which makes it very difficult to use legal means to hold the military accountable . First, there is Article 204 of the Egyptian constitution (Manshurat, 2019), which stipulates that members of the Armed Forces and the General Intelligence Services can only be tried by military courts for crimes committed in the line of duty. The nature of the crimes is not specified, and hence can plausibly be extended to cover financial misconduct and fraud. The military judicial system is hardly impartial in this set-up since the judges are themselves officers. Indeed, this provides army officers with an extra layer of protection in the form of a highly sympathetic judicial system. Second, there are two legal amendments issued before the coup of 2013; ironically the most relevant, namely the amendment to Law 25, was issued in April 2012 by the Parliament dominated by the Muslim Brotherhood, when an uneasy alliance was in place between the military and the Islamist group. The amendment to Law 25, originally issued in 1966 and amended in 2012, laid down that an officer in the Armed Forces could only be summoned before a military court on charges of financial misconduct after that officer's retirement (El Abd, 2018). This makes it very difficult to prosecute on grounds of corruption, not only because of the sympathetic nature of the military judicial system, but also because of the length of time required to bring such charges forward. In addition, the top brass is shielded from prosecution if they are recalled for lifelong service by the President, since, in practice, they never retire. This amendment in essence provides the military with an official green light for mass graft and financial misconduct. Finally, there is the amendment to Law 133, issued in 2011, called the 'Exceptional Legal Rule', which states that any member of SCAF who were serving during the 25 January revolution has to remain in reserve military service even after they reach retirement age (Basal, 2018). This ensures that those who were members of SCAF during the first transitional period have a safe exit from power, since they cannot stand trial in front of civilian courts for acts of violence committed in the period between 2011–12.

This array of unprecedent laws has a number of significant consequences, the most notable of which is the creation of a parallel legal system, which acts to shield the military from civilian oversight or control. This not only creates a state within a state but also allows the military to operate in a legal vacuum, where acts of political violence and financial graft are almost impossible to prosecute. This dual legal system also allows the military to extend its power within the state apparatus, since they are not accountable for acts of repression, which are directed against their political opponents. Finally, and arguably most importantly, the Egyptian constitutional and legal system closes all avenues for holding the military accountable within the existing legal structures. As such, there is no other option than to act outside the legal system, through public protests, heightening the likelihood of social unrest. Indeed, the military establishment has constructed a legal system that leaves the populace no choice but to defy it, leaving blunt repression as the only method to ensure the regime's stability. The heart of this system is the ideological belief in the supremacy of the military establishment, which no civilian, no matter what his position, is allowed to contest, even by legal means. This is a perfect recipe for mass upheaval.

The militarization of the public space

The dominant position of the military establishment within the Egyptian political system ushered in a process of militarization of the public space. A number of laws were issued, either by the Interim President Adly Mansour or under the Sisi presidency, that completely closed the public space and unleashed the security apparatus to carry out repression at will. This is not to argue that the security apparatus under Mubarak was humane or restrained, but there has been a clear qualitative shift in the legal framework in which it now operates. This shift has led to a penetration of the state into the lives of millions of Egyptians, in an unprecedent fashion. In a Gramscian sense, the state grew to encompass the private sphere, with the state's tentacles evident everywhere.

The first law issued to restrict access to the public space was Law 107, introduced by the Interim President Adly Mansour (Carlstrom, 2013). The law is called 'Organising the Right to Public Meetings, Processions and Peaceful Demonstrations', better known domestically as the 'Protest Law' (Manshurat, 2013). The law was promulgated by the transitional government under Prime Minister Hazem El Beblawi (Amer, 2013), which was dominated by secular liberals and leftist political figures. The argument made at the time by these politicians was that there was an urgent need to restore 'order' and 'stability' after years of upheaval, familiar arguments used by autocrats to justify the repression of dissent. The law severely restricts the right to protest, imposing heavy fines and prison sentences on those who break it, while giving the security forces the green light to use lethal force to disperse such protests. This signalled the beginning of the consolidation of the power by the military and the restriction of the ability of the opposition to exert pressure on the regime through popular action.

The first restriction appears in Article 5 of the law, which criminalizes the use of places of worship as places of protest or gathering points for demonstrations. This might appear reasonable to some, but places of worship played a critical role in the mass protest of 2011, where they acted as gathering points for the planned marches. The importance of mosques and churches is that they provide a semblance of protection against the violence of security forces, as the authorities are more hesitant about storming such buildings, thereby giving protestors, by default, a safe haven to assemble. Article 5 was followed by Article 7, which criminalized any acts that involved 'disturbing the public order', affecting 'production' or trespassing on public building or roads: in essence, any act of protest that has a tangible effect on the public space was outlawed. This also includes the criminalization of strikes, sit-ins or walk-outs, since they directly affect production. It is important to remember that industrial action and strikes were an important element in Mubarak's downfall, with waves of strikes paving the way for the 2011 mass protests and in the decision of the military to push Mubarak out (Alexander and Bassiouny, 2014).

The law also grants the security forces considerable leeway in cancelling protests and the use of repressive tactics. For example, Article 10 of the law gives the Minister of the Interior or the local head of security the right to cancel protests, if information comes to hand that suggests that the planned protest will negatively affect public order. This article was deemed unconstitutional by the Supreme Constitutional Court (SCC) on 3 December 2016. It was then rephrased and approved by the Parliament on 10 March 2017 (Lasheen, 2017), with the amendment stating that a judge had to approve the cancellation of a protest. This was not considered to be a major victory for regime opponents, since the SCC held that the other provisions of the law were constitutional, but it was nonetheless a rare sign of dissent within the ranks of the state apparatus. This was before the constitutional amendments of 2019, which heavily restricted the independence of the judiciary. The power of the security forces was further extended by Article 14, which gives the Minister of the Interior the power to designate certain areas as 'Secure Zones', where protest and gathering are prohibited. This power is absolute, with no clear specification as to what qualifies a certain area to be worthy of such designation, nor is the size of the proposed 'Secure Zone' mentioned in the law. In January

2017 the Ministry of the Interior issued a decree designating a distance of 800 metres around government buildings in Cairo as 'Secure Zones' (TIMEP, 2018), severely restricting the right to protest and access to public space. The law also has highly punitive aspects, in particular heavy jails terms. For example, breaking Article 7 carries a two- to five-year prison sentence coupled with a heavy fine ranging from Eg£50,000 to Eg£100,000. Articles 12 and 13 of the law specify the methods that can be used to disperse protests, which includes the use of live shotgun pellets, something that has been documented to cause severe injury and even death and among peaceful protestors, since the eruption of mass protest in 2011 (Amensty, 2012).

The Protest Law was followed by the introduction of the 'Anti-Terror Law' in August 2015, and its amendment in 2021 (Manshurat, 2021), which is widely used to repress dissent and imprison pro-democracy activists. Indeed, the standard package of charges available for use against peaceful activists includes that of 'joining a terrorist organization', regardless of the affiliation of the person arrested. The pretext for issuing this law was the assassination of the Attorney General, Hesham Barakt, on 29 June 2015 in a bomb attack (BBC, 2015), the highest government official killed in the spate of violent attacks after the coup of 2013. The most prominent and worrying feature of the law is its vague definition of what constitutes a 'Terror Act', a definition so malleable that is can be applied to any act of dissent, from organizing a protest to a critical post on social media. The definition mentioned in Article 2 of the law defines a terror act as including obstruction of government operations, occupation of private and public buildings, as well as damaging national security, social peace and national harmony – a coded reference to sectarian strife. According to this law, a terror act also includes acts that damage the national economy, the communication network and the banking system. The definition is further broadened by declaring the aiding, supporting and preparation of these actions to be acts of terrorism. Based on this definition, a critical post on Facebook can be considered to be a terror act, as indeed has been the case, since, in the eyes of the regime, it negatively affects social peace. A notable example of the application of this law is the case of prominent activist Alaa Abdel-Fattah, who was arrested in September 2019 and charged with joining a terrorist group (OMCT, 2021), a veiled reference to the Muslim Brotherhood. The evidence cited against him was a Facebook post. Abdel-Fattah was sentenced in December 2021 to five years in prison (BBC, 2021). He had already spent five years in prison for breaking the Protest Law, and was only released in the summer of 2019 before being rearrested a few months later. Indeed, acts of peaceful protest can also fall foul of this law, since they necessarily affect government operations and might include the occupation of public buildings.

The broad definition of terrorism contained in the law is coupled with complete legal immunity granted to member of the security services. Article 8 states that members of the security forces cannot be prosecuted for the use of force when acting in their official capacity. The article does not specify when force should be used, nor to what extent. Indeed, the article reads like a blanket immunity granted to members of the security forces. This immunity had immediate consequences, with 755 people killed in alleged shootouts with the security forces (HRW, 2021) between January 2015 and December 2020, with only one suspect arrested. The police alleged that all of those killed were militants belonging to the Muslim Brotherhood, but very few details were provided in police statements. There is considerable evidence that these were in fact cases of extrajudicial killings (HRW, 2021), with some of the men killed already held in custody according to the testimony of relatives. Torture marks were sometimes visible on the bodies of the victims. Human Rights watch stated that 'documented incidents demonstrate a clear pattern of unlawful killings and cast serious doubt on almost all reported "shootouts"'.

In addition to the immunity of the security forces, the law was amended in November 2021 (RT, 2021) after the State of Emergency was lifted – exceptional circumstances that gives that security forces wide power of arrest, and which will be discussed in detail below. Article 53 was now added to the law, granting the President the power to take necessary measures to maintain 'Public Safety', including the depopulation of certain areas, isolating them and applying a state of emergency in the designated areas. This decision has to be approved by Parliament within seven days of being made, enough time to ensure that the security forces had already stamped out any forms of protest.

A law closely related to the terrorism law is Law 8, issued in February 2015 and entitled 'The Regulation of Terrorist Entities and Terrorists' (Manshurat, 2015). This law gives the Public Prosecutor the power to issue lists of supposed terrorist and terrorists entities, without the need for a prior conviction. The list has to be approved by the special criminal judicial circuit at the Cairo Appeals Court, based on the evidence provided by the Public Prosecutor. The list is valid for three years, and if the persons or entities are not convicted of terrorism during this period, then their names are removed from the list. However, the Public

Prosecutor is free to add their names to a new list to be confirmed by the court. This law gives the security services a wide array of powers against those named on the terror lists, including the right to ban entities named on the list, seize their assets and prohibit fund raising for them. The same applies to individuals named on the list, where besides having their assets seized, they lose their political rights, their passports can be confiscated or not renewed, and they can be banned from leaving the country, all without a conviction for a crime. Even though it was issued a few months before the 'Anti-Terror Law', the Regulation of Terrorist Entities and Terrorists law shares the same vague definition of what constitutes terrorism, allowing the Public Prosecutor to place anyone on the list who is engaged in dissent. This includes, for example, one of the most beloved sports figures in Egypt, retired footballer Mohamed Aboutrika, who was added to the terror list in January 2017 (BBC, 2017), accused of financing the Muslim Brotherhood, a charge that was never proved in court. In 2021, Aboutrika was again added to the list, a decision that will remain in effect until 2023 (Kahzan, 2021). The football star now lives in exile in Doha. Other prominent individuals to fall foul of this law is the businessman Safwan Thabet and his son Seif, the owners of Juhayna, a local, family owned, consumer good company specializing in dairy products, who were added to the list after alleged disputes with the security services over the ownership of their company (HRW, 2021). This is the clearest example of the regime using its dominant position in the state apparatus, and its complete control over the repressive organs of the state, to secure economic benefits.

The tentacles of the state and the security apparatus also extends to the realm of civil society, where a new law was issued that severely restricted its operations, namely Law 149, issued in 2019 (Manshurat, 2019). The first version of the law was issued in May 2017 (Manshurat, 2017), but was so heavily criticized for its draconian punishments (including harsh prison sentences) that it was replaced with a milder version, issued in August 2019. The less severe version, which will be discussed here, kept most of the restrictions in place but removed the most draconian prison sentences. The most restrictive aspect of this law is mentioned in Article 3, which states that the charter of all civil society organizations should state their respect for 'public order', 'National Security' and 'Public Morals'. This is coupled with Article 14, which prohibits NGO activities in areas that are deemed to negatively affect these three taboo topics, in essence outlawing organizations that are involved in human rights work, since these might be deemed by the government to be violating 'National Security', and any organization that is concerned with issues that are considered to be taboo in Egyptian society, like LGBTQ+ and sexual rights. Article 14 also prohibits NGOs from conducting surveys and field research and publishing the results until these activities have been approved by the Central Agency for Mobilization and Statistic (CAPMAS), a government agency. Moreover, there are severe restrictions placed on the ability of an NGO to raise funds. For example, NGOs are only allowed to raise funds with government approval, both domestically and internationally, while any funds received without such approval are subject to confiscation (HRW, 2019). This allows the regime to choke the supply of funds to an NGO if deemed appropriate. There are also severe restrictions placed on the ability of foreign NGOs to work in Egypt, where licenses can be revoked if the work of the NGO is deemed to affect 'National Security' or 'Public Order', based on Article 74 of law. In addition, local NGOs are prohibited from working with foreign experts or volunteers unless approved by the relevant minister. All of these restrictions have had a major negative impact on the ability of NGOs and civil society organizations to work in the country. The most notable example of this impact was the closure of the Arab Network for Human Rights, founded by the prominent human rights defender Gamal Eid. Eid explained that the closure was due to the unprecedent repression and harassment that he and his staff had faced, even though he had attempted to comply with the new NGO law (Selim, 2022). He stated that the informal message received from the regime was that the Arab Network should stop working on human rights and freedom of expression topics, prompting Eid to close the NGO rather than become, in his phraseology, 'complicit' in the regime's repression.

No analysis of the regime's legal framework of repression would be complete without inclusion of the Emergency Law, originally issued in 1958, a reincarnation of the martial law first declared by the British in 1914 to allow the British commander in Egypt to act as military governor during the First World War (Manshurat, 1958). The Emergency Law comes into effect on the declaration of a State of Emergency, a power granted to the President, and reviewed by Parliament, which can be extended every three months on parliamentary approval. The State of Emergency became infamous during the rule of Mubarak, as it was in effect for almost thirty years (BBC, 2012), the entire duration of his period in power, and was the main legal tool he used to repress dissent (HRW, 2008). It was only allowed to lapse in 2012, in a time of popular mobilization. A State of Emergency was declared by Sisi in April 2017 (Brown, 2017), after the bombing of two churches which led to the death of forty-five people (HRW, 2017). It was amended by Sisi in 2020, making it even more draconian. The law gives the security forces wide powers, including the power to detain suspects for one month without charge, a period that can be extended indefinitely after approval from a court; the power to restrict public gatherings and demonstrations with no judicial oversight; and the power to confiscate and close down publications and newspapers. It also gives the President the power to assign the task of maintaining order to members of the Armed Forces, with the military prosecutor having jurisdiction over all violations of the law in areas under the protection of the military – in essence, turning the military into a tool of internal repression. However, the most important aspect of the law is the creation of a parallel system of courts, called the State Emergency Courts, whose verdicts cannot be appealed. These courts are notorious for harsh sentences and violation of due process. The law also gives the President the power to appoint military officers, with the rank of captain and above, as judges in the State Emergency Courts, thereby transforming these courts into a branch of the military's judicial system.

In October 2021 the State of Emergency was lifted, in what was hailed by the regime as a sign of success in achieving stability (Reuters, 2022). However, after the State of Emergency was lifted, a number of amendments to existing legislation were passed to ensure that the State of Emergency became permanent, making the law redundant. This included the amendment to the Law for Protection of Public and Vital Entities, discussed earlier. The amendment now made the originally temporary law permanent, allowing the President to assign the military tasks for maintaining regime security, in effect permanently transforming it into a tool for internal repression and facilitating the further encroachment of the jurisdiction of military courts into civilian life. The anti-terror law was also amended, giving the President the power to designate the security agency that was to implement his directives, a thinly veiled reference to the military, once again ensuring that the military could be deployed to repress dissent without legal hinderance.

The militarization of the public space is not limited to physical space, but also extends to social and traditional media. The long arm of the regime leaves no stone unturned. There were two laws issued in August 2018 that were concerned with the regulation of social and traditional media. The first was Law 175, also known as 'The Law to Combat Cybercrime' (Manshurat, 2018). Article 7 of the law gives the security services the power to block websites and media outlets that are deemed to be a threat to 'National Security', a decision that needs to be confirmed by the relevant court. The blockages of websites critical of the government predates the introduction of this law, with the first batch of websites blocked in May 2017 (SAYADI, 2018). The list has been growing ever since, exceeding 500 websites by July 2018 (Open Observatory of Network Interference, Association for Freedom of Thought and Expression, 2018). There is no evidence of judicial involvement in this process, and some of the most notable websites, like news outlet Mada Masr which was blocked in 2017, remain blocked, without any criminal conviction. The law also stipulates, in Article 34, that the maximum prison sentences are handed down if the law is violated with the intention of harming 'National Security', 'National Unity' or 'Social Harmony'. Article 25 of the law also stipulates a minimum of six months in prison if 'Egyptian Family Values' are violated, a vague term used to repress those with different sexual orientations and religious beliefs.

The second piece of legislation concerned with the regulation of social and traditional media is the law for the 'Regulation of Journalism, Media, and the High Media Council' (Manshurat, 2018), issued two weeks after the 'The Law to Combat Cybercrime' was approved. The 'Regulation of Journalism' law is concerned with the regulation of different forms of media, at the discretion of the High Media Council, a body created in the constitution of 2014 with the principal task of regulating the operation of the media and exercising wide-ranging powers detailed in this law. For example, Article 4 of the law gives the High Media Council the right to ban media material if it is deemed harmful to 'National Security', without any form of judicial review being required. In addition, any media material that offends 'Public Decency' is to be banned. Article 19 states that media outlets and websites are prohibited from publishing 'False News', with the definition of media outlets covering social media accounts that have more than 5,000 followers, in effect the Facebook and Twitter accounts of prominent activists. Accusations of spreading 'False News' would become a staple in the charges levied against peaceful activists, with evidence including Twitter and Facebook posts. For example, in January 2022, Haitham El-Banna, a member of the El-Dostour Party, was arrested at his home because of a tweet reminiscing about the mass protest of 2011. He was charged with joining a terrorist organization, spreading false news and misusing social media (The New Arab, 2022) – a standard set of charges drawn from a mind-boggling array of repressive laws.

Hence, the regime has built a comprehensive legal framework that allows it not only to repress dissent but also to deeply penetrate the public space and control the public discourse. Besides the obvious repression meted out against its opponents, the regime has the power to penetrate the lives of millions of its subjects, creating an environment with very little room to publicly protest or even express dissenting views on social media for fear of retribution by the authorities. This is all in the name of preserving the organic unity of the people and ensuring the primacy of the military as the guardian of the nation and the state.

A state undone

The complex legal framework which has provided the military with vast powers and has allowed it to colonize the public space is the product of a process of state restructuring, in which the security and intelligence services have systematically undermined the independence of the legislative and judicial branches of government. This process not only ensured the concentration of power in the hands of the military, paving the way for the legalization of its repressive practices, but also undermined the very foundations of the Egyptian state, fundamentally transforming it into a blunt tool of repression. This is not to argue that the state under Mubarak was not repressive, but the degree of qualitative transformation that Sisi introduced represents a radical break between the two regimes. Indeed, the most repressive period under Mubarak did not witness such a sustained attack on the principle of the separation of powers as the one witnessed under Sisi. In a hallmark of direct military rule, other civilian organs of authority were hollowed out and made subordinate to the military and its policy directives. The coercive apparatus of the state not only penetrated the public space but cannibalized other state organs, undermining its very foundations.

This is most notable in the legislative branch, and the political system that emerged from it. The defining feature of this system is that, unlike under Mubarak, Egypt currently does not have a ruling party in the traditional sense, a role filled by the National Democratic Party (NDP) during the Mubarak years. The NDP played a major role in the Mubarak regime, not only dominating the Parliament but also populating the government, including the position of Prime Minister, with Mubarak acting as the head of the party (Carnegie Endowment, 2011). The party was responsible for formulating public policy and also acted as a vehicle for the presidential ambitions of Gamal Mubarak, a source of friction with the military establishment (Al Ahram, 2011). Under Sisi, the situation is radically different. For example, unlike during the Mubarak years, Sisi is not the head of any political party, and ministerial positions are not filled by members of civilian parties, even pro-government parties. For example in the government formed by Prime Minister Moustafa Madbouli in June 2018 (State Information Service, 2018), not a single minister belonged to an existing political party represented in Parliament, most of them being technocrats, military generals or career diplomats (American Chamber of Commerce, 2022). Hence, rather than develop a civilian façade, in a power-sharing deal with a political party, the military opted to concentrate power in its own hands, instilling a puppet civilian government. This has had a number of important consequences, the most notable of which is the severe restriction on the regime's scope for political manoeuvre and its ability to absorb shocks in the event of social upheaval. For example, during the early days of the mass protest of 2011, the regime was able to siphon off some of the popular anger by acting swiftly, forcing a large number of senior NDP figures to resign, including Gamal Mubarak (France 24, 2011). As the protest grew larger, the military stepped in to remove Mubarak, an action that allowed it to reduce the protest even further and garner enough goodwill to survive the turbulence with its institutional interest intact. The NDP was later dissolved by the Administrative Court in April 2011 (France 24, 2011). The existence of the NDP allowed the military to absorb popular anger in a way that is not possible today, successfully distancing itself from the regime, even though it was a major component of it (Abu Al Magd, 2018). This room for manoeuvre no longer exists due to the hyper-concentration of power in the hands of the military establishment. This makes repression, rather than co-option or concession, a more likely response to popular demands for reform. Simply put, changing the government or replacing the Prime Minister will no longer appease popular anger, since in the popular mind, the military, personified by Sisi, is in charge. This is, once again, a ramification of the military's belief in its own supremacy and its contempt for civilians.

The absence of a civilian ruling party occurred not by accident but by design – written into the Egyptian constitution. Article 146 of the constitution (Manshurat, 2019) gives the President the power to form the government, and there are no restrictions in terms of the criteria for selection of its members. Once formed, the Parliament is required to hold a vote of confidence. If the government does not gain the Parliament's confidence, an unlikely scenario, then the party or coalition with the largest number of seats is allowed to nominate the Prime Minister. This, in essence, means that winning a parliamentary election does not guarantee the formation a government, or, considering the heavy interference by the security services in the electoral process, even the ability to influence the process of government formation. Indeed, in addition to the constitutional framework that concentrates power in the hands of the President, the security services have interfered to a significant degree in parliamentary elections, most notably in 2015, which produced the first post-coup Parliament. This was revealed by Hossam Bhagat, one of Egypt's top investigative journalists, when he exposed the role of the security services in engineering the 'For the Love of Egypt' electoral coalition, which ran in the 2015 elections (Bahgat, Mada Masr, 2016). The coalition was formed by ten parties, all of which professed support for regime. They were able to sweep the election, winning 120 seats allocated to the party list, accounting for 100% of the allocated seats under the winner-takes-all system. The system was in fact designed to ensure complete domination of the list (TIMEP, 2016). The local media referred to the ten-party group as the 'coalition to support the Egyptian State' (Saeed, 2015), with an ex-intelligence officer, Sameh Sief El-Yazal, acting as its general coordinator. The coalition is said to have included a total of 317 members of Parliament (Essam El Deen, 2018), including independents, forming a clear majority in the 568-seat chamber. It was later renamed as the 'Support Egypt Coalition'. An indication of the malleability of the new Parliament was provided in its first session, when the newly elected body approved forty laws issued since July 2013, when President Morsi had been ousted (Middle East Eye, 2016). The laws approved included the 'Protest Law' and the 'Anti-Terrorism Law', both fundamental to the regime's repression.

The 2020 parliamentary election followed a similar pattern, albeit with more extreme results, with a new party emerging as the most dominant pro-Sisi force, namely 'Mostaqbal Watn' or 'Nation's Future'. The party has close ties to the President and former members of the disbanded NDP (TIMEP, 2016). Similar to 2015, an electoral coalition was created, now called the 'National List' containing twelve parties, under the umbrella of supporting the regime and Sisi. As part of the new coalition the largest winner was 'Mostaqbal Watn', which saw its number of seats increase from 57 to 315, accounting for 55% of the available seats, officially forming the parliamentary majority (Reuters, 2020). The party benefited from a change in the electoral rules that allocated 284 seats to party lists, under a winner-takes-all system. The party won 145 seats from those lists, with the rest distributed amongst its coalition partners. The result was another Parliament that only acts to rubber-stamp the regime's policies and comprising of parties that have a limited popular base.

The manipulation of Parliament and the total erosion if its independence is accompanied by a continuation of a Mubarak-era policy, which is often overlooked, namely the penetration of local government by ex-military officers and retirees. This policy was examined by Yezid Sayigh, who demonstrated the extent to which the apparatus of local government was filled by ex-officers during the Mubarak era (Sayigh Y., 2012). This penetration was not limited to the position of governors, but extended to cover all levels of local governments, right down to local councils, which are appointed by the executive. As Sayigh explains, the entire edifice is heavily populated by ex-military officers, providing them with post-retirement financial security, as they act as the local representatives of presidential power – a clear case of 'coup-proofing'. It is important to note that the structure of local government in Egypt is deeply hierarchical, with power flowing from top to bottom and most appointments made by the executive, with the President appointing the governors, the Prime Minister appointing the heads of cities and boroughs, and the governors appointing village heads. There is no semblance of democratic procedure, including elections. Sayigh's analysis demonstrates how deeply entrenched the military is in the local government apparatus:

> One example suffices to encapsulate the wider picture. On February 22, 2012, the minister of military production, Major General Ali Ibrahim Sabri, signed an agreement to develop the Giza governorate's wholesale market. Signing for the other side was the wholesale market's executive head, Major General Mohammed Sami Abdul-Rahim. In attendance were the deputy governor of Giza, Major General Usama Shama'ah; the secretary general of the local council, Major General Mohammad al-Sheikh; and his assistant secretary-general, Major General Ahmad Hani. This illustration notwithstanding, even if only one former officer holds a post in every executive body at each level of local government – a highly conservative assumption, evidently – then the nationwide total adds up to some 2,000 posts filled by former EAF officers.

Due to the difficulties of conducting research in Egypt and the lack of available information, it is hard to provide concrete data on the situation under Sisi, but there are some proxy indicators that can be used. One such is the number of governors with security backgrounds appointed by the President. In August 2018, Sisi appointed twenty-seven new governors, nineteen of whom either had a military or police background. In November 2019, sixteen new governors were appointed, eleven of whom had a security background (Al-Monitor, 2019). This trend dates back to 2015, when eleven new governors were appointed, all but two of whom had a security background (El-Shiekh, 2015). The penetration of local government was further enhanced by a law issued in July 2020, namely Law 165 (CNN, 2020). This is an amendment to an existing law concerned with popular defence, originally issued in 1968. The amendment to the law stipulates that each governorate should have one military advisor, with an appropriate number of aides, appointed by the Minister of the Defence. The advisor in question has the power to follow-up on ongoing development projects, act as the local representative of the Ministry of Defence and directly communicate with the local community to solve local problems. The language used is very vague, giving the military advisor extensive powers to act as a representative of the military establishment at the local level. This set-up not only militarizes local government but also facilitates mass corruption, considering the legal immunity of members of the armed forces, previously highlighted. It also increases the ability of the military to penetrate every aspect of civilian life to an unprecedent degree.

This trend is intensified by the penetration of other public agencies and public sector companies by senior retired officers, by means of what is known as a 'loyalty allowance'. This was a practice established in the days of Nasser, which saw senior officers appointed to senior positions in the public sector after retirement – in order to guarantee their loyalty. This not only allows the retirees to augment their income, but also extends the influence of the military over the public sector, even when it is not under its direct control (Sayigh Y., 2019). This creates a symbiosis between the formal military economy and a shadow military economy run by military retirees. This trend has continued since the coup of 2013: for example, in 2018 out of seventy-two general authorities, retired military officers were the head, deputy heads or board members in forty (56%) (Sayigh Y., 2019).

The overt dominance by the security establishment of the legislative branch and local government is compounded by a complicated relationship with the judiciary, who, albeit with some instances of discord, played a critical role in the regime's repression. This tension manifested itself in the legal battle over the transfer of the two islands in the Red Sea, Tiran and Sanafir, from Egyptian to Saudi sovereignty, when the judiciary briefly defied the regime. However, the overall tendency of the judiciary was to comply with the regime's repression to such an extent that the principle of judicial independence was severely compromised. This tarnished image stems from a number of cases in which the judiciary violated due process by meting out harsh sentences against opponents of the regime in mass trials. This was more blatant in the period directly following the coup, when repression of the Muslim Brotherhood was at its height and the polarization of the political system was at its most extreme. For example, in March 2014 an Egyptian court in the southern governorate of Minya sentenced 529 members of the Muslim Brotherhood to death in a mass trial that lacked due process (HRW, 2014) (Alsharif, 2014). The verdict was so shocking that the UN Secretary General at the time, Ban Ki Moon, expressed his concern (BBC, 2014).[5] The verdict was later commuted by a higher court to life imprisonment for 492 defendants, while confirming the death sentence for thirty-seven others (France 24, 2014). In another infamous case, in June 2021, the Court of Cassation, the highest court in the country, confirmed the death sentence for twelve members of the Muslin Brotherhood. They were part of a mass trial of 739 members of the organization concerning participation in anti-government protests in 2013. The death sentences were final and could not be appealed. The trial was considered to be unfair by a number of international human rights organizations (Amnesty International, 2021).

In addition to these mass trials, there is also considerable evidence of judicial collusion with the regime's repression of senior figures in the Muslim Brotherhood, most notably the late President Morsi. The ousted President was charged with a number of charges that seemed to defy logic, the most notorious of which was the charge of conspiring with the foreign armed groups Hamas and Hezbollah, of which he was found guilty and sentenced to life imprisonment in May 2015. The sentence was overturned in November 2016 and a retrial was ordered. Another case involving Morsi, in which he was sentenced to life imprisonment and the sentence was confirmed, involved a charge of leading an illegal group, a ludicrous accusation considering that the 'illegal group' in question was the Muslim Brotherhood, which had been democratically elected to office, and that he was being tried by a regime that came to power as the result of a coup d'état (BBC, 2019). These are all blatant examples of the general willingness of the judiciary to accommodate the regime's repression at the cost of their own institutional independence.

The militarization of the Egyptian state, which evolved from the political dominance of the military and the political system that it spawned, has led to a considerable erosion of the foundations of the modern state. In essence, the legislative and judicial branches have become a mere extension of the security apparatus, while the trend of militarization of local government has intensified. The militarization of the civilian organs of the state has severely weakened and securitized the responses of the state to possible public crises. This was starkly demonstrated with the advent of the Covid-19 pandemic.

A militarized response to a public health crisis

The regime's response to the outbreak of the Covid-19 pandemic is a clear example of not just the regime's ruthlessness but of the impact on public policy of the militarization of the state and the public space. Indeed, the regime viewed the pandemic as a threat to regime security rather than a public health emergency, with devastating consequences for the citizenry. This view is not universally shared amongst commentators and analysts. For example, Amr Hamzawy and Nathan Brown have argued that, in a break with Sisi's traditional policy, the regime allowed the civilian government to take the lead in the pandemic response, led by Prime Minister Mostafa Madbouly (Hamzawy and Brown, 2020). This break in policy, they argue, might have some long-term effects, moving the regime in a more technocratic but not democratic direction. This would occur on two levels: first, policy coordination would drop down one level from the presidency to the cabinet; second, a limited return to the pre-2011 period would be possible, where 'state institutions had more autonomy within their own realms and in which strong leaders in specific sectors emerged'.

Even though the argument that the civilian government took the lead in the pandemic response is indeed correct, the responses of government overall followed Sisi's blue print of heavy-handed repressive tactics. In essence, the civilian government's response did not differ much from what would have been expected from a security agency, a by-product of the militarization of the state and the public space. The response rested on three different pillars. First, was the engagement of different government officials in a bizarre propaganda campaign, to either shift the blame for the spread of the virus to the citizenry, to minimize the threat of the pandemic or to attempt to boost public confidence in the regime's response. Second, a wide range of repressive tactics against critics of the government's response was deployed. The victims of the regime's repression included medical professionals as well as activists and journalist. Third, a partial and limited lockdown and aid package was introduced, which failed to prevent a large death toll, much higher than official government figures.

The government started early with the propaganda campaign, with the onset of the pandemic seeing the Health Minister Dr Hala Zayed make a number of trips abroad, in which she offered aid to other countries in the form of medical supplies, in what appeared to be a public relations campaign aimed at touting the strength of the regime. For example, in January 2020, Zayed sent 10 tons of medical supplies to China to help combat the pandemic (Egypt Today, 2020), with a follow-up visit in March (Al Masry Al Youm, 2020). In April, Zayed went to Italy with a shipment of medical supplies based on Sisi's directives. Two planes full of supplies were sent as part of the aid package (Egypt Independent, 2020). This was followed by another shipment of aid to the United States. This aid package consisted of one plane filled with anaesthetics, antibiotics, body bags, masks and testing swabs (Middle East Monitor, 2020). This might be seen by some as clever diplomacy, but it played another role domestically, namely the propagation of an image of national strength among the regime's base. The problem with this approach was that it did not correspond to facts on the ground, specifically the domestic shortage of medical supplies, which left the regime open to criticism (Farouk M., Al-Monitor, 2020), especially from medical personnel who complained about the lack of Personal Protection Equipment (PPE) and testing kits at the beginning of the pandemic (Guardian, 2020). This was the same material donated abroad by the government as part of its propaganda blitz.

The regime's propaganda policy included a set of bizarre statements, which seemed to be aimed variously at minimizing the severity of the crisis, shifting the blame for the pandemic to the 'negligence' of the populace or to instilling confidence in the government's ability to handle the outbreak. For example, in March 2020, Zayed expressed her confidence in the strength of the Egyptian health care system and the ability of the government to deal with the pandemic. This statement can only be described as blatant propaganda (Al Masry Al Youm, 2020). The Egyptian health care system is extremely fragile, as a cursory review of some figures reveal. For example, in January 2020, before the onset of the pandemic, the number of ICU beds in the country stood at 132,000, or an equivalent of one ICU bed per 813 citizens (Roqaya, 2020). Placing this figure in context, the same figure in Italy, where the health care system collapsed at the beginning of the pandemic, stood at one bed per 363 citizens, based on 2013 data (WHO, 2022). The shortages of ICU beds was also compounded by a shortage of medical personnel due to poor working conditions. For example, out of 220,000 locally trained doctors, 120,000 were working abroad (Ahram, 2019). The same shortage applied to nurses, with a reported 55% shortage of highly skilled ICU nurses, crucial at the time of a pandemic (Roqaya, 2020). These issues were primarily caused by chronic government underspending on the health sector. For example, in the 2018–19 budget, the total public health care spend per citizen stood at US$25 per annum (Al Araby, 2018), a ridiculously low amount. Hence, the statement by the Health Minister seemed disconnected from the realities of the health sector and can only be described as fantastical propaganda, aimed at increasing public confidence.

As the virus started to spread, government officials changed track, now blaming the citizenry for the outbreak, while minimizing its impact. For example, in May the head of the Preventative Medicine Sector in the Ministry of Health, Ala Eid, stated that the pandemic situation was 'stable', while praising the response of his own ministry. The only concern he had was the behaviour of the citizenry, who, he claimed, were not following the guidelines laid out by the ministry (Al Masry Al Youm, 2020). The Ministry of Health continued to issue statements blaming the citizenry for the spread of the virus, arguing that the lack of adherence to the guidelines and lack of awareness of the threat were the real problems. This approach included a statement by the head of the Covid-19 scientific committee, Doctor Hossam Hosni, who blamed the public for the spread of the virus (Al Masry Al Youm, 2020). The propaganda statements continued until June, when the advisor to the Minister of Health, Dr Sherif Wadea, stated that the strong immune system of Egyptians gave the ministry the needed 'breathing room' to handle the pandemic (Al Masry Al Youm, 2020). The latter statement was not based on any scientific research, but can be seen simply as a continuation of a campaign of deliberate misinformation. The government even went so far as to develop a statistical model, presented by the Minister of Higher Education, Khaled Abdel Ghaffar, which predicted that the number of positive cases would reach a maximum of between 37,000 and 40,000 cases, after which the number of cases would start to decline. This point was expected to be reached by the end of May 2020 (Mohamed, 2020). This model proved woefully inaccurate, with the total number of cases, based on official estimates, reaching 513,468 positive infections in May 2022, an inaccuracy that can be attributed to incompetence or more likely wilful disinformation (Reuters, 2022).

This misinformation campaign went hand in hand with a broadening of the regime's repressive tactics. For example, in April 2020 three doctors were arrested and accused of spreading false news, misuse of social media and joining a terrorist organization. The reason for their arrest revolved around social media posts criticizing the government responses to the pandemic, most notably the lack of PPE, which was necessary to protect doctors from infection (Reuters, 2020). The lack of PPE led to a high death toll amongst medical personnel, with the number exceeding 500 by May 2021, based on the best available estimates (EIPR, 2021). In May 2020 the confrontation between medical personnel and the government reached its apex, with the death of Dr Walid Abedel Halim in Al Monira hospital after he contracted Covid-19. His death sparked mass resignations by doctors in protest over the lack of PPE and medical supplies (Al Hurra, 2020), while the medical syndicate accused the government of a failure to protect doctors (CNN, 2020). The response of the government was to initiate a defamation campaign against the doctors. For example, Zayed called doctor resignations 'treason', while at the same time acknowledging the legitimacy of their demands (Hawary, 2020). Zayed anchored her accusation in the regime's deeply nationalist rhetoric that equated protest with national betrayal. The attack on doctors by the Minister of Health was accompanied by a media campaign accusing the resignation organizer, Dr Mahmoud Tarek, of belonging to the Muslim Brotherhood, thus portraying the protests as a plot against the state (El Balad, 2020). The accusations were repeated by Parliament member Mohamed Farag Amer, a prominent business tycoon (Cairo24, 2020). The defamation campaign also included the accusation that Turkey – a regional backer of the Muslim Brotherhood – was planning to incite the medical staff against the state in cooperation with the Islamist group (Kamel, 2020). The regime also used the outbreak of the pandemic as a pretext to amend the aforementioned emergency law and make it more draconian. As discussed above, the law was amended in May 2020 (Napoleon, 2020), when a state of emergency was still in effect . According to Gamal Eid, the net results of the regime's repressive tactics was the arrest of at least 500 people, including eleven journalists, by the end of May 2020.

It is important to note, however, that the regime did attempt to implement some non-repressive measures to counter the pandemic. These included an economic stimulus package which provided Eg£100 billion to support the industrial sector, as well as Eg£2 billion to support exporters and a 3% reduction in interest rates (Al Bawaba News, 2020). The government also imposed a partial lockdown, as well as the closure of places of worship, in an attempt to limit the spread of the virus. The partial lockdown lasted till end of June 2020 (Al Arabiya, 2020). Overall, however, the government's response was heavily securitized and focused on the repression of dissent, which led to a devastating death toll. Based on official government figures, the total death toll reached 24,606 cases in May 2022 (Reuters, 2022). However, there is reason to believe that the actual death toll is much higher and that the government has deliberately falsified the number. This is due to the fact that Covid-related deaths are only included in the official death toll if the deceased was treated in public hospitals, excluding those that went to private hospitals or died at home. Based on a report issued by the BBC, comparing deaths in the period May/June/July 2020 to the same period in 2019, there is an increase of 60,000 deaths, most likely Covid-19 victims, in a time span of just three months. Placing this in context, Dr Mohamed El-Nady, a member of the Covid-19 task force, stated that the real death toll was most likely ten times greater than the official figures (Abou Taleb, 2020). In May 2022, the WHO estimated that the real death toll in Egypt is likely 11.6 times higher than the official figures, making it closer to 280,000 dead (Grimley, Cornish and Stylianou, 2022).

The response of the civilian-led government to this situation helped to underline the fundamental militarization of the state under Sisi. In essence, the government engaged in a propaganda campaign combined with heavy repression in dealing with the pandemic, treating it as a security threat rather than a public health crisis. This essentially transformed the civilian organs of the state, like the Ministry of Health, into integral components of the regime's policy of repression, eroding their independence and capacity to deal with similar crises in the future. It is apparent that the coercive arm of the state is no longer limited to the security services, but has encompassed its technocratic aspects, threatening the very foundations of the modern Egyptian state.

Dissent in the ranks

The process of state militarization was not resistance-free; on the contrary, there were two incidents where there was significant dissent against Sisi from within the elites of the state apparatus. These were the transfer of the two Red Sea Islands from Egyptian to Saudi sovereignty, and the presidential election of 2018, when Sisi was challenged by men from the military establishment. Both challenges, however, were unsuccessful and the regime responded with hallmark repression. The end result was an acceleration of the process of state militarization and consolidation of Sisi's position at the head of the regime.

In April 2016, during a visit to Cairo by King Salman, Sisi announced the transfer of two islands in the Red Sea, Tiran and Sanafir, from Egyptian to Saudi sovereignty (Fahmy and Noueihed, Reuters, 2016).

The news, in Sisi-like fashion, came with no public debate on the topic, leading to a public outcry and the first mass protest against Sisi since he officially took power. The regime responded with a clampdown and mass arrests (Maslin, 2016), as expected. However, what was more notable about this episode was resistance within the state apparatus, namely the judiciary and elites within the military establishment, in a rare case of dissent against Sisi. Resistance within the judiciary revolved around a court case filed by the ex-presidential candidate and prominent human rights lawyer Khaled Ali to annul the transfer of the islands. The case was filed with the Court of Administrative Justice (CAJ), part of the State Council, the judicial body responsible for litigation against the state. In June 2016, the court issued a verdict annulling the transfer of the islands (BBC, 2016). The regime then appealed the verdict before the Cairo Court for Urgent Matters, which approved the transfer of the islands in September 2016 (Maspero, 2016). However, in January 2017, the Supreme Administrative Court (SAC) delivered a decision rejecting the appeal and upholding the CAJ's nullification of the transfer (Haitham and Reda, 2017). The contradictory rulings allowed the regime to take the case to the Supreme Constitutional Court (SCC), which accepted the case even though the commissioners' report, a non-binding legal opinion by the court commissioners, argued against accepting it, since it did not fall within the court's jurisdiction (Bassal, 2017). Regardless, the court considered the case and ruled in favour of the transfer of the islands in June 2017 (Euro News, 2018). Sisi would later ratify the treaty for the transfer of the islands on 24 June 2017 (Al Jazzera, 2017).

The struggle over the transfer of the two islands between the judiciary and the regime was a last-gasp attempt by the former to maintain a semblance of independence, even though it had played a significant facilitating role in the regime's early repression. The judiciary had resolved to challenge the regime on this matter due to two intertwined factors: first, the public outcry that had followed the announcement of the transfer of the islands; and second, and closely connected to the first reason, the notion that the transfer was a clear breach of the nationalist narrative propagated by the regime, a radical break with its own ideological construct, which drove a number of elites to oppose it.

The regime responded swiftly to the challenge. The immediate reaction was to make adjustments to the 'Judicial Authorities Law', in April 2017, which allowed Sisi to select the heads of Judicial Authorities from a pool of three candidates based on seniority (Goma, Masrawy, 2017). Previously, the most senior judge was nominated by each authority, and the President simply approved the nomination in a largely ceremonial process. The adjustment to the law allowed Sisi to bypass Yehia Dakroury for the position of Head of the State Council. Dakroury was the CAJ judge responsible for the verdict annulling the transfer of the two Read Sea islands. He was the most senior judge at the time, and, based on the previous procedure, would have been automatically selected as Head of the State Council (Magdy M., 2017). Instead, Sisi appointed Judge Ahmed Abu al-Azm (Aboulenein, Reuters, 2017). The State Council judges attempted to challenge the appointment of Al-Azm by unanimously nominating Dakroury as their sole candidate for the head of the State Council position (Mada Masr, 2017), and Dakroury also attempted to appeal the decision (Gamal El-Din, 2017), but to not avail. Abu al-Azm was sworn in as Head of the State Council on 20 July 2017 (Egypt Today, 2017). The changes in the law would later be codified in the 2019 constitutional amendments discussed at the beginning of the chapter, which would drastically reduce the independence of the judiciary and ensure that challenges like this one were not repeated.

Opposition to the transfer of the two islands was not limited to the judiciary, as it also extended to the mostly docile Parliament and even within the military establishment itself. As the legal battle over the transfer of the two islands dragged on, the regime attempted to bypass the judicial system by asking Parliament to approve the treaty, which was submitted to it in June 2017, before the final verdict of the SCC was issued. Even though there were court orders annulling the transfer of the two islands, the head of the Parliament, Ali Abdel Aal, stated that the legislative body was not bound by the courts, basing his assessment on the notion that the Administrative courts did not have the proper jurisdiction to review acts of sovereignty (Egypt Independent, 2017). This led to considerable resistance in Parliament, with members of the '25–30' parliamentary coalition threatening to resign if the treaty was approved (Mansi, 2017). The coalition represented a group of independent MPs who had taken more of a nuanced position in the parliament, with some members being broadly supportive of Sisi and other taking more of an oppositional stance. However, this did not stop the Parliament from approving the treaty on 14 June, a week before the SCC final verdict (Mourad and Hamdy, 2017). After approval had been given, 119 MPs sent a letter to Sisi, asking him to postpone the final ratification of the treaty (Adeeb, 2017). The letter was ignored. No mass resignation from Parliament was triggered by the final ratification of the treaty. There were also opposition from former members of the military establishment, who were openly critical of the transfer of the two islands, a group that included two former Chiefs of Staff, Sami Anan and Magdy Hatata. Anan had served in this role from 2005 to 2012, while Hatata had held the position between 1995 and 2001. In his criticism, Anan went so far as to state in a Facebook post that to suggest that the two islands were not Egyptian was treasonous (Annan, 2017). Another prominent figure to criticize the transfer of the islands was the last Prime Minister of the Mubarak era, Air Force General Ahmed Shafiq. In an appearance on a popular talk show, Shafiq was openly critical of the move (Al Araby, 2017). Ultimately, none of this was sufficient to stop the transfer of the islands, and Sisi was able to emerge from the crisis unscathed.

The other incident that saw some resistance to the consolidation of power by Sisi was the presidential election of 2018, when he was challenged by Shafiq and Anan, the two members of the military establishment who were openly critical of the transfer of the two Red Sea islands. However, this challenge should not be read as a conscious attempt to reverse the process of state militarization or to democratize the state, but rather reflected the assumption that power could be transferred and contested peacefully, albeit amongst military elites and in a controlled fashion. This assumption was one of the last vestiges of the 2011 mass protests and the downfall of Mubarak that followed. Sisi, however, responded in a manner that shattered this assumption completely. Shafiq, who was living in the UAE when he announced his intention to run in the election, was arrested and deported to Egypt (BBC, 2017). Upon landing, he was held incommunicado, prompting speculation that he had been kidnapped by the security forces, something that he later denied (BBC, 2017). Shafiq subsequently withdrew his candidature (BBC, 2018) and has kept a low profile ever since. Anan, on the other hand, was treated even more harshly. He was arrested in January 2018 (BBC, 2018) and charged with violating Egypt's military code, attempting to run for public office without permission, forging official documents and inciting the public against the military establishment. His arrest was founded on his breach of the 'Exceptional Legal Rule', referred to at the beginning of this chapter, which states that those who were members of SCAF during the 2011 revolution are to remain in reserve service after they retire, a rule that seems not apply to Sisi himself, who was also a member of SCAF in 2011. Anan spent two years in military prison, before being released in December 2019 after suffering a stroke (Maged, 2019). In fact, so successful was Sisi in eliminating all opposition ahead of the election that the regime had to call on Moussa Moussa, the head of the Ghad Party, to stand against the Sisi, with his candidature registered just a few hours before the deadline (Mumbere, 2018). Moussa had been a vocal supporter of Sisi, even organizing electoral events for the President (Ibrahim, 2018), before he was called to run against him. It was a truly farcical spectacle. The results were not surprising, with Sisi winning 97% of the vote (Tolba and Davison, 2018).

The principal consequence of these challenges was further militarization of the state and the consolidation of Sisi's position as the head of the regime. An important aspect of the constitutional amendments mentioned at the beginning of this chapter was in response to the challenge from the judiciary over the transfer of the Red Sea islands to Saudi Arabia, ultimately ensuring that the judiciary became completely subservient. Furthermore, the 'Law for Treatment of Senior officers of the Armed Forces' was issued to ensure that men like Anan and Shafiq could not challenge Sisi in the future. By the end of 2019 the regime had completely consolidated its grip on the state apparatus, fully militarizing it, while colonizing the public space to an unprecedented degree.

The end game

The militarization of the state apparatus and the public space has a number of important consequences, besides the obvious stifling of democratic aspirations, which will prove fundamentally transformative. The most notable of these consequences is the radical transformation of the state apparatus to become an appendage of the security services, which reduces the capacity of the state to provide public good to the population, transforming previously technocratic organs of the state into a tool for repression. This modus operandi became apparent in the Ministry of Health's responses to the Covid-19 pandemic. In the long term, this is bound to reduce the effectiveness of civilian organs of the state, which in turn will reduce public trust in the entire state edifice, not just the regime. Another significant consequence is the complete erosion of the independence of the judiciary and the legislative branches of government. This process created strong institutional interests within the state apparatus to oppose even the most modest reforms, since these will not only threaten the paramount position of the military establishment within the state but might also weaken the position of judges and members of Parliament who participated in the regime's repression. Resistance to reform becomes endemic, which in turn makes social upheaval more likely. Finally, the legal framework that enabled the process of state militarization poses a significant hurdle to the prospect of democratization, since the legal system, including the constitution, would require a complete overhaul in order for any reform to be effective.

The most worrying dynamic, however, is the regime's colonization of the public space and the extension of its tentacles into the lives of millions of Egyptians, in a truly totalitarian fashion. This process not only represses democratic aspirations but also affects the nature of the Egyptian state and its social role, as well public attitudes towards it. Indeed, under Sisi the state has been radically transformed into a tool of repression, much more so than under Mubarak, with daily violence meted out to the population. This not only serves to keep the regime in power, but also to keep social and class conflict at bay. This strategy is anchored in the fear of social upheaval entrenched in large segments of the regime's support and Sisi's version of Nasserism. This, in turn, has transformed attitudes towards the state among large segments of the populace. Regime supporters are in favour of the regime's repression, its brand of chauvinistic nationalism, the militarization of the public space and most importantly the model of the state that it propagates. On the other hand, the regime's violence has created strong opposition amongst large segments of the populace, who detest the regime's totalitarian vision of the state. This has fundamentally transformed the struggle for democratization into a struggle over the state itself – its nature and its social role. This struggle is seen by both factions as existential, with regime supporters viewing Sisi's vision of the state as a lifeboat in the middle of a turbulent sea of social upheaval, while the regime's opponents abhor the state in its current form. This has only served to increase polarization, and justify state violence on an unprecedent scale, as the next chapter will show.

Chapter 3

THERE WILL BE BLOOD

'There are no political prisoners in Egypt.'

— Abdel Fattah El-Sisi

On 6 January 2019, President Sisi appeared on the American Television show *60 Minutes*. In a rather uncharacteristic performance, Sisi seemed nervous, with visible beads of sweat appearing on his forehead. When asked about the estimated 60,000 political prisoners languishing in Egyptian prisons, the nervous dictator denied that there were any political prisoners in the country (HRW, 2019). Sisi's performance was so poor that the Egyptian government contacted CBS in an attempt to block the episode being aired (VOA news, 2019). CBS ignored the request and showed the interview. Sisi's denial of regime repression does not change the facts on the ground, namely that his regime presided over a campaign of mass repression, the likes of which Egypt had not witnessed since the founder of the Egyptian state, Mehmed Ali, came to power in the beginning of the nineteenth century. Indeed, the regime's violence has resulted in thousands of victims, including political prisoners, torture victims, citizens subjected to forced disappearances and victims of extrajudicial killings – a deliberate policy aimed at creating what Ramy Shaath, a prominent activist, called a 'Republic of Fear' (CNN, 2022).

Indeed, the most obvious aim of the regime's repressive campaign was the complete eradication of dissent and the closure of the public space.[1] The logic of repression employed by the regime appeared to be simple, namely that any acts of defiance were to be handled with extreme prejudice, making the cost of dissent extremely high, regardless of the act of dissent itself. For example, terror charges were levied against those who were critical on social media, as if they had committed acts of violence. By equating violent and non-violent opposition to the regime, the authorities created the possibility of future waves of violent radicalism in the country. Indeed, the regime has invested heavily in building a complex infrastructure of repression, from a mega prisons to surveillance systems, and urban infrastructure projects. All to ensure that the regime can repress dissent at will. However, state violence has had a number of other, less apparent but not less critical, consequences for the functioning of the regime. State violence has in fact allowed the regime to consolidate support amongst its base and to bind the security services to it, in a bond formed in the crucible of mass social upheaval.

This can only be understood if one looks at the bloody events of the summer of 2013 and the massacre of protestors by security forces. This moment of genesis was built on a simple but powerful narrative, namely that there was a fundamental threat facing the Egyptian state, the only bulwark against complete chaos, and that the military as the defender of the state and the nation had to intervene to counter it. This is framed as an existential threat, which can only be dealt with through popular participation in repression and support for the regime. As such, the regime was able to solicit mass popular support, not only from it base but also from large segments of the populace who fell prey to the fear of social anarchy. In essence, state violence became a tool for the regime to tether its base to it. Indeed, this has become an ideological imperative for a regime whose raison d'être is to protect the state from collapse, countering conspiracies and fifth columnists – or other code words for the opposition – in the regime-legitimizing narrative. Hence, state violence has now become an integral part of the regime's ideological edifice and its hegemonic apparatus. Indeed, Sisi's passive revolution necessitated exorbitant levels of mass violence, not only to cement his rule but to act as an ideological glue, holding the entire regime together.

The unleashing of the campaign of mass repression, however, had two effects: one intended, while the other, in my analysis, was a side effect that the regime cannot control. The intended result was the expansion of the power of the security services within the state apparatus and the tethering of the security services and some members of the judiciary to the regime, as partners in the military's repression. The unintended side effect is a process of repression decentralization, in which the centre can no longer control the periphery, and the level of repression can no longer be moderated based on political expediency. Indeed, the case of the Italian PhD student Giulio Regeni, which will be examined below, is an illustrative example of this logic in play.

This means that even if the military elites attempt to moderate repression, there are a number of obstacles in the way, such as the ideological imperative to keep an internal enemy that needs to be repressed, in order to solicit support from the regime's base. There is also the prospect of possible resistance from within the security services, which have been thoroughly indoctrinated in the regime's ideological worldview. This makes repression endemic to the Sisi regime, even if it slightly moderates its stance over time, making any hopes of elite-led reform unlikely. Indeed, this means that the regime needs high degrees of state violence to remain in power, even if it has mass popular support, since arguably a large part of this support stems from the regime's repression – a vicious reinforcing cycle. This does not augur well for the prospects of democratic transition, since the regime requires a high level of social polarization to sustain its position in power, as a system of direct military rule. In simpler terms, if the internal enemy disappears then the entire ideological edifice on which the regime's claim for legitimacy lies will collapse and the argument against democratic transition becomes less plausible. The regime has created an image of itself as the antithesis of the demands of the 2011 mass protests, in a manner that it cannot escape, locking itself and the opposition in a cycle of violence that might lead to mass social upheaval that the regime and it supporters dread.

This chapter starts with the case of Giulio Regeni as an exemplar of the regime's modus operandi at work, and the decentralized and ideological nature of the regime's repression. Using this case as a starting point, the rest of the chapter will detail the regime's repressive tactics, including the physical infrastructure that the regime has constructed to carry out its campaign of mass violence, as well as the deadly insurgency that emerged, partly in response to the regime's repression. The chapter closes with an examination of the consequences of the regime campaign of violence for the prospect of democratic transition, as well as the way that state violence acts as an ideological straitjacket, limiting the regime's policy options and the prospect of elite-led reform.

The curious case of Giulio Regeni

On 4 February 2016 the bloodied body of the Italian Cambridge PhD student Giulio Regeni was found in a ditch beside a desert road in Cairo (BBC, 2016). Regeni was half naked, with visible marks of torture, including broken bones, signs of cigarette burns, deep wounds and electrocution marks, with mysterious letters carved into his flesh. His body was so badly mutilated that his mother could only recognize her son by the tip of his nose (Al Jazzera, 2017). Regeni had disappeared on 25 January, the fifth anniversary of the eruption of the mass protests that led to the downfall of Mubarak, a time of heightened tension for the security services. Regeni had entered the country the previous year to conduct field research on independent trade unions in Egypt, where he immediately came to the attention of the security forces. Once Regeni's body was discovered, the regime's media apparatus went into overdrive, producing a number of stories explaining his horrific death. The first, was that he died in a hit-and-run incident; another theory was that Regeni was a homosexual and that he was murdered by a lover; and the final explanation was that he was murdered by the local branch of the Islamic State (IS) in an attempt to disrupt Italian–Egyptian relations (Veto Gate, 2016). And then, in March 2016, the Egyptian security forces gunned downed five men in an alleged shootout. The security forces claimed that those killed were part of a criminal enterprise that specialized in abducting and robbing foreign nationals. Regein's personal belongings were found in the possession of the his alleged killers. However, a few days after the alleged shootout, the Italian government rejected the latest coverup attempts by the Egyptian security forces (DW, 2016). The Egyptian government later recanted its version of events and the investigation of the case continued (Shorouk News, 2016).

As the investigation continued to run its course, it became apparent that Regeni was tortured to death by the Egyptian security forces. In December 2018, the Italian Prosecutor named five members of the Egyptian security forces as suspects in the murder, including two National Security Agency (NSA) officials, Major General Tarek Saber and Major Sherif Magdy, as well as three members of the Egyptian police: Colonel Hesham Helmy, Colonel Acer Kamal and junior police officer Mahmoud Negm. Tarek Saber, who was retired, had been a senior security official in the NSA at the time of Regeni abduction, while Sherif Magdy was a mid-level official in the NSA and in charge of the team dealing with the Regeni case. At the time of the abduction, Colonel Hesham Helmy was serving in a police station in Cairo's Dooki district, where Regeni lived, and Colonel Acer Kamal was head of a police department in charge of street work and discipline (AP, 2018). In October 2021, the trial of four out of the five suspects – Major Sherif Magdy, General Tarek Saber, Colonel Hisham Helmy and Colonel Acer Kama – started in Rome in their absence (CNN, 2021). However, the case was adjourned after an argument was put forward by the court-appointed defence that since there was no evidence that the suspects knew that the case was ongoing, the proceedings should be suspended (Balmer, 2021). Regeni's case offers a unique insight into the operation of state violence in Egypt, its logic, goals and dynamics, since it is the only case that has been documented in some degree of detail. Regeni got caught in an already existing repressive apparatus, whose operation was beyond the control of the regime's elite. Indeed, Regeni's death was probably not intended, considering the diplomatic cost that the regime incurred, but there was always a risk of something like this happening due to the character of the regime and the systematic nature of its repression. If the main concern of the security forces was the nature of Regeni's research, he could simply have been deported, but the regime's repressive apparatus took over with tragic consequences.

In order to understand Regeni's murder, we need to retrace his path from when he entered Egypt in September 2015 to his death in February of the following year. Based on a statement made by the Egyptian Attorney General, Nabil Sadeq, in September 2016, Regeni came to the attention of the security services on 7 January 2016, after an informant, Mohamed Nabil, reported him to the NSA as a suspected spy. Nabil was Regeni's contact in the street vendor labour union, the subject of Regeni's research. Based on the statement made by the Attorney General, the results of the investigation revealed that Regeni was not considered to be a national security threat, and, as such, was no longer followed by the NSA (Guardian, 2016). When he disappeared a few weeks later, the Egyptian authorities denied that he had been detained or questioned. However, ICCTV footage from the metro station where Regeni was abducted, which were handed over to the Italian prosecutor, showed signs of tampering, with some gaps in the tape, raising the suspicion that the security services were involved (Reuters, 2018). A video also later surfaced, leaked by the Egyptian security services, showing Nabil trying to solicit money from Regeni in an attempt to entrap him, which Regeni refused (BBC, 2017). The purpose of the video remains unclear, since, if anything, it shows that Regeni was not a spy and that he adhered to ethical research practices. However, this didn't seem to dissuade the security services from arresting and torturing him to death, as one security official was overheard in a security conference in an African country admitting to kidnapping and torturing Regeni, on suspicion of being a British spy (Middle East Eye, 2019). The security official in question was heard bragging about punching Regeni during his arrest.

A pattern emerges in the case, one that is both simple and horrifying, namely that Regni fell victim to the regime's ideological construct, which saw conspiracies and foreign plots to destroy the state everywhere. The security forces are deeply indoctrinated with this construct, which, coupled with a complete lack of accountability, provided the preconditions for the torture and murder of Regeni. This episode also attests to the decentralized nature of repression in Egypt, where a handful of security officials could drag the regime into a major diplomatic incident, a clear case of the periphery taking the centre hostage.

Indeed, in the face of growing Italian pressure, the regime showed remarkable resistance to the notion of calling its security officials to account. For example, in April 2016, Italy withdrew its ambassador to Egypt in protest over the failure to provide evidence to solve the murder of Regeni (Scherer, Reuters, 2016). The ambassador only returned to Cairo in August 2017 (Scherer, Reuters, 2017). In August 2018, the Italian Parliament increased the pressure by unilaterally ending diplomatic relations with its Egyptian counterpart (Egypt Today, 2018). The diplomatic pressure seemed to pay off when in July 2018 President Sisi proclaimed the regime's commitment to finding Regeni's killers (Al Ahram, 2018). However, this all proved to be part of a process of delays and obfuscation, with the Egyptian General Prosecutor, Hamada El-Saweey, closing the investigation in December 2020 (El Fass, 2020). The General Prosecutor's statement exonerated the five security officials charged by Italy with Regeni's murder. The statement also reiterated the notion that the Egyptian authorities had fully cooperated with the Italian prosecution and that there were third parties attempting to disrupt relations between the two countries. The statement was promptly rejected by the Italian government (RT, 2020). Despite constant pressure from a close European ally, the regime refused to call to account any of its security officials, of any rank, in the Regeni murder case. Granted, there were no real sanctions introduced against the regime and that economic ties between Egypt and Italy actually increased during this time,[2] but still, the diplomatic pressure on the regime was continuous. This can be contrasted with the response of Saudi Arabia in the case of Jamal Khashoggi, where a number of security officials were scapegoated, under the guise of a rogue operation that went wrong. The Sisi regime did not even contemplate a cover-up.

In choosing the path of protecting its petty security officials, an important insight can be gleaned from the otherwise black box that is the working of the security apparatus, namely that an unwritten pact exists between the regime elites and the lower-level security officials protecting them. The terms of the pact are straightforward, yet monumental in their impact. Simply put, security officials are allowed to repress at will, using any means necessary, in exchange for which the regime offers them immunity at any cost, even a major diplomatic incident. The terms of the pact are consistent with the regime's ideological raison d'être, as it sees itself as the protector of the state against the forces of chaos – a powerful narrative that has not only seeped into the consciousness of the regime's supporters but has also reached members of the security apparatus, with horrifying effects. It is the same old story of men of violence locked in an existential struggle for the salvation of a nation. However, this pattern has the unintended side effect of decentralizing repression in a way that the elites cannot control, so rather than deport Regeni, the more sensible approach, he ends up being tortured to death, exposing the regime to unnecessary risks.

The act of killing

The gunning down of five men who were presented as Regeni's murderers was part of a larger pattern of killings committed and sanctioned by the state. This deliberate policy was enabled by the legal structure and the collusion of the judiciary explored in Chapter 2, which provided the security forces with the needed legal immunity to unleash waves of deadly repression on an unprecedent scale. Indeed, the policy followed by the regime revolved around four, closely interconnected, tactics, with devastating consequences for the targets of repression. The tactics in question are extrajudicial killings in alleged shootouts; forced disappearances; medical negligence in prisons that leads to a slow death; and the widespread use of executions in trials that lacked due process. The long-term impact of these policies is not only the deep social polarization that it produces, but also the need to restructure the security apparatus completely in order for any democratic transition to be successful. This will be an extremely difficult task considering the central position that the security services occupy in the current edifice of the Egyptian state.

Evidence of mass extrajudicial killings started to become public within a few years of the military takeover. For example, in April 2017 a video was leaked on the Muslim Brotherhood-affiliated television channel, Mekammleen, which showed the extrajudicial killing of two teenagers by militias affiliated with the Egyptian military in Sinai. The two young men, Daoud Sabri al-Awabdah, aged sixteen, and Abd al-Hadi Sabri al-Awabdah, nineteen, were brothers and they were both arrested by the security services in the town of Rafah and forcibly disappeared in July 2016, only to appear in the videos showing their executions (HRW, 2017). They were both shot at point-blank range, while the evidence of a firefight was planted after their execution, based on the leaked video. The two teenagers later appeared in a regime video showing the bodies of eight men that the military claimed had been militants killed in alleged shootouts with the security forces, raising the question of whether the other six men were killed in similar fashion to the al-Awabdah brothers. This was not the first public exposure of men allegedly being executed by security forces while in regime custody. For example, in February 2017, several tribes based in the North Sinai city of Arish declared partial civil disobedience, after a raid that killed ten alleged militants. The families of five of those men alleged that they had been held in the NSA headquarters in North Sinai at the time of the alleged raid (Sakr, 2017). Like the killing of the five men in the Regeni case, there was no investigation of the allegations and no members of the security forces were held accountable. This pattern was not confined to Sinai, with similar incidents occurring in the Delta. For example, in December 2018, less than twenty-four hours after a bomb attack on a tourist bus near the Pyramids in Giza that killed four tourists (Guardian, 2019), the Egyptian security forces announced that they had killed forty suspected militants in Giza and North Sinai. After the raids, photos were leaked showing what appears to be the extrajudicial execution of suspected militants, with a man bound and shot in the back of the head (Middle East Monitor, 2018). The same man appeared later in a photo released by the security forces, this concerning a staged gunfight, replicating previous cases.

These killings are part of larger pattern of extrajudicial killings, which has claimed hundreds, if not thousands, of victims. This spate of killings kicked into high gear in the summer of 2015, when the anti-terrorism law came into force, providing the security services with immunity from prosecution as long as any killing was performed in the line of duty. Indeed, based on an analysis conducted by Reuters of social media posts made by the Ministry of the Interior, between July 2015 and December 2018 (Reuters, 2019), 465 people were killed by the security forces in 108 alleged shootouts. Only six men survived these encounters, representing a kill ratio of 98.7%. Of the 471 victims, 302 were not named in the statements issued by the ministry, making it extremely difficult to verify the regime version of events. The ministry, however, classified the dead, with 320 categorized as terrorists; 117 listed as members of the Muslim Brotherhood; and 28 described as common criminals (Reuters, 2019). The causalities on the side of the security forces stood at five killed and thirty-seven injured, casting doubt on the regime's version of the events, since one would expect higher levels of casualties considering the high number of those killed by the security services. The case of two cousins, Souhail Ahmed and Zakaria Mahmoud, illustrates the arbitrary and cruel nature of the regime's violence. The two men, both in their twenties, went on a road trip from their hometown of Damietta to Sharm El-Shiekh in July 2017. Based on their families' testimonies, they were not politically active and not affiliated with the Muslim Brotherhood. Five days later, the Ministry of the Interior announced in a Facebook post that the men were killed in an alleged shootout with militants, when the security forces approached their hideout in Ismailiyah. However, it was the opinion of independent experts that the bullet wounds on the bodies of the two men indicated a point-blank-range execution. Another report issued by Human Rights Watch estimated that 755 people were killed between 2015 and 2020, in 143 shoot outs, with only one suspect arrested. It is important to note that these numbers are only estimates, based on statements made by the Ministry of the Interior; the real number is probably much higher. For example, based on the work of the El-Nadeem Centre, a local leading NGO, the number of extrajudicial killings in 2017 alone reached 1,029 cases (El Nadeem, 2017).

The systematic use of extrajudicial killings is closely linked with another tactic, namely forced disappearances, in which people are arrested by the security forces but their whereabouts are unknown, with the security forces sometimes denying that they are holding them. They are in legal limbo with no access to lawyers or support from their families; in other words, they are at the total mercy of the security forces. They sometimes reappear after false confessions are extracted from them under brutal torture. Children as young as fourteen have been subjected to this horrendous practice. For example, based on a report issued by Amnesty International (Amensty International, 2016), the case of Mazen Mohamed Abdallah, a fourteen-year-old boy at the time of his abduction, stands out for its brutality. Mazen was forcibly disappeared in September 2015 and was repeatedly raped with a wooden stick in order to extract a 'confession'. There is also the case of Islam Khalil, twenty-six at the time of his abduction in March 2015, where he

> …was subjected to 122 days of enforced disappearance. He was blindfolded and handcuffed for the whole of that time and was brutally beaten, given electric shocks including on his genitals, and suspended naked by his wrists and ankles for hours at a time by NSA interrogators in Tanta, a town north of Cairo, until he lost consciousness.

There are cases in which those that have been forcibly disappeared do not reappear. The most notorious case of a person that was suspected to have been forcibly disappeared, with his whereabouts unknown, was that of Mostafa El Naggar, a political activist, ex-Member of Parliament and one of the icons of the mass protest of 2011. El-Naggar was convicted and sentenced to three years in jail for insulting the Judiciary in December 2017, a verdict that he appealed before the Court of Cassation. Before the courts decided on his appeal, El Naggar disappeared in September 2018 (CNN, 2018) and has been missing ever since. There were rumours that he had been arrested, but the regime has denied that he is being held (Al Ahram, 2018). He is officially considered a fugitive. There is a widespread belief that El Naggar has been forcibly disappeared, but his fate remains unknown despite repeated pleas from his family. There is also the case of Asmaa Khalaf, a doctor at the Women's Health Hospital and deputy resident at the Assiut University Hospital, in the south of Egypt (El-Sadany, 2017), who was arrested on her way home, in July 2014, and forcibly disappeared. Her whereabouts remain unknown, in spite of a verdict issued by the Supreme Administrative Court, in July 2017 (Al Araby, 2017), requiring the security forces to reveal her whereabouts. Interestingly, the security forces have not denied Khalaf's arrest, but her name has not been found in any official database, indicating foul play; she remains missing. The practice of forced disappearances has claimed thousands of victim; in 2016 there were 980 cases documented, increasing in 2017 to 1,274 (El Nadeem, 2017) and escalating again in 2020 to 1,917 cases (Committee For Justice, 2021), indicating an intensification of repression.

The policy of extrajudicial killings was also creatively extended, to include those detained by the regime, employing deliberate medical negligence combined with poor prison conditions and torture – a policy designed to kill as many inmates as possible. There are no reliable estimates for the total number of victims, but the figures that are reported show a deliberate and consistent policy that started during the coup and has continued ever since. For example, from the beginning of January of 2021 until September of the same year, there were thirty-six documented cases of death in detention centres (Al Araby, 2021). Another estimate, based on a statement made Ahmed Mofrah, the head of the Committee for Justice, a Geneva-based NGO, is that the number of those who died in Egyptian prisons due to deliberate medical negligence reached 825 between June 2013 and March 2019 (Al Araby, 2019). Other estimates place the number of those killed at 1,000 victims, between June 2013 and February 2022 (Middle East Monitor, 2022), confirming a deliberate policy that has claimed the lives of hundreds, if not thousands. The most famous example of death due to deliberate medical negligence combined with poor prison conditions is that of the ousted President, Mohamed Morsi, who died in court in June 2019 (Guardian, 2019). The former President was held in a maximum security prison the Tora prison complex, where he was detained in solitary confinement for a period of six years, only allowed to leave his cell for an hour a day. During his detention, Morsi slept on a concrete floor and was denied access to medication, which was severely damaging to his health due to his diabetes and high blood pressure. His prison conditions were described by a UN panel of experts as 'brutal'. Indeed, the results of his maltreatment were clear to see, as a UN report stated (OHCR, 2019):

> Dr. Morsi was held in solitary confinement for 23 hours a day. He was not allowed to see other prisoners, even during the one hour a day when he was permitted to exercise. He was forced to sleep on a concrete floor with only one or two blankets for protection. He was not allowed access to books, journals, writing materials or a radio. Dr. Morsi was denied life-saving and ongoing care for his diabetes and high blood pressure. He progressively lost the vision in his left eye, had recurrent diabetic comas and fainted repeatedly. From this, he suffered significant tooth decay and gum infections. The authorities were warned repeatedly that Dr. Morsi's prison conditions would gradually undermine his health to the point of killing him. There is no evidence they acted to address these concerns, even though the consequences were foreseeable.

This has prompted the UN panel of experts to describe his death as a 'state sanctioned killing'. One might say that Morsi was executed by the regime without the intervention of a hangman.

Another case that garnered wide attention was that of Shady Habash, a filmmaker and photographer. Shady was arrested in March 2018 because of his participation in the making of a satirical song mocking Sisi. At the time of his death, in May 2020, he had been in pre-trial detention, without a conviction, for more than two years, which is the maximum limit in Egyptian law. According to the Public Prosecutor's statement, Shady's death was due to alcohol poisoning (France 24, 2020), insisting that he had received the required medical attention. A UN Special Rapporteur on arbitrary detention expressed concern in an official letter to the Egyptian government about the nature of Shady's death and the failure to provide adequate medical care (OHCR, 2020). Shady was twenty-four when he died.

In addition to the rampant rise in extrajudicial killings, in its various forms, the regime has also resorted to legal executions, which have increased dramatically since the coup of 2013. The executions were handed down in what was described by Amnesty International as '[g]rossly unfair mass trials' (Amnesty International, 2020). Even though there are no official statistics available, local NGOs have laboured under difficult conditions to collect data that, though incomplete and probably an underestimation, can provide some insight into the expansion of the use of the death penalty in Egypt. For example, based on the tally from the Egyptian Commission for Rights and Freedoms (ECRF), the number of executions has skyrocketed from fifteen in 2014–15 to 176 in 2020–1 (ECRF, 2021). Even though most of the executions were criminal cases, there was a substantial proportion that had a political dimension. For example, of the 176 executions carried out in 2020–1, thirty-two were classified as political. There are a number of cases in which there is considerable evidence that confessions were extracted under torture and the defendants not afforded a fair trial. For example, in the Arab Sharks case, six men were executed in May 2015 after they were convicted of attacking military forces in March 2014 and belonging to Wilayat Sinai, the local Islamic State (IS) affiliate (Mada Masr, 2015). Their conviction was delivered by a military court in October 2014. The details of the case are horrifying, revealing a draconian system at work. Besides the fact that the suspects claimed that their 'confessions' were extracted under torture (Mada Masr, 2015), three of the defendants claimed that they had been arrested and forcibly disappeared in the Al-Azouly prison, three months before the attack on the military forces took place. Hence, they were already in custody at the time of the attack. Even though there is no concrete evidence, there are a number of reports that claim that the prison, which is part of the Galaa military camp, was used by the military to detain and torture suspects. The state has not acknowledged the existence of the prison, and the men were duly convicted and executed (Bahgat, 2014). Another case involves the execution of nine men in February 2019. They were accused of assassinating the Public Prosecutor, Hesham Barakat, in a car omb in 2015. There was considerable evidence that the confessions from these men were extracted under torture (Amnesty International, 2019). The suspects alleged that after they were forcibly disappeared, they were tortured for days. Their claims were dismissed by the presiding judge, without proper forensic examination (Egyptian Initiative for Personal Rights, 2018). These are just two cases where execution can be classified as state-sanctioned killing, with a legal veneer, but they re not far removed from cases of explicit judicial killing by the security forces.

The regime was able to unleash unprecedented levels of arbitrary mass violence not only to repress dissent but to keep social conflict at bay, raising the cost of minor acts of defiance to unprecedent levels. A critical social media post was sufficient to send someone to jail for years, where a combination of medical negligence and torture could lead to a slow and deliberate death. This wave of violence was anchored in the legal and constitutional framework that the regime has built since the coup, as well in the state of political polarization that conjured up public support for these acts of killing.

Sisi's dungeons

The escalation in the level of state violence was also accompanied by a radical transformation of the Egyptian penal system, which witnessed a metamorphosis into a system of indiscriminate repression, designed to punish dissent with brutal severity. Indeed, under Sisi, the Egyptian prison system, which was already horrific under Mubarak, developed a lethal combination of endless cycles of detention, solitary confinement and horrid conditions, swallowing up thousands of victims. Placing this in context, the total number of prisoners in Egypt increased from 66,00 inmates in 2011 to 106,000 in 2018, incarcerated in seventy-eight prisons across the country (World Prison Brief, 2022). Out of these, there is an estimated 60,000 political prisoner languishing in the regime's dungeons (HRW, 2019). The conditions in these prisons, as well as the treatment of the inmates, is truly horrific. For example, even though the regime has embarked on a prison-building spree, constructing a total of thirty-five prisons between 2011 and 2021 (Arabic Network For Human Rights Information, 2021), overcrowding remains an chronic problem, with some of the most densely populated prisons exceeding their capacity by 300% (CIHR, 2020). This overcrowding has had severe detrimental effects on the physical and the mental health of the incarcerated. In addition to the overcrowded conditions, the regime has also relied on the extensive use of solitary confinement of political prisoners for years on end, with reported beatings, restriction of movement and lack of food (Amnesty International, 2018). Solitary confinement is also used as a punishment for those who protest against their maltreatment by the security forces in the regime's prisons. These conditions, combined with a policy of deliberate medical negligence, elaborated above, and torture have radically transformed the Egyptian penal system into a tool for slow executions. There are some prisons, most notably the Tora maximum security prison, also known as the Scorpion prison, that have become synonymous with prisoner abuse. Ibrahim Abd al-Ghaffar, a former warden in the prison, stated in a television interview in 2012 that the Tora prison 'was designed so that those who go in don't come out again unless dead. It was designed for political prisoners' (HRW, 2016).

These practices are combined with two other policies, namely the heavy use of pre-trial detention and the revolving-case policy, which allows the regime to imprison its opponents indefinitely, without the need for a conviction. According to Aly Badr, a member of the Human Right Committee in the Egyptian Parliament, in April 2017 60% of the prison population was held in pre-trial detention (Kamal, 2017). It is worth noting that during the Mubarak presidency, the comparative figure was 10% of the total prison population. The Mubarak regime even introduced legal reforms in 2006 and 2007 aimed at limiting the period of pre-trial detention, with a maximum six-month period for misdemeanours, eighteen months for felonies and two years for crimes that carried a life imprisonment or death sentence (Manshurat, 2006, 2007). Such moderation is not exercised under Sisi, with a large number of documented cases of defendants being kept in pretrial detention even after the maximum period of their detention has lapsed. For example, in May 2016, the Egyptian Initiative for Human Rights documented 1,464 cases of suspects, across four governates, held in pre-trial detention for periods exceeding the legal limit (EIPR, 2016). These cases were tried before special terrorism and violence circuit courts, as well as before military tribunals. In addition, many of those who were eventually found not-guilty and released by the courts had spent a substantial amount of time in pre-trial detention. In a sample of 2,700 cases in the period between 2013 and 2016, 58% had spent between six and eighteen months in pre-trial detention, while 4% had spent more than the two years in detention (Hamama, 2018). Even in cases where the suspect is released by the court, the Pubic Prosecutor tends to appeal the decision, usually resulting in a renewal of the detention. For example, Safwat Abdel Ghani, a prominent member of the Islamist legitimacy coalition, which opposed the overthrow of President Morsi, completed four years of pre-trial detention in 2018. During this period he was released four times, but the Public Prosecutor appealed each decision and Ghani's detention was extended. There is also the case of Mustafa Kassem, an Egyptian American who died in January 2020 from heart failure while serving a fifteen-year prison sentence. Kassem had been arrested in August 2013 directly after the coup and was held in pre-trial detention for five years. He was sentenced in September 2018 to fifteen years in prison, as part of a mass trial of 700 defendants that lacked due process. He was on a liquids-only hunger strike when he died in an attempt to garner more robust intervention from the Trump administration (CNN, 2020).

Closely connected to the use of pre-trial detention is the revolving-case policy, wherein a defendant is released from pre-trial detention in one case, only to immediately face charges in another case brought forward by the Public Prosecutor, the charges in the new case being very similar, if not identical, to those that applied in the first case. This practice opens up the possibility of endless detention without need of a conviction, all within the bounds of the law. For example, Mohamed Qasas, vice-president of the Strong Egypt Party, an officially recognised and legal political party with Islamist leanings, was arrested in February 2018, just before the presidential elections, as part of crackdown on the opposition. Charged with having links to the banned Muslin Brotherhood and spreading false news, Qasas was kept in solitary confinement and not allowed to leave his cell. After twenty-two months he was released from pre-trial detention by the Public Prosecutor (Al Araby, 2019), but before he could even leave his cell, fresh, almost identical, charges were levied against him in a new case. This allowed the security apparatus to keep him in pre-trial detention (Al Araby, 2019). Qasas was also released in the new case, in August 2020, only for the same process to be repeated, with a new case brought against him involving almost identical charges (Mada Masr, 2020). The same tactic was used against the leader of the Strong Egypt Party, Abdel Mounim Abou El Fotouh, a prominent opposition figure, ex-presidential candidate and ex-member of the Muslim Brotherhood. He was also arrested in February 2018, upon his return from a trip to London, after he gave an interview to Al Jazeera that was critical of Sisi (Egypt Independent, 2018). He was charged with having committed terror-related offences and remanded in pre-trial detention. Similar to Qasas, after twenty-three months in pre-trial detention Abou El Fotouh was charged in a new case, involving his alleged leadership of a terrorist organization, a veiled reference to the Muslim Brotherhood (Al Araby, 2020). In August 2021, he was charged with five new but very similar terror-related charges (Middle East Monitor, 2022). Since his arrest in February 2018, Abou El Fotouh has been kept in solitary confinement, in conditions that have seen his health rapidly deteriorate (Committee For Justice, 2022). On 29 May 2022, he was sentenced to fifteen years in prison, while al-Qassa received a ten-year prison sentence (Al Jazeera, 2020).

This revolving-case practice is not aimed solely at prominent members of the opposition, but also extends to members of the general public. Ahmed Sabry was first arrested in January 2018, when he was eighteen years old, and since then has been held in pre-trial detention, without a criminal conviction, in spite of being released by the courts on multiple occasions. The Ministry of the Interior simply refrained from releasing him, while the Public Prosecutor levied fresh charges each time the maximum pre-trial detention period was reached. He was even found not-guilty by a court in April 2022, only to be held by the security forces and charged in a new case, with almost identical charges. All the charges were terror-related, including that of joining a terrorist organization. In total, Sabry has faced charges in four different cases since 2018, spending years in jail without a single conviction (EIPR, 2022). This policy is extremely pervasive, with at least 2,299 cases documented by a local NGO between 2020 and 2021. This number is probably a substantial underestimation considering the great difficulty in collecting data on this matter (Transparency Center for Archiving Data Management and Research, 2022).

The horrid conditions in the regime's prisons have transformed them into hotbeds of radicalism. These conditions, combined with a policy of not separating radical elements, mostly members of the local IS branch, from more moderate Islamists or bystanders caught up in the regime's repressive sweeps, have facilitated the process of radicalization. The suspects are grouped according to their charges, and since radical elements face the same charges as moderate Islamists or secular activists, the result is the possible radicalization of thousands. Indeed, the regime's penal policy is a super-spreader of radicalism amongst those that survive its cruelty, similar to the way in which Nasser's repression was the harbinger of the first wave of Jihadists in 1960s under Sayyid Qutub. The most prominent example of this kind of development is Mahmoud Shafiq Mohammad Mostafa, who in December 2016 blew himself up in a suicide attack on a church in the middle of Cairo, killing thirty-one people and injuring dozens more. Mahmoud Shafiq had been one of those arrested in the summer of 2013, after the coup. He was held in Fayoum prison, in pre-trial detention, where he was exposed to jihadi elements and ideas. He was released in May 2014, finishing his high school degree and joining the Department of Natural Science in Fayoum University. However, in summer 2014 he was sentenced to two years in prison in absentia since he failed to attend the court hearing. He was charged with illegally protesting. He went on the run and disappeared only to reappear in the attack on the church in 2016, when he was identified as the attacker. It later became apparent that he had travelled to North Sinai where he joined Wilayat Sinai, the local IS branch, and participated in the attack. He was twenty-two when he died (ARIJ, 2022).

The systematic reliance on mass incarceration as a matter of long-term policy became apparent in September 2021, when President Sisi announced on a popular television talk show the opening of a new prison complex, called New Wadi Al-Natrun (Egypt Today, 2021). The new complex is the largest in the country's history, covering 216 hectares and with an estimated capacity of 34,000 inmates. It is so large that the Ministry of the Interior announced, in October 2021, the closure of twelve prisons across the country (Badry, 2021), to be replaced by the new complex. New Wadi Al-Natrun has a high degree of self-sufficiency, with large water containers, greenhouses for food production, industrial workshops and a court complex, as well as an NSA headquarters. The inmates no longer need to leave the prison to attend court, limiting their exposure to the outside during prolonged periods of pre-trial detention. The prison complex is located on the desert road between Cairo and Alexandria, 162 km north of the capital and away from populations centres – a literal a fortress in the desert. The feature of the prison that has raised some concerns are the four maximum security buildings that appear to be designed in a similar fashion to the Scorpion prison, with an apparent abundance of solitary-confinement cells. The location and size of New Wadi Al-Natrun indicate an intensification of repression, with the regime creating the necessary infrastructure to keep thousands incarcerated in an isolated location (We Record, 2021). This not only increases the hardship of thousands of families who have loved ones imprisoned, but also gives the security forces greater latitude to abuse the inmates since they are even more removed from the public eye. It also ensures that the mass prison breaks that took place in 2011 will be much more difficult to repeat, allowing the regime to keep thousands hostage in case of mass social upheaval. New Wadi Al-Natrun is not the only one of its kind, with news appearing in early 2022 of another prison complex with a capacity to house 20,000 inmates being built in North Sinai, a very remote area, certainly for any inmates from the Nile Valley, making it extremely difficult for family members to visit and for lawyers to have access to their clients (Mada Masr, 2022).

The launch of the new New Wadi Al-Natrun prison complex was accompanied by an Orwellian propaganda campaign, touting the regime's humane treatment of prisoners. This included, a ten-minute propaganda video showing the inside of the prison, its state-of-the-art medical facilities and a number of hobbies that inmates could pursue, from painting to sculpting and sports (YouTube, 2021). Considering the actual conditions of Egyptian prisons, it had the feel of a fantasy film, rather than an infomercial. It was even accompanied by the launch of a music video for a song called a 'Chance for Life', showing one of the inmates painting a picture of Sisi (Sky News, 2021) – a truly Orwellian scene. In a feeble rebranding effort, the prison authority was also renamed as the 'Social Protection Authority' (Nawafez, 2021). This great fanfare was all part of the regime's attempts to give its penal policy a new image – one focused on rehabilitation rather than punishment.

In fact the regime has deliberately transformed the penal system into a tool for mass incarceration and repression of its opponents, a systematic policy that show no signs of abating. For example, in addition to the 60,000 political prisoners noted above, local NGOs have claimed that at least 16,064 people were subjected to arrest for political reasons in 2020 and 2021. This number is a modest one due to difficulty of collecting relevant data, and also due to exclusion of North Sinai from the report due to complete lack of data in that area. The NGO report further notes that 90% of those arrested were charged with having joined a terrorist group, 44% were accused of the misuse of social media and 35% accused of illegal protest. The transformation of the penal system has become one of the darkest chapters of Egypt's deepening social crisis (Transparency Center for Archiving Data Management and Research, 2022), a development that will further reduce the prosect of democratic transition and reconciliation.

The costs of an insurgency

The mass state violence unleashed in the aftermath of 2013 precipitated an insurgency of varying intensity across the country, with a plethora of groups claiming attacks against the security forces, and civilian targets, leaving behind thousands of dead. The total number of security force personnel killed reached 3,277, based on a statement made by Sisi in April 2022 (Essam, 2022). The response of the regime, however, was extremely repressive and indiscriminate, especially in Sinai, where reports of the use of heavy weaponry, airstrikes and extrajudicial killings abound, some already discussed above. This has only served to intensify the insurgency, and increase the number of civilian causalities, while heightening the level of social and political polarization in the country to an unprecedent degree. The insurgency also provided the regime with a justification for broadening and deepening its repressive practices to an unprecedented degree.

Interestingly the hazards of using the military to repress the militants in Sinai was well known to Sisi. During the Morsi presidency, Sisi was asked to use the military to confront the growing insurgency in North Sinai, a request that he refused stating that 'my mission is not to combat terrorism'. He is also reported to have highlighted the dangers of using the military to combat the militants, as this would lead to 'very grave dangers' to civilians in Sinai, arguing that in the end '[y]ou would create an enemy against you and against your country, because there will have been bad blood between you and him' (Kirkpatrick, 2019, p. 175). However, Sisi did not heed his own prudent advice, deploying the military with full force against the insurgents, leading to a large number of civilian casualties while fuelling the insurgency through the military's heavy-handed tactics. This heavy-handedness failed to completely end the uprising, at least at the time of writing.

The most important of the militant groups is Wilayat Sinai, previously known as Ansar Beit El Maqdas. The group is thought to have formed in 2011, but it pledged allegiance to IS in April 2014. It was already carrying out attacks before the coup of 2013, but the intensity of the insurgency increased exponentially after the coup. The main base of the group's operation is North Sinai, but it has claimed attacks across the country, including the worst terror attack in modern Egyptian history. This took place in November 2017 and claimed the lives of over 300 civilians in an attack on a Sufi mosque in Sinai (TIMEP, 2017). The group is also responsible for a large number of attacks against the security forces, especially in Sinai, where the number of attacks reached a frequency of at least one per day at the height of the insurgency. For example, in the third quarter of 2016, the number of attacks claimed by the group reached 133, with an average of forty-eight per month for the first six months of 2016, compared to twenty-eight attacks per month for the last six months of 2015 (TIMEP, 2016). This large number of attacks was carried out by a small number of dedicated insurgents, with the Central Intelligence Agency (CIA) (State, 2015) and the Israeli Defence Forces (IDF) (IDF, 2016) estimating the size of the group at around a thousand members. In spite of its small size, Wilayat Sinai has carried out a significant number of successful large-scale attacks against the Egyptian security forces, especially against stationary targets. For example, in January 2015, thirty-two members of the security forces were killed in a wave of attacks carried out by the militant group on army bases and police stations (Kingesly and Abdo, 2015). In July 2107, twenty-three members of the security forces were killed in a similar attack (Guardian, 2017). This trend continued up to May 2022, with the death of eleven members of the security forces in an attack on a checkpoint guarding a pumping station in Sinai (Al Jazeera, 2022). The group even claimed an attack on the Arish International Airport in December 2017 (Higazy, 2017) during an unannounced visit by the Interior Minister Magdy Abdel Ghaffar and the Minister of Defence Sedky Sobhy (Khalil, 2018), illustrating the ability of Wilayat Sinai to compromise the regime's security protocols and target its senior officials. It was even able to deal a significant blow to the Egyptian economy when it planted a bomb on board a Russian commercial jet, killing all 217 passengers (Hanna, 2015). This led to the suspension of Russian flights to the Red Sea resorts towns Sharm El Shiekh and Hurghada for six years, with flights only being restored in August 2021 (Reuters, 2021).

The response of the security forces to these attacks was ferocious, employing collective punishment, depopulation, the use of heavy weapons in civilian areas, and extrajudicial killings, with catastrophic consequences for the civilian population. The military launched a number of large operations over the years, including Operation Eagle in 2012 (Eleiba, Al Ahram, 2012), Operation Martyr's Right in 2015 and the Comprehensive Military Operation also known as Operation Sinai in 2018 (Eleiba, Al Ahram, 2018), all of which failed to end the insurgency. However, the intensity of the insurgency seems to have abated over time, at least based on media reports. The reaction of the regime to the attack on the Arish International Airport is a clear example of its heavy-handed approach. In January 2018, Sisi announced the creation of a safe zone around the airport of 5 km to the east, west and south of the airport and 1.5 km to the north. This entailed the removal of a large number of residential buildings, farmlands and villages around the city. This buffer zone included the erection of a large concrete wall, separating the city of Arish from the proposed safe zone, cutting off the city from swathes of farmland. Extensive tracts of farmland were indeed erased to create the safe zone (Mada Masr, 2018), an indication that winning the hearts and minds of the locals was not on the regime's agenda.

The heavy-handed counter-insurgency tactics also included a policy of depopulation when necessary. For example, in June 2014, in its attempt to control its border with the Gaza Strip, the security forces decided to create a buffer and isolation zone of 79 km^2, stretching along the Gaza border. This included the entire town of Rafah and a substantial area of farmland around the town. Between July 2013 and August 2015, the regime, carried out the destruction of 3,250 residential buildings around the Gaza border, and the razing of 675 hectares of farmland, without appropriate compensation or alternative housing provided for the residents (HRW, 2015). This policy scattered thousands to places as far away as the Delta and Cairo, with many of the displaced living in tents or sheds, reminiscent of IDF policy in the occupied Palestinian territories. By July 2020, the total number of residential buildings that had been destroyed totalled 12,350, while some 6,000 hectares of farmland had been taken out of commission – a mass act of depopulation and displacement (HRW, 2021).

The policy of depopulation is combined with the use of heavy weaponry in civilian areas and the use of extrajudicial killings, leading to large number of civilian casualties. Simple arithmetic reveals the deadly logic at play. A year after the commencement of Operation Martyr's Right, which began in September 2015, the military claimed that it had killed 2,539 militants (TIMEP, 2016), two and a half times the size of the Wilayat Sinai, based on the estimates of the CIA and the IDF (David Kirkpatrick puts the total tally of Wilayat Sinai casualties at 6,200, based on a government press release – six times the estimated size of the group (Kirkpatrick, 2019, p. 287)). If true, this should have ended the insurgency completely, unless the reported dead militants, at least to some extent, included civilian casualties that the security forces claimed to be militants, a manipulation of the figures for which there is considerable evidence (New Humanitarian, 2013). There are also reports of the use of heavy weaponry and air strikes in civilian areas, with villages associated with the militants suffering almost total destruction from heavy shelling (Afify, 2015). For example, in 2016 the Nadeem Centre, a leading local NGO, reported a total of 1,384 cases of extrajudicial killings, with 1,234 cases reported in Sinai. Airstrikes account for most cases of death in these incidents (451), followed by extrajudicial execution (443 reported cases). Death from artillery shelling was considerably lower, but still stood at 56 cases (El Nadeem, 2016). Another feature of the counter-insurgency is the constant state of emergency and curfew imposed on the civilian population, which started in June 2014, after thirty-one soldiers were killed by militants (Al Jazeera, 2014), and was most recently extended, in April 2022 for an additional six month (Egypt Today, 2022). This policy only serves to alienate the local population that found itself between the hammer of the state and the anvil of the militants (Mikhail, 2016).

Wilayat Sinai was not the only group to emerge from Sisi's repression. Hasm is the other main militant group, mostly operating in Cairo and the Delta (Cummings, 2017). The ideology and affiliation of this group is not clear, but its deadly intent certainly is. Hasm was assumed to be responsible for a deadly ambush against the security forces in October 2017, resulting in the death of fifty-four police officers (Zaki, 2017), who were said to have been killed when they approached the group's hideout, around 135 km south-west of Cairo.

The regime's repression has therefore fed a burgeoning insurgency, which in turn only served to justify the state's mass repression, in a vicious cycle of violence. Sisi's heavy-handed tactics not only failed to eradicate the insurgency, but has had long-term social and political consequences of increased polarization that will far outlive Sis and the regime that he has built.

Haussmann in Cairo

In March 2021, President Sisi declared what he called a 'New Republic' (Essam El-Din, 2021). The occasion for the announcement was the inauguration of the New Administrative Capital (NAC), a US$58 billion mega project, the most expensive of the regime's white elephants. The new city was designed to replace Cairo as Egypt's capital. It contains a business district, government buildings and presidential palaces, with an estimated capacity of six million residents (Egypt Independent, 2022). The NAC is the most tangible manifestation of the regime's fear of a mass urban uprising in congested, rebellious Cairo. The ghost of 2011, when attacks on police stations across the city were critical for the success of the mass protests and the removal of Mubarak, still haunts the regime and its security apparatus. Indeed, some ninety-nine police stations across Egypt were looted in this period (Ismail S., 2012), incapacitating the domestic security apparatus that was critical to Mubarak's survival. This was coupled with the occupation of the public space, which was of critical importance for the regime's ability to function, most notably Tahrir Square. Mona El- Ghobashy explains the terror facing the police on the eve of the 2011 mass protests, with protest groups roaming the streets and threatening to severely disrupt the government's ability to operate:

> The exceptionally compact layout of the city centre explains police commanders' terror at the prospect of roaming demonstrations. Visualize a plaza, Tahrir Square, ringed by several important

> buildings: The American University in Cairo Campus; the higher government complex of Al- Mugamma; the Arab League Headquarter; the Nile Hilton; the government's National Democratic Party (NDP) headquarters; and the Egyptian Antiquities museum. Within half a mile of the Plaza sits more sensitive buildings: The Maspero state radio and television headquarter to the north; the two houses of parliament to the south; the Interior Ministry to the southeast, the British and US embassies to the southwest, and the bar association, High Court, press syndicate, and the judge club to the southwest. West of the square are two bridges connecting central Cairo to the teeming western neighbourhoods of the mega city.
>
> El Ghobashy, 2021, p. 5

The NAC will ensure that a similar scenario is unlikely to occur, as the regime attempts to move the centre of government away from the urban masses, in a large-scale social engineering experiment, transforming Cairo into a slum for the poor and those left behind in the middle class.

The first indicator of the regime's strategy is the price of the flats in the NAC, which stands at US$62,000 for a two-bedroom flat (Guardian, 2018), a price tag that puts it beyond the reach of most Egyptians. To put this in context, the Egyptian GDP per capita hovers around US$3,000, or 5% of the price of a two-bedroom flat in the NAC. Therefore, moving to the new capital is only a possibility for the elites, while the urban poor and the middle class are left behind. This will allow the regime to surround the centre of government with a supportive social base, one that is unlikely to revolt. It also reduces the ability of Cairenes to exert pressure on the regime through mass protests that would block government operations, since, simply, the government is no longer there. The regime is creating a new urban space that is easier to control, unlike Cairo with its urban poor and narrow twisted streets. The second indicator of the regime's strategy is the location of the NAC, and the accompanying transportation infrastructure. Located 65 km east of Cairo, and 60 km from Ayn El Sokhna, it occupies a strategic location in the desert, far enough from rebellious Cairo to make it difficult for the protestors to reach, but close enough to the Red Sea in case of the need for a quick escape (El Sakty, 2021). The NAC will also have its own airport, with plans for a fast-rail link, at an estimated cost of US$23 billion (Abu Zaid, 2021), connecting the Red Sea and the Mediterranean coasts, passing through the NAC (Egypt Project Map, 2022), again ensuring a quick escape if required. The first phase, at an estimated cost of US$3 billion, began in February 2021 (Egypt Independent, 2021).

Coupled with the NAC, the regime also embarked on a policy of mass urban engineering, with the apparent goal of altering the urban landscape in a manner that would allow the security forces to tighten their grip over Cairo, moving thousands of urban poor away from the city centre into new urban settlements that can be easily policed. For example, the urban slum of the Maspero triangle, located in a strategic location by the Nile and very close to the Foreign Ministry and the headquarters of the National Radio and Television – important government buildings that project the regime's power – was the sight of one of the earlier massacres committed against protesters, when twenty-eight Coptic demonstrators were killed by members of the security forces in the summer of 2011 (Khalifa, Amr, 2014), with the state-owned TV broadcasting calls for citizens to defend the armed forces, a call with sectarian undertones. The development project at this location involved the complete destruction of the existing slum, to be replaced by an investment and residential hub, with an estimated budget of US$222 million. The residents of the slum were offered three options: either relocate to the Asmarat neighbourhood in the south-eastern outskirts of the city; return to the area after the completion of the project where they can buy or rent accommodation at in increased cost; or accept financial compensation of Eg£100,000 (= US$5,300) (Farouk M., Al Monitor, 2017). Almost 70% of the residents accepted the financial compensation. This process allowed the regime to change the social composition of a vital area of the city, replacing the original urban poor with upper-middle-class elites that are less likely to revolt or to clash violently with the security forces.

The Maspero triangle development is part of a comprehensive policy with an estimated cost of Eg£318 billion (= US$17 billion) under the control of the Slum Development Fund (Abdu, 2020). There are other examples of residents being allowed to return after a development project was complete, but as tenants rather than owners, placing them at the mercy of the regime and subject to arbitrary eviction. For example, Tala Al Aqarib slum – one of the oldest in the city, founded by rural migrants in the 1920s – was torn down in 2015 as part of the urban development scheme, with the residents returning in 2019 as tenants. The developed slum, however, was easier for the security forces to control and penetrate, as residents of the slums have reported (Tarek, 2021). This is very different from the Mubarak-era policing policy, when the security forces tended to limit their presence in slums to larger thoroughfares rather than smaller alleyways. The police tended to patrol bridges at night, requesting the identity cards of youth leaving or entering the slum, with residents believing that to return home after

11 pm meant risking an unpleasant encounter with the police. In essence, residents were under siege and their movements tightly controlled (Ismail S., 2006, pp. 155–6). Now, however, there is a clear policy to relocate the urban poor away from the city centre and towards the outskirts, with some 850,000 residents earmarked for relocation between 2016 and 2021. As of 2020, 750,000 people have been relocated (Farouk M., Reuters, 2020). This is a massive undertaking, aimed at fundamentally altering the social composition of entire neighbourhoods and allowing the regime to tightens its grip on Cairo.

The other side of the coin is economic, in which, under the pretext of urban development, prime areas of real estate are taken over by the regime, transforming them into areas of luxury real estate, like the Maspero triangle. The other prominent example of area transformation is Warqa Island, located in the middle of the Nile. The residents here have a long history of resistance against attempts to dispossess them under the guise of development during the Mubarak era, a resistance that has continued under Sisi. The island was earmarked as a site of luxury real estate development, part of a joint project between the government and the Army Engineering Corps. In July 2017, during an attempt to demolish 700 houses on the islands, clashes erupted between the security forces and the residents, leading to the death of one resident and injury to thirty-seven members of the security forces (Mada Masr, 2017). The clashes led to the arrest of thirty-five residents and their trial before a terrorism court. The sentences that were handed down in December 2020 were draconian, with one defendant sentenced to life imprisonment, thirty sentenced to fifteen years in prison and four sentenced to five years in prison (Manshurat, 2020).

The regime's drive for urban development was accompanied by heavy investment in transport infrastructure, which would allow military and paramilitary troops to be quickly deployed across the unruly city. Indeed, the regime engaged in a bridge-building frenzy, with forty bridges constructed at an estimated cost of US$895 million, concentrated in the eastern part of the city (Woof, 2020). The top-down and heavy-handed nature of the projects became apparent in the case of Terat El-Zomor bridge, which was built a mere 50 cm away from the balcony of some of the residents (El-Shamaa, 2020), and completed in spite of the objection of those residents. Even the historic part of the city was not spared the heavy-handedness of the regime, with a large part of the historic Mameluke Cemetery demolished as part of the Paradise Axis project, a road development through the slums of Mansheyat Nasir and Duwaika (Al Monitor, 2020).

The regime has, indeed, laid out a staggering plan of urban control. Learning the lessons of 2011, when protestors attacked police stations across the city, exhausting the security forces and leading to their collapse, it has created a new urban reality. The regime has restructured the urban landscape of the city, locating large sections of the troublesome urban poor away from the centres of government and has proceeded to build an urban transportation network that will allow the security forces to repress protests with greater ease. The fast deployment of troops and the demographic buffer was accompanied by a much more radical solution, namely a new capital city populated by the elites. This would allow the regime to remain in power even if it loses control of large urban centres like Cairo and Alexandria. However, and most disturbingly, these changes will allow the regime to unleash mass repression on urban centres if needed, while shielding the elites from scenes of mass slaughter. Indeed, Sisi has laid out the necessary infrastructure for a Syria-like scenario in Egypt, if that should be necessary.

A regime held hostage

Empowered by a draconian legal system, and in complete control of the state apparatus, the military has cast its repressive net far and wide. Its victims include researchers and academics like Ismail El Eskandrany; activists like Ala Abdel Fatah; politicians like Abdel Moneim Aboul Fotouh, and ordinary citizens that caught in repressive machinery of the regime, like the Tik Tok girls. The regime's repression appears to have a clear logic: by raising the cost of minor acts of dissent to the extent that it guarantees the complete closure of the public space, continuation of direct military rule is ensured. It is a policy aimed at making the regime impervious to change from below. However, a closer examination shows a much more complex dynamic at play, one that holds the regime hostage to its own repressive policies, reducing its ability to manoeuvre and its ability to absorb popular shocks. This reduces the regime's resilience and makes repression rather than co-option its default policy choice.

The most glaring characteristic of the regime's repression is its ideological imperative, not just to maintain its popular appeal but to maintain the cohesion of the security forces. The regime's raison d'être, based on the its own narrative, is to protect the Egyptian state from collapse by combating traitors, terrorists and foreign agents. This logic not only helps the regime to consolidate its support base but it also justifies the complete closure of the public space, and the intense repression required to do so. Hence, any attempts at easing repression would raise questions about the need to completely close the public space, the necessity for the continuation of military rule, and, most importantly, the truthfulness of the regime narratives that are used to solicit popular support for its repression. Indeed, a simple question from its base, such as why release accused terrorists from prison, would be extremely difficult to answer. The regime is therefore under pressure from its own base to continue its repression. Indeed, popular support for the regime exists *because* of its repression, not in spite of it.

The pressure, however, is not limited to the base alone, as it also comes from within the security apparatus, especially from the petty security official and judges, the ones on the front lines in the regime war against dissent. These men have been indoctrinated in the regime's chauvinistic version of nationalism, which is founded on the existence of an internal enemy, threatening the fabric of the nation. This became apparent in the Regeni case. When he was believed to be a spy by the regime's security officials, the standard operating procedure was applied, namely severe torture which led to his death. Hence, any attempts at easing repression jeopardizes the credibility of the regime narrative – which is essential for maintaining the cohesion of the security apparatus – and is bound to be strongly resisted by its members. This brings us to the second characteristic of the regime's repression, namely its decentralized nature. In essence, the ideological indoctrination and the widespread popular support, as well as the legal immunity of the security forces, have made repression and torture endemic and decentralized. Indeed, the use of state violence has become a standard operating procedure, rather than a tool employed by the security forces to protect the regime, a feature that Human Right Watch has called 'an assembly line of torture' (HRW, 2017). This means that the centre can no longer control the periphery, and even if Sisi wished to rein in the repressive apparatus, he would struggle to do so.

The regime's reliance on repression, and Sisi's inability to rein in the security apparatus at will, stems from another structural feature, namely the lack of a civilian counterweight to the military and the security apparatus. Unlike Mubarak, Sadat or Nasser, Sisi does not seem interested in establishing a ruling party, which he could then use to hold in check the military and the security forces. Indeed, his main strategy seems to revolve around tightening his grip over the security apparatus and intelligence agencies through the appointment of loyalists, rather than developing a civilian counterweight to the military's dominance.

The most prominent example of this feature of the regime was the appointment of Abbas Kamel, a close confidant, as the head of the General Intelligence Services (GIS) in June 2018 (Egypt Today, 2018). The absence of a mass ruling party, along the lines of Mubarak's NDP or Nasser's Arab Socialist Union (ASU), significantly reduces the ability of the regime to co-opt the citizenry, making repression the primary tool for managing dissent. This situation is exacerbated by the regime's success in decimating and discrediting the moderate opposition, most notably the Muslim Brotherhood, which had a long history of working with the regime and the military establishment in moments of crisis (Gerges, 2018), most notably in the 2011–12 period (Kandil, 2015). This is very similar to the role that the secular opposition played in the aftermath of the coup of 2013, when the first post-coup government included secular and leftist figures like labour activist Kamal Abu Eita (Al Ahram, 2013) and the liberal figure Ziad Bahaa El-Din (Gulhane, 2013), helping to legitimize the coup. This has a simple yet significant consequence, namely the inability of the regime to negotiate with an organized, moderate opposition at times of mass social upheaval, making mass repression the only possible policy option. Indeed, the Muslim Brotherhood has been so thoroughly vilified that any attempts at reconciliation or negotiating with the group would lead to a disintegration of the regime's ideological edifice and the rapid loss of popular support, which would have catastrophic consequences for the regime. The same applies to the secular opposition, albeit to a lesser extent. Repression has become endemic and is unlikely to abate due to ideological and structural constraints that are beyond the control of Sisi and his generals. This would explain cases where repression seemed senseless, and more costly than beneficial for the regime. Such a case is that of the economist Ayman Hadhoud, who was arrested and forcibly disappeared in February 2022 (Egypt Watch, 2022). His body was found in April 2022, in Al- Abbasiya mental hospital, bearing what appeared to be torture marks, including bruises, cuts and dislocated bones (DAWN, 2022). Hadhoud had been a member of the Reform and Development Party, led by Anwar El-Sadat, the nephew of Egypt's ex-President. Sadat was a member of the parliamentary human rights committee at the time of Hadhoud's abduction, and was leading the negotiations with the regime for the release of a small number of political prisoners. Hadhoud was by no means a radical, but rather a member of a legal political party, which, by all counts, was close to the regime and the security apparatus – part of the domesticated opposition. His death baffled many, but considering the endemic nature of repression in Egypt, it should have come as no surprise. The regime's policy of repression has clearly gone beyond its control, in a manner that will prove costly to Egypt and Egyptians.

The end game

The regime's policy of mass repression will have long-term consequences that go beyond the misery sweeping the country. The most obvious consequence is the mass loss of life and its long-term traumatic effects. The victims are numbered in the thousands, including those killed and those that are imprisoned for years. This has created deep wounds in Egyptian society that will be very difficult to heal. The complicating factor is the public support that the regime's repression has enjoyed, especially the first wave of repression and massacres in 2013, under the influence of mass propaganda campaigns. Popular participation in the regime's repression has created substantial barriers to possible reconciliation between regime supporters and the opposition, especially the Islamists who have been particularly targeted. These barriers will be difficult to overcome and will make the prospect of peaceful coexistence between the bulk of the regime's support base and the opposition a remote one, which in turn will further delay the prospect democratic transition.

These barriers are made more formidable by the regime's success in debilitating the opposition, making the prospect of an elite-managed gradual transition to democracy ever more unlikely. Indeed, if a popular mass uprising erupts, the regime will have no viable policy choice but to repress it, since, simply put, there is no organized opposition to negotiate with. Even the moderate Muslim Brotherhood, which was a willing negotiating partner in 2011, can no longer fulfil that role, since it would simply disintegrate under pressure from its own base. The regime has in effect created a zero-sum game, through its use of extremely repressive tactics, making a head-on, direct confrontation more likely. This zero-sum logic, combined with mass repression over several years and horrific prison conditions, has created the perfect conditions for the rise of radical groups on an unprecedented scale. Granted, the potential insurgency facing the regime, although deadly, is not strong enough to threaten it, but it can evolve rapidly in the case of mass social unrest, taking advantage of a security vacuum that might develop . One only needs to remember Syria, where mass repression over years, combined with mass social unrest and the weakness of the secular opposition, paved the way for the rise of extremely violent radical groups, leading to the collapse of the state in large areas of the country. In some ways, the regime narrative of impending state collapse might prove prophetic, as a direct result of its own repressive policies.

This zero-sum logic, the ideological necessity of repression, combined with its extremely violent nature also make the prospect of elite-led reform from within the military establishment unlikely. Indeed, the structure of the regime, with its lack of a civilian ruling party, the decimation of the opposition and the complete dominance of the security establishment, means that repression has become endemic. This means that the response to any signs of social unrest will necessarily be extremely repressive. Indeed, unless the regime experiences an external shock, like the military defeat of 1967 or a deep economic crisis, then the likelihood of a peaceful transition to democratic rule is unlikely. The regime has now become beholden to its own repressive practices, limiting its policy options. This, in turn, will, most likely, make the security officials and the regime's support base more radical, as the level of violent repression escalates. This will be accompanied by an intensification of the regime's chauvinistic forms of nationalism, solidifying yet another barrier to democratic transition. The impact of the regime's repression is multifaceted and complex, and its long-term social and political impacts are legion. Sisi and his regime have transformed Egypt into a harsher, darker place, and his legacy, similar to that of Assad or Saddam, will linger for decades to come.

Chapter 4

POTS, PANS AND GUNS

> 'The Egyptian Army is a great patriotic army. The Egyptian Army is a very noble and tough army, and it's toughness comes from its nobility.'
>
> — Abdel Fattah El-Sisi

The coup in 2013 not only ushered in a concentration of political power without precedent in the hands of the military establishment in Egypt, but also entailed a transformation of the Egyptian political economy on an unprecedented scale. Indeed, the ability of the military establishment to take complete control of the state apparatus has allowed it to become the dominant economic actor in the country, not only in terms of direct economic activity, but, more importantly, as the policymaker. In essence, the military establishment, using the apparatus of the state, is now able to determine the socio-economic process of capital accumulation in Egypt. This, in turn, will affect social and class structures in the country, with long-term consequences that will far outlive Sisi and his regime.

The new role of the military establishment as a policymaker in the economic sphere is one consequence of the change in its status from prominent stakeholder and policy influencer, during the Mubarak era, to direct ruler, with economic policy geared towards enrichment of the military establishment and its elites.

The process of capital accumulation in Egypt is historically state-centric, in which the state has played an essential role, either as the main economic actor in the country during the Nasser era, or as an appropriator of public funds on behalf of state-dependent bourgeoisie during the Mubarak years. However, Sisi has introduced a new variant to these patterns which has led to a historic increase in poverty and the exploitation-rates faced by the poor. This, in turn, has led to the expansion of military-economic enterprises, which both enjoy multiple tax exemptions and lie completely outside civilian control. A militarized form of aggressive state capitalism, devoid of any principles of social justice or provision for the public good, now prevails. This has transformed the coercive apparatus of the state into a profit-making business enterprise, incentivizing it to repress the labour movement and any potential social unrest. Arguably, this is will be the most enduring legacy of Sisi's passive revolution, ushering in a new phase of state capitalism that is extremely resistant to reform.

This expansion has been primarily driven by multi-billion-dollar mega-infrastructure projects – of dubious economic benefit – in which the military plays a direct role. Control of the levers of the state and economic policy is critical for this process. The spending spree involved in this process has been financed through debt accumulation, both domestic and foreign. Furthermore, this debt has not only financed the growth of the military itself but was one of the tools used by the regime to entrench itself in the global financial system, thereby, in effect, tying its survival to those of global financial interests. This expansion was accompanied by a drastic change in the legal and constitutional framework of public institutions, aimed at weakening their supervisory and anti-corruption roles so that the military's chokehold on the economy could not be challenged.

The concentration of economic power in the hands of military elites has been accompanied by an extensive transfer of wealth from the lower and middle classes to the upper classes, especially to the military elites. This was achieved through a combination of a reduction in social spending, a regressive taxation system and debt interest repayments, a system that was also used to finance the mega-infrastructure projects, thus directly financing the military's economic expansion.

These processes, which will be discussed in detail in this chapter, should be viewed as an integrated and comprehensive whole. Indeed, the military's quest for economic dominance should be seen as part of its overall goal of complete control over politics and the state. The aim was to ensure that no rival power-centre with an independent economic base could emerge to challenge the military's position. General economic development, welfare and the provision of consumer goods are not prioritized in this system, which will have devastating long-term economic and social consequences.

Before proceeding with the rest of the chapter, a note on the theoretical framework used in the analysis is in order. In his seminal work *Rule of Experts*, Timothy Mitchell argued that the dominant feature in the story of capitalism is that of a universal free-standing object, with its own internal logic, regardless of the local variations and social relations in which it is embedded. In essence, bestowing upon it a universal nature, transcending local conditions. As Mitchell argues, this only conceals more than it reveals but also obscures the impact of local market and non-market conditions, which affects the nature and dynamic of the local version of capitalism (Mitchell, 2002). Therefore, the rest of this chapter will look at the development of capitalism under Sisi, not as a stand-alone object, but within the broader social relations in which the economy is embedded, including the role of international actors and financial markets as critical components in the development of a militarized variant of Egyptian capitalism.

The first part of this chapter will examine the expansion of the military's economic footprint a the alteration in the legal framework and hollowing out of state institutions accompanying this expansion. The second half of the chapter will examine the impact of these policies on overall economic performance, poverty rates, elite enrichment and capital formation. Finally, the chapter will conclude with a review of the role of international capital in the regime's economic model, and the long-term impact of these policies on Egypt's economic prospects.

The military's economic expansion

Even though the military's economic role in Egypt is not new, since it dates back to the late 1970s, with its production of civilian products reaching US$300 million by the early 1980s (Richards and Waterbury, 2008), the advent of direct military rule ushered in a spectacular growth of the military's economic footprint. This has been primarily driven by the massive, debt-financed investment drive for major infrastructural projects, and for other projects in which the military plays a prominent role, either directly implementing the project in question or managing that project with a civilian partner. The total value invested in such projects reached US$200 billion over a five-year period, as President Sisi made clear in November 2019 (Ghali, Hosni and Bedawi, 2019). To put this figure in context, the size of Egypt's GDP at the end of 2019 was US$319 billion (Trading Economics, 2020), so that the investment total was equivalent to two-thirds of GDP, a massive tally. In October 2022, the *Financial Times* estimated that US$400 billion was invested by the regime in infrastructure projects, double the amount stated by Sisi in 2019 (England, 2022).

The level of investment involved was reflected in the total number of civilians employed in these projects. For example, in December 2016, Kamel El Wazeer, the head of the Army's Engineering Authority at the time, stated that military-run infrastructure projects were directly and indirectly employing more than two million engineers and technicians. This included projects that covered road and transportation development, housing, and water treatment (Abdulallah, 2016). In September 2019, the military spokesperson Colonel Tamer Rafai put forward an even larger figure, claiming that the military was managing 2,300 projects employing five million civilians nationwide (El Naggar, 2019). Assuming that both figures are accurate, this indicates that there has been a rapid rise in military economic activity within the span of three years.[1] Since the total Egyptian labour force has hovered around 30 million workers during the same period (World Bank, 2020), then the share of civilian employment controlled by the Egyptian military has risen from 7% to 17%, an astounding increase. It also makes the military the second largest national employer after the Egyptian public sector, which employed 5.6 million workers as of 2018 (Emam, 2018).

There have been several high-profile projects of dubious economic benefit, which were touted by the regime as economically transformative. The most notable of these have been the New Suez Canal and the new administrative capital. The new US$8.2 billion Suez Canal project (Habib and Cunningham, 2015) was completed in August 2015, amidst much fanfare including a lavish ceremony, with President Sisi appearing in full military attire (Abdel Khaliq, 2017). It was touted as a major achievement, completed in adverse conditions, which would serve as the bedrock for Egypt's economic revival. Indeed, the head of the Canal authority, Muhab Memsih, stated in November 2014, when the project was still under construction, that he expected the new canal revenues to reach US$100 billion per annum (Hagag and Gendy, 2014). This proved to be extreme hyperbole, since the revenue increase over the first five-year period, from 2015 to 2020, has turned out to be a mere 4.7%, a total of US$27.2 billion, compared to US$25.9 billion for the previous first five-year period from 2010 to 2015, before the project had been completed (Reuters, 2020). The failure of the project was also reflected in a statement made by President Sisi, who declared in June 2016 that the main purpose of the project was to 'raise national morale', not achieve a tangible economic benefit, thus contradicting the earlier narrative (Abdel Salam M., 2016). The project had been completed by the military in one year, rather than the original estimate of three years, under orders from the President (Tantawi, 2015).

As has been the case with similar projects, debt was the primary tool for raising financing. This was done through the issuance of investment certificates (JOC Group, 2014) worth US$6.8 billion with a rate of return of 12%, which was later raised to 15.5% in November 2016 (Al Arabiya, 2016), in addition to US$1.4 billion worth of bank loans. In March 2019, when the bank loan instalment was due to be repaid, the Suez Canal Authority had to reach an agreement with the Ministry of Finance to repay US$600 million on its behalf due to the inability of the Authority to meet its debt obligations (Amar, 2019). The military, therefore, effectively used debt to finance a project with dubious economic benefits, which it used as a tool to expand its economic footprint. Public funds were expropriated, since they had to be used to repay the debt.

The new administrative capital is another similar mega-project but on a much larger scale, with an estimated budget of US$58 billion (Lewis and Abdellah, Retures, 2019). As already noted, the project aims to create a new Egyptian capital away from troublesome Cairo, with its propensity for demonstration and revolt. The project is being handled by the Administrative Capital for Urban Development Company, 51% of which is owned by the military through the Armed Forces National Land Projects Authority and the National Service Products Organization, and 49% owned by the Housing Ministry (Egypt Independent, 2019). The source of funding for the new capital remains a mystery, with state officials claiming that the funds required are not coming from the government's public budget (State Information Services, 2020).[2] In June 2018, Ahmed Zaki, the Chairman of the Administrative Capital for Urban Development Company stated that the project was being financed through the sale of public land, hence it did not need to draw of the state budget. Of course, this logic ignores the fact that the sale of public land is a form of public financing. If true, the sale of US$58 billion-worth of Egyptian public land would be truly astounding. This comes amidst news of the failure to attract foreign developers to invest in the project, and growing difficulties over financing. For example, in 2017 a US$3 billion deal between the government and the Chinese State Construction Company failed to materialize because of commercial disagreements (Knecht, 2017). This had been preceded by the United Arab Emirates developer, Emar, which was supposed to lead the development, quitting for similar reasons. This, in turn, was followed in 2018 by the failure of a US$20 billion investment deal with China Fortune Land Development (Magdy M., 2018), which fell through, again due to commercial disagreements. Even though the source of funding and the expenditure remain a mystery, the military's control of the project and its use of it to expand its economic footprint is very obvious. Closely connected to this project are several other grandiose construction projects in the new administrative capital, which also double as propaganda tools for the regime. This includes the construction of the largest cathedral in the Middle East, as well as a massive new mosque and the tallest tower in Africa.

The military's economic activity is not limited to administering mega-infrastructure projects, but also includes commercial ventures for the production of items for civilian and military use. Such ventures range from food production to cement and steel manufacturing. To put this in context, Yazid Sayigh has provided some estimates of the size of military production capacity compared to national production capacity in certain sectors. For example, in the water bottle market, the military production capacity is 50 million bottles per year, compared to a national capacity of 435 million bottles, constituting 11.5% of the total. In the gasoline sector, the military's own petrol stations sell 1 billion litres per year, compared to a total capacity of 25 billion litres, controlling 4% of the market. In construction-related industries, the picture is starker. In the cement industry, the military controls 19.5 million tons of capacity, compared to an industry total of 83.5 million tons, controlling 23% of the nation's production capacity. Finally, in marble and granite production, it controls 1.44 million tons of production capacity, out of a national total of 4 million tons, hence controlling 36% of the national capacity (Sayigh Y., 2019). The military, in short, is a major supplier for the domestic economy.

The military economic expansion has raised complaints that it is effectively crowding out the private sector. The most notable example of this is the cement industry, with an annual demand of 50 million tons annually in 2013 and 2014, rising to 54-to-55 million tons in 2015–18 with the advent of Egypt's mega projects. This sector suffers from chronic oversupply, with estimates of production capacity ranging from 68.5 million tons a year according to official figures, to 83.5 million tons according to the Cement Association of the Egyptian Federation of Industries. Until 2018, 92% of the market was in the hands of private enterprise, with the publicly owned National Cement Company and the military-controlled Al Arish cement company supplying the remaining 8%. In 2012, the military doubled the capacity of the Al-Arish cement company to 6.5 million tons, and then in 2018 added another 12.5 million tons by building an entirely new plant in Bani Suef, at a cost of US$1.12 billion (Sayigh Y., 2019). This was at a time when the state-owned National Cement Company had had to shut down in November 2017 after suffering heavy losses, while the German-owned Suez Cement company saw its losses in 2017 double to Eg£1.14 billion, and the Greek-owned Alexandria Cement suffering losses amounting to

Eg£513.9 million (Reuters, 2018). The vertical integration of the supply chain allows the military to make profits at both ends, as a supplier of cement as well as a consumer, given its infrastructure projects. It also creates incentives to keep up the demand for cement, through a continuous slew of infrastructure projects based on the appropriation of public funds, even if the economic benefits are dubious – a clear case of the tail wagging the dog.

The military has also become involved in the provision of medical supplies to the Ministry of Health, indeed becoming the exclusive supplier to the ministry in 2016. A crisis in the supply of baby formula was the starting point, when on 25 September 2015, the state-owned Egyptian Pharmaceutical Trading Company took out a paid advertisement stating that the import of baby formula had moved to a sovereign body, imploring President Sisi to intervene. The Ministry of Defence confirmed that it had stepped in to counter increased price gouging by middlemen, while General Assar, the Minister of Industrial Production at the time, stated that the military would produce baby formula locally. However, the military merely ended up importing the product on a monopolistic basis. As of February 2019, baby formula was sold with a 28% mark-up under the label of the Long Live Egypt Fund. Over the following year the military would aggressively expand into the market after sensational news from regime-affiliated media outlets and officials of crises of supply, price gouging and the import of low-quality medical supplies, all blamed on the greed of middlemen (Sayigh Y., 2019).

The size of this military economic activity is notoriously difficult to estimate, given the nebulous and opaque networks of ownership and patronage that permeate the Egyptian military economy. President Sisi stated in late 2016 that the military's economic output was Eg£3–4 trillion which constituted 1.5–2% of GDP (Reuters, 2016). This, however, ignores military-owned businesses that are nominally private and hence would not be considered in the tally. An example of this is the involvement of the General Intelligence Services (GIS) in the import of natural gas from Israel, through several shell corporations registered offshore in 2018. The US$15 billion deal was labelled by the Ministry of Petroleum as a 'private sector negotiation or agreement', as it declined to comment further on the transaction. In reality the deal was done through a shell corporation owned by GIS in cooperation with a number of Egyptian businessmen, so that the gas is bought from Israel and sold to the Egyptian state for a profit, which includes transportation fees. The use of a shell corporation registered in a European tax haven, such as Switzerland, the Netherlands and Luxembourg, allows the GIS to avoid paying Egyptian taxes through its 'privately' owned company. Hence the profits flow directly to the GIS, with little public oversight (Hossam, 2018). On 23 February 2022 the Egyptian Parliament approved legislation that formally permitted the GIS to establish commercial enterprises, a move that simply legalizes an already long-established practice (Al Qudus El Araby, 2022).

The line between the civilian and the military economy is also sometimes not very clear cut, as many former military officers transition to roles as heads of private companies whilst maintaining close relations with the security apparatus. This trend is manifested most clearly in the media market, through the Falcon Group and the Egyptian Media Group, for example. The Falcon Group, originally a provider of private security services, became a major player in the media market with a 4.9% market share (Reporters without borders, 2019). The company is owned by General Khaled Sherif, an ex-military intelligence officer. Falcon purchased the Hayat TV channel in 2017, for an estimated US$79 million (New Arab, 2017). The Egyptian Media Group, on the other hand which controls, 12.2% of the media market, is owned by Eagle Capital, a state-owned investment firm, which is in turn owned by the GIS. The Media Group was founded by businessman Ahmed Abu Hashima, who is known for his close links to the security service; he later sold the company to Eagle Capital in 2017 (Reporters without borders, 2020).

Therefore, even though the size of the Egyptian military economic footprint is difficult to estimate and is subject to debate, its influence over economic affairs and policy is incontestable. Indeed, the military has been able to marshal state and public resources for its own enrichment. It also wields its influence to shape economic policy and capital accumulation patterns in a manner that benefits military elites at the expense of the mass of the citizenry, a clear consequence of direct military rule.

The legal framework

As part of the military's power grab, supervisory state bodies, nominally responsible for combating corruption and graft, have been systemically weakened to ensure that there are no other power centres that could arrest the military's economic ascendancy. What we see, in essence, is a process of 'hollowing out' state institutions to ensure the complete dominance of the military. This was evident in the case of Hesham Genina, the ex-head of the Central Accounting Organization (CAO), one of the top state auditing agencies in the country. The CAO is responsible for auditing the administrative apparatus of the state, as well as the public sector and the local municipalities. In 2015, the CAO issued a report claiming that corruption had cost the Egyptian state Eg£600 billion between 2012 and 2015 (Abdel Salam M., 2016). The claim was roundly criticized by the government, along with accusations by state security and the Administrative Monitoring Authority (AMA), the military-controlled auditing agency, of exaggeration and the deliberate use of false data. The report, however, detailed allegations against 'sovereign' bodies, such as the GIS and AMA, accusing them of corruption (Al Araby, 2016).

In response, Parliament issued Law 89 (Egylaw, 2015), to allow the President to remove the heads of state watchdogs if they 'jeopardize the state' or if they cause harm to 'national interests' – deliberately vague grounds for dismissal. This law was also at variance with the 2014 constitution, which guarantees the independence of anti-corruption watchdogs (EIPR, 2015). After parliamentary approval of the law in January 2016, Genina was promptly removed from his post. The State Prosecutor issued a gag order preventing publication of the 400-page report, so it has never been made public. Hesham Genina was arrested in March 2016, charged with spreading false information (BBC, 2016) and ultimately sentenced to five years in prison by a military court (Ismail A., 2019). This was after he had joined the presidential campaign of Sami Anan and claimed to have evidence of the involvement of military intelligence in the killing of protestors (El Ghobashy, 2021, p. 225).

In addition, Law 207, issued in 2017, restricted the jurisdiction of the AMA to the civilian sector of the state, and made it directly answerable to the President. It is worth noting that the jurisdiction of the AMA was already, de jure, restricted to the civilian sector. This de jure restriction was made de facto by this law. In addition, the AMA is under the control of the military. Thus, for example, in 2020 the head of the AMA was General Hassan Abdel Shafi, who replaced General Sherif Seif El Din. General Abdel Shafi was director of the Department of Military Engineers and Chief of Staff of the Armed Forces Engineering Authority (Egypt Today, 2020). The AMA had always been led by officers, giving it the characteristic of an intelligence agency rather than an auditing institution. Military control of the AMA not only exempted it from oversight, but also allowed it to be used as a tool to punish civilian opponents (Sayigh Y., 2019). For example, it was Major General Mohamed Erfan Jamal-al-Din, the head of the AMA at the time, who led the investigation against Genina (Sayigh Y., 2019).

The erosion of the independence of state-oversight bodies was compounded by the erosion of the independence of judicial bodies, which could have, potentially, acted as a bulwark against cronyism and corruption. In 2019, as the result of an amendment to Article 193 of the Constitution, the State Council, a judicial body responsible for adjudication of disputes between the state and the citizenry, had its responsibility for reviewing contracts signed by the state, and other public institutions, removed. No replacement body or process was designated to perform this task (Mandour, 2019). This weakened another oversight mechanism which might have acted as a brake on the power of the military to make decisions and opened the way for more graft. Another development has been the increased use of 'direct bidding', which allowed government and military agencies to award contracts of defined values without a competitive bidding process, based on Law 89, issued in 1998. This law was amended in 2013 by the interim president, Adly Mansour, greatly expanding the upper limit of the amount that could be awarded through direct bidding 'in case of emergencies'. No limit was placed on non-competitive transactions, and the law has been used to award military-administrated contracts in government-funded projects to civilian contractors, with no oversight. It has also prevented third-party challenges to the process of awarding state contracts (Sayigh Y., 2019). Since a large proportion of the projects led by the military are subcontracted to civilian contractors, the scope for graft and cronyism has increased further.

The military, in short, has created a legal framework within which it can expand its economic reach without the hindrance of civilian oversight, and has, effectively, used its control of the state and a labyrinth of laws and bylaws to increase its economic footprint. This was very apparent in the area of real estate and land development. For example, in 2016, President Sisi issued a decree which designated twenty-one national roads as strategic zones, giving the military control of them, including potential commercial development in their vicinity. Furthermore, decrees 378 and 380, issued in 2019, placed desert land with tourist potential under the control of the military, designating them as strategic zones with military importance. Finally, the most direct example of direct expropriation is Prime Ministerial Decree 1657, which required the approval of the Ministry of Defence for the extraction of mineral wealth anywhere in the country and gave the ministry the power to levy fees on the output from such production sites.

This power is coupled with a plethora of tax exemptions, covering income tax, customs duties and property tax . These exemptions go back to Law 204 (1957), which exempted the military from taxes, customs and duties related to armament contracts, all the way to Presidential Decree 66, issued in 2017, which exempted the military from the new IMF-inspired valued added tax (VAT). Indeed, even though senior defence industry officials have stated that the military's economic activity is subject to normal taxation, this is patently not true. For example, there is no evidence that the revenues which accrued to the military from managing public projects have been subject to taxation, with the status of military-owned public sector companies and joint ventures remaining ambiguous (Sayigh Y., 2019).

In essence, the military has used its control of the state to weaken other state institutions that could, potentially, act as barriers to its expansion. Indeed, the military has created a legal framework that has severely curtailed the independence of other state organs, instead concentrating power in its own hands and, in the process, weakening the very foundations of the state as an institution and as a vehicle of monitoring and control.

Economic underperformance and capital deformities

In March 2015, during an international investment conference aimed at attracting foreign investment and loans, President Sisi stated that Egypt needed US$200–300 billion of investment to develop (Reuters, 2015). At the time, this number seemed fantastical and hyperbolic. However, the regime was to claim that it was able to invest the targeted amount within five years. Yet, the result of this massive investment flow has been at best modest. Indeed, there is a strong case to be made that it has led to economic deformities and capital accumulation in unproductive sectors, mainly construction, as well as a systematic transfer of wealth from the lower and middle classes to the business and military elites. The accumulation of such assets was reflected in gross capital formation as a percentage of GDP, which rose from 14.21% in 2013 to 17.6% in 2019 (World Bank, 2020).

From a macro perspective, GDP growth averaged 4.47%, from 2014 to 2019, which was lower than in the last year of the Mubarak regime, which had reached 5.15% in 2010 (World Bank, 2020). Placing this in context, as a percentage of world GDP the Egyptian economy's share shrank from 0.32% in 2013 to 0.25% in 2018, despite the major investment spree. When one digs deeper into the source of this claimed growth, the structural deformities become apparent. For example, the manufacturing sector as a percentage of the GDP dropped from 16.61% in 2013 to 15.91% in 2019, showing that the manufacturing sector was not the source of the growth. Manufacturing added value remained almost stable, with a slight increase from US$47.9 billion in 2013 to US$48.23 billion in 2019. The service sector as a percentage of the GDP did not fare any better, with the percentage dropping from 52.3% in 2013 to 50.47% in 2019, following a similar trend to the manufacturing sector. Growth, therefore, did not derive from a rise in the manufacturing or service sectors. On the contrary, these sectors' contributions to the economy decreased (Global Economy, 2021).

In terms of export performance, the Egyptian economy did not fare better either, even though the regime decided to float the pound in November 2016 (BBC, 2016), which caused it to lose half of its value almost overnight (Atkinson, 2016). The devaluation should have led to an improved export performance, but exports as a percentage of GDP remained steady at their 2013 levels, with a slight increase from 17.02% in 2013 to 17.5% in 2019. Imports, on the other hand, increased from 23.36% to 25.77%, despite the increase in the price of imported products due to the currency devaluation. This led to a worsening trade balance, which as a percentage of GDP deteriorated from -6.34% in 2013 to -8.27% in 2019 (Trading Economics, 2020), indicating that the global competitive position of Egyptian manufacturing and services has not improved and that the source of GDP growth is not increased external demand. The weakness of the Egyptian economy's international competitive position was also seen in the country's current account as a percentage of GDP, which increase from -2.2% in 2013, the year of the coup, to -4.6% in 2021 (Trading Economics, 2020)

The performance of the non-oil private sector followed a similar pattern, which was driven by a drop in local consumption, indicating a reduction in the size of the domestic market. In the Central Agency for Mobilization and Statistics' (CAPMAS) report of June 2019 on spending and consumption from 2015 to 2018, a substantial drop in consumption was evident, with average national family consumption dropping by 9.7%. Urban areas showed the greatest decline, with a drop of 13.7%, while consumption in rural area dropped by 5.1% (Central Agency for Mobilization and Statistics (CAPMAS), 2019). The drop in the level of consumption was reflected in the performance of the non-oil private sector, which as of December 2019 had only shown growth for six out of the previous thirty-six months (Reuters, 2019). Indeed, October 2020 was the first time in ten months in which the private sector had showed growth (IHS Markit, 2020).

The weakness of private sector performance, combined with the weakness of the manufacturing and the service sectors, indicates that the massive investment drive did not lead to a more dynamic and innovative economy, nor lay the foundation for a long-term economic revival based on a durable competitive advantage. The source of growth stemmed from large-scale investment in infrastructure, which led to a boom in the construction sector. In 2018 the construction sector grew by 8.9%, making it the largest contributor to GDP growth in that year (Egypt Today, 2019). The then Housing Minister, Mostafa Madbouly, stated in November 2017 that the construction sector had been the driver of the Egyptian economy, providing 3–4 million new jobs over the previous three years (Ministry of Housing, Utilities and Urban Communities, 2017), confirming that economic growth was due to the mega-infrastructure projects, which were implemented with no or limited feasibility studies and with dubious economic benefits. This should not come as a surprise, since President Sisi had declared in December 2018 that if he had relied on feasibility studies then only 20–25% of what had been 'achieved' would have been possible (Al Jazzera, 2018).

The heavy reliance on infrastructure projects as a method for capital accumulation and surplus value extraction has had several negative consequences. Most notably, it has led to the accumulation of capital in non-productive assets, in other words an accumulation that is not based on a durable economic base which relies on innovation and market dynamics. On the contrary, it can only continue through the appropriation of public funds and heavy reliance on debt. This reinforces the political economy of cronyism and buttresses the central role that the state plays in the process of capital accumulation, leading to long-term structural deformities. Moreover, the heavy investment in these projects diverts financial resources away from potential investment in the manufacturing and services sectors, which could become the base of sustainable economic development. In addition, the continued reliance on public funds for capital accumulation makes it necessary to exploit the lower and middle classes in order to sustain the capital accumulation cycle. In effect, wealth is transferred from the lower and the middle classes to the military elites, through major publicly-funded projects. Finally, the consequent shrinkage in local consumption and the accompanying drop in living standards become inconsequential, for capital accumulation is no longer reliant on the growth of the local market nor on increased international demand for Egyptian goods and services. In other words, capital accumulates independently of the market, through the control of the state and its coercive apparatus, effectively shielding the military from competitive market pressures and reducing any incentive to innovate. Capitalism prevails independently of the market!

The weak suffer what they must

In June 2019, CAPMAS issued its bi-annual report on 'Income, Expenditure, and Consumption', noted above. The findings of the report were damning, in terms of the success of the regime's economic policies in raising the standard of living. In fact, the level of poverty had risen from 26.3% in 2013 to 32.5% in 2018,[3] with millions driven into destitution. The greatest increase was between 2015 and 2018, with the advent of the IMF-inspired economic reform programme, which saw poverty rates rise from 27.8% to 32.5%. The level of extreme poverty had also increased from 4.4% in 2013 to 6.2% in 2018. The national poverty line in this report was set at Eg£735 per month (US$47), while the level of extreme poverty was defined as Eg£490 per month (US$31), extremely low figures by international standards. The rise in the level of poverty has been particularly remarkable in some parts of the country. For example, Cairo saw the poverty rate almost double in the span of three years, from 17.5% in 2015 to 31.1% in 2018. This highlighted the drastic impact that the regime's policy had had on the level of urban poverty. The south of the country, however, is the most impoverished, with governorates such as Assuit, Sohag and Luxor at the top of the list, with poverty rates reaching 66.7%, 59.6% and 55.3% respectively (Central Agency for Mobilization and Statistics (CAPMAS), 2019).

In terms of consumption, which is a good indicator of the levels of income inequality, the picture also remains stark. In urban areas the lowest decile of the population accounts for 3.8% of total consumption, compared to the top decile which accounts for 27.2%. In rural areas, consumption is more even, with the lower decile responsible for 4.7% of consumption and the top decile responsible for 20.6% (Central Agency for Mobilization and Statistics (CAPMAS), 2019). In terms of income inequality, the top decile claims 28.3% of national income, compared to 3.6% for the bottom decile. A new report issued in 2020 corroborates this trend (Central Agency for Mobilization and Statistics (CAPMAS), 2020), with the top decile claiming 25.6% of national income, slightly lower than the previous figure, compared to the bottom decile, which claims a mere 4.2% of national income. It is worth mentioning that

CAPMAS report is based on self-reporting surveys rather than more reliable sources such as tax records. Self-reporting is likely to conceal levels of poverty, and most importantly wealth and income inequality, since top earners are less likely to report their real incomes and more likely to be excluded from the survey (Piketty, 2020). Therefore, the figures quoted are most likely understated and the real level of social deprivation much starker. For example, the income inequality database, run by a number of renowned economists, provides much higher figures for income and wealth inequality. It estimates that in 2020, the top decile claimed 49.9% of the national income, with the top 1% alone accounting for 19.9% of income, while the bottom 50% of the population claimed just 14.6% of national income. Wealth inequality is even more striking, with the top decile claiming 62.5% of national wealth and the top 1% accounting for 30.5%, while the bottom 50% accounts for a meagre 4.8% of national wealth (World Inequality Database, 2022). These estimates are based on surveys, with corrections applied to compensate for the lack of tax records, essentially facing the same issue as the CAPMAS report, difference being that the CAPMAS report makes no adjustment for poor data quality, hence making it a less reliable source. The poor data quality means that the above figures should be taken as indicators, not precise statistics. Nonetheless, the data presented provides a useful yardstick with which to evaluate the level of inequality in Egypt.

The dramatic rise in poverty levels is the result of a systematic policy of wealth transfer from the lower and middle classes to the elites, which is in accord with the regime's prevalent logic of capital accumulation. Indeed, its use of mega-infrastructure projects as a vehicle for capital accumulation using public funds isolates the military from the market, allowing it to continue to accumulate capital even if exports falter or if the size of the local market decreases as a result of lower levels of income. This frees the military to exert enormous pressure on the lower and middle class, stepping up exploitation, unhindered by the need to maintain a minimal level of local demand to ensure that commercial activity did not suffer, as indeed was the case with the non-oil private sector. Egypt's political economy, in short, has been designed to exploit the country's lower and the middle classes for the benefit of the elites.

There are three interconnected policies used to transfer this wealth to the elites. First, there is the heavy reliance on debt, in lieu of taxation, to finance the regime's investment spree and to finance the government's operations. A substantial dependence on debt not only acts to insulate the regime from the demands of a tax-paying populace, but also acts as a vehicle for wealth transfer, since the borrowed funds have to be repaid with interest to international and domestic debt holders from taxes and other public revenues. The second policy is the reliance on an extremely regressive taxation system, which shifts the tax burden to the middle and lower classes and is integral to the process of wealth transfer. The heavy reliance on debt combined with a regressive taxation system ensures that the debt burden falls on the shoulders of the middle and lower classes who not only finance the growth of the military's economic empire but also transfer their wealth to public debt holders, who are either domestic elites or international creditors. The final policy involves the regular cuts in the level of social spending, resulting in increased economic pressure on the poorest segments of the society.

The increase in the level of debt has been meteoric, rising from 80% of GDP in 2012 to 88% in 2020, reaching an all-time high of 108% in 2017. This increase was driven by a considerable increase in the level of external debt, which reached 39% of GDP in 2019 (Global Economy, 2021), up from 14% in 2012. Placing this in context, the level of debt as a percentage of GDP in neighbouring Morocco and Tunisia reached 66% and 72% respectively in 2019 (Trading Economics, 2020). The loans were procured from regional allies, international organizations like the IMF and the World Bank, and international markets through the issuance of financial instruments. The regime's borrowing spree has made it the largest issuer of bonds in Africa, issuing US$22 billion-worth in the span of two years (New Arab, 2019). This does not include the largest Eurobond release in the country's history, valued at US$5 billion, in May 2020 (Enterprise, 2020). These loans were, at least partially, used to expand the military's economic footprint. For example, in 2015 the World Bank extended a US$500 million loan to the Egyptian government for social housing projects managed by the military (Sayigh Y., 2019). The trend of a heavy reliance on debt was expected to continue in 2022, with S&P predicting that Egypt would overtake Turkey as the largest issuer of sovereign debt in emerging markets in the Middle East and North Africa (MENA), with an expected total of US$73 billion-worth of bonds (Reuters, 2022)

This dependence on debt has had significant consequences for the state budget, where loan and interest payments consume large parts of planned expenditure. For example, the 2020–1 budget earmarked Eg£555 billion for loan and interest repayments, out of a total planned outlay of Eg£1.7 trillion, constituting 32% of planned expenditures. Placing this in context, the same budget allocated Eg£335 billion for public sector wages (Egypt Today, 2020). In other words, one third of the budget is used to repay loans, which places significant constraints on the ability of the state to invest in public services. In the 2022–3 budget, based on the figures presented by the government, loan and interest repayment are planned to consume 54% of state expenditure, an astronomical figure (Kassab B., 2022).

Besides acting as a tool for wealth transfer to the elite, debt allows the regime to offer a wide range of tax exemptions, not only to the military but to large civilian corporations as well, and to shift the burden of taxation to the lower and middle classes (Sayigh Y., 2019). This weakens the overall tax base of the state. Mohamed Maati, the Minister of Finance, stated in September 2019 that tax revenues as a percentage of GDP stood at 14%, with plans to increase it to 16.5% in the next five years while maintaining the 'stability' of tax policies (Daily News Egypt, 2020). In other words, the regressive nature of the taxation system is to continue. Yet the current average for tax revenues as a percentage of GDP amongst OECD countries is 34%, while Morocco, Tunisia and South Africa stand at 28%, 32% and 29% respectively. The current African average stands at 16.5%, placing Egypt at the lower end of the scale in terms of tax revenues, by regional and international standards (OECD, 2020).

The weakness of the tax base is combined with a highly regressive taxation system, which, as already noted, serves to shift the majority of the tax burden to the lower and middle classes, thus effectively transferring wealth to elites. This is due to the regime offering tax exemptions and loopholes to the elites and using debt instead of taxation to finance government operations and investments. The debt, in turn, is then repaid, with interest, from the pockets of the middle and lower classes. In 2017, 47% of all tax revenues were derived from taxes on goods and services, as well as value added tax – both regressive forms of taxation, since they tax consumption. The parallel ratio for the OECD totalled 32%. In terms of tax rates on personal income and corporate tax rates, the regime has imposed very modest rates. Corporate tax rates stand at 22.5% at the time of writing, which is the fourth lowest in Africa (Trading Economics, 2020). In April 2020, the Egyptian Parliament approved a new tax law which placed the highest rate of personal income tax at 25% for an Egyptian earning more than Eg£400,000 pa (US$22,000), a very modest rate by regional standards, placing Egypt fourth on the list of African countries with the lowest personal income taxes (Refeat, 2020).

The final leg of the triangle, which completes the crushing circle around the middle and lower classes is the regular cuts in social spending, encouraged by the IMF, especially after the US$12 billion

IMF loan to Egypt in November 2016 (IMF, 2016). This, followed by a decision to devalue the pound and by a reduction in social spending and subsidies saw inflation soar to 29% in 2017, before dropping to 14% in 2018 (World Bank, 2020). There are still indications that inflation remains high. For example, in May 2019, driven by the increased price of food and non-alcoholic beverages, urban inflation rates reached 14.1%, as food prices rose by 15%, disproportionately affecting the poor (Arab News, 2019). In June 2020, the price of electricity was increased by 19%, the seventh increase since President Sisi officially took power in 2014 (Middle East Monitor, 2020). This is part of the overall government strategy to completely eliminate electricity subsidies by 2022, as part of the IMF economic reform programme. This was followed in August 2020 by an increase in the price of Metro tickets in Cairo for the second consecutive year. The price of the cheapest ticket was increased from Eg£3 to Eg£5 ticket, while the price of the nine-to-sixteen-stops ticket increased from Eg£5 to Eg£7 and that for the sixteen-to-forty-stops tickets rose from Eg£7 to Eg£10 (Egyptian Streets, 2020). In another measure which targets the poor, in August 2020 the regime cut the size of subsidized bread loaves by 20 grams. Egypt has a large food subsidy programme, which supports 60 million people (Nadine, 2020), but on 3 August 2021 Sisi announced his intention to increase the price of subsidized bread (Fahmy O., Reuters, 2021), breaking a promise he made not to do so five year earlier. According to Heba al-Laithy, head of CAPMAS, this would increase poverty rates by a further 4–5% (Seif El-Din, 2021).

In short, the increased levels of poverty and social deprivation are the result of the deliberate and systemic policies of wealth transfer to the elites, which themselves are a core element of the regime's political economy and the process of capital accumulation. The long-term consequences of these policies are many, and will be discussed below. However, first we must consider the role of international capital in the increased pauperization of Egyptians and in helping secure the dominant position of the military regime.

International capital flows

Besides the increased level of poverty and social deprivation that the vast majority of Egyptians are subjected to, due to the regime's economic policies, the regime has also entrenched itself in the global financial system in a manner that links its survival to global financial interests.

This structural dependence implicates international partners – who include allies, international monetary organizations and international financial markets – in the process of surplus value extraction and increased social deprivation. In effect this creates a symbiotic relationship between Egypt's military elites and international capital and, in essence, implicitly makes international capital a direct accomplice of the military elites, not only in terms of economic exploitation but also in the repression of dissent and in the regime's human right abuses. This, in turn, creates a situation where demands for democratization directly clash with the interests of international capital, partly explaining the lavish international support that the regime has received, despite its atrocious human rights record.

Debt plays a significant role in this process. Egypt's level of external debt reached US$123.5 billion in June 2020, with an estimated payment of US$20 billion as its external debt obligation in the 2020–1 financial year (Moneim A., 2020). The level of external debt had risen from US$43.2 billion in June 2013 (Al-Wali, 2020) to a whopping US$145.5 billion by the end of 2021 (Egypt Today, 2022), a 237% increase. The rapid rise in debt levels was accompanied by a rapid expansion of short-term debt instruments, known as 'hot money'. The value of these short-term debt instruments had increased from US$60 million in mid-2016 to US$20 billion by December 2017 (Zikrallah, 2018). The rapid increase in the inflow of 'hot money' was driven by the high interest rates offered by the regime, hovering at around 13%, as well as by the perceived 'stability' of the country, earning Egypt the nickname 'darling of the emerging markets' (Laessing, Arnold and Barbuscia, 2020). This type of short-term investment is the form most sensitive to political upheaval.

External debt serves not only as a vehicle for the military's economic expansion, but also invests international capital in regime survival. Simply put, were there to be mass social unrest, the regime would be unable to meet its debt obligations since its ability to collect taxes would be impaired, as would its ability to 'roll over' its debt, since the perceived 'stability' of the regime would vanish. Hence, international creditors, from financial markets to international financial organizations, have a direct interest in the maintenance of the status quo. In addition, international creditors thereby also become direct accomplices in the process of militarization of the Egyptian economy, and the increased level of social deprivation of the mass of the citizenry, since the extracted surplus is partly transferred to them. In other words, the process of loan and interest repayment involves wealth transfer to international creditors, as the regime uses tax revenues and other public sources of income to make those payments. It also furthers cronyism and moral hazard since it helps insulate the regime from the market and from popular demands for democratization. The interest rates offered on Egyptian debt instruments were the highest in the world, making it extremely attractive to international investors (Magdy and El-Tablawy, 2022)

Beyond the regime's investment spree in infrastructure, it has also embarked on what can only be described as a single-horse arms race. Indeed, a number of multi-billion-dollar arms deals has made it the third largest arms importer in the world in the period from 2015 to 2019, with a 212% increase in arms imports compared to the figures for 2010–14. Only India and Saudi Arabia imported more arms. The largest arms suppliers to the regime are France, Russia and the United States, in that order, with France supplying 35% of the regime's purchased armaments (Pieter, Aude and Kuimova, 2020). The importation of weapons is not restricted to conventional arms, but also includes crowd-control and surveillance equipment (Middle East Eye, 2016), which is used in the direct repression of dissent (Jeannerod, 2019).

The importation of billions of dollars-worth of arms also implicitly implicates Western arms industries and their States in the regime's acts of repression, making them less likely to pressure the regime to curtail its human rights abuses. Indeed, there is an argument to be made that continued human right abuses are integral to the sales of Western arms to the regime. In some cases, debt is used to finance the purchases of these weapons, creating an Orwellian scenario in which Egyptian citizens subsidize the Western arms industry through the purchase of arms used to repress them. This was apparent in 2015, when the regime concluded a deal worth US$5.2 billion for the purchase of French Rafale fighter jets. The deal was partially financed by a US$3.2 billion loan from the French government (Reuters, 2015). However, the financial sources for most of the arms deals are obscure, since the official defence budget does not reflect this increase in expenditure. Defence expenditure as a percentage of GDP stood at 1.2% in 2019, a minuscule amount compared to the size of the arms deals actually concluded (Kuimova, 2020). Considering the size of these deals, one can only speculate that the use of debt as a financing tool has been rampant.

In addition to the involvement of multinational corporations in the regime's mega-projects, direct foreign investment plays a significant role in the regime's international entrenchment. In 2019, direct foreign investment reached US$9 billion (Egypt Independent, 2020), making Egypt the largest recipient of direct foreign investment in Africa. Most of these inflows were focused in the oil-and-gas sector, driven mainly by the Shorouk natural gas concession, which contains the Zhoro field, the largest natural gas discovery in the Mediterranean. The field was discovered by Eni in 2015, with an estimated capacity of 30 trillion cubic feet. Eni owns 50% of the concession, with the rest divided between Rosneft, British Petroleum and Mubadala Petroleum. The level of investment by Eni is substantial – US$13 billion between 2015 and 2018 (Ahram online, 2019), with the President himself voicing support for Eni's continued expansion (State Information Service, 2020). In an attempt to increase investment in the sector, the regime introduced a new type of contract in 2019, where the foreign producer is no longer obliged to sell the extracted fossil fuel to the government but can dispose of his share as he pleases (Energy Voice, 2019).

Multinational corporations have also been involved in the regime's investment spree, most notably Siemens. In 2020, the German corporation signed an agreement to build a 1,000 km high-speed electrical railway connecting the Red Sea to the Mediterranean and passing through the new administrative capital. The deal is estimated to be worth US$23 billion (Al Arabiya, 2021). This is in addition to a previous project, in which Siemens was engaged to build three power stations worth US$7 billion in 2015.

In order to fully appreciate the wider impact of the regime's global financial entrenchment, one need look no further than the case of Giulio Regeni, the Italian doctoral student from the University of Cambridge who was abducted and tortured to death in Cairo in January 2016. From the onset there were strong suspicions that the regime's security forces were responsible. In December 2018, the Italian prosecutor named five members of the regime's security forces as suspects (BBC, 2018), and in December 2020 four members of the security forces were formally charged with his murder, as discussed above (Michaelson and Tondo, 2020). In spite of this, the Italian government continued not only to invest in the oil and gas sector through Eni, but to sell arms to the regime. This included a tripling of arms sales in 2019 compared to 2018, to a total of €238 million (Middle East Monitor, 2020). As late as 2020, the regime was in talks with Italy regarding a massive arms deal, worth US$12 billion, dubbed 'the deal of the century'. This would have included four frigates, twenty-four Eurofighter Typhoon jets, twenty-four trainer aircraft and a satellite. The status of the deal remains unclear, as public pressure mounted in Italy to halt it. However, in June 2020, a US$1.2 billion deal was approved by the then Italian Prime Minster, Giuseppe Conte, which included the sale of two frigates (Michaelson and Tondo, 2020).

Other European countries did not behave any better, most notably France, where during a state visit in December 2020, President Sissi received the country's highest honour, the Grand Cross of the Legion of Honour (France 24, 2020). The French President, Emmanuel Macron, stated that arms sales and economic cooperation with the regime would not be conditional on Egypt's human rights record, remarking that, 'It is more effective to have a policy of demanding dialogue than a boycott which would only reduce the effectiveness of one of our partners in the fight against terrorism' (France 24, 2020). This lavish support will ensure that the regime will survive longer than it otherwise would or indeed should!

A mirage in the desert

Playing devil's advocate, some might argue that there are positive economic indicators that need to be considered in order to provide a comprehensive analysis of the regime's economic model. This includes, for example, a reduction in unemployment rates from 13.5% in 2013 to 7.4% in 2019, but rising to 9.16% in 2020 due to the Covid-19 pandemic (World Bank, 2020). The unemployment rate dropped again to 7.4% in 2021. The budget deficit also decreased from -12.4% in 2016 to -7.8% in 2020 (Statista, 2022), which, according to neo-liberal orthodoxy, should promote private investment. There is also the introduction of the minimum wage for the first time in the private sector, which was set at Eg£2,400 (US$131), and the increase of the minimum wage to Eg£2,700 (US$147) in the public sector in early 2022.

A closer examination of these figures, however, reveals a different dynamic. For example, the reduction in the level of unemployment was accompanied by a dramatic increase in the level of poverty and lowers level of consumption, which can only be explained by extremely low wages. The poor performance of the private sector would also indicate that the drop in unemployment is driven by the regime's mega-projects, hence it illustrates the failure of the regime to create well-paying jobs in miliary-managed projects. A closely connected figure is that of the budget deficit, which saw a dramatic fall. This decrease, however, did not lead to an improved private sector performance; on the contrary, the growth of the private sector has been weak. There is also good reason to doubt the reliability of these figures, since they exclude the regime's arms spending spree (Kuimova, 2020) and some of its mega-projects, the most notable being the Administrative Capital. The real budget deficit is mostly likely much higher.

The most important criticism that can be levelled against the regime model for economic growth is its inability to provide sustainable growth and alleviate poverty. Its failure on both these counts became apparent on 21 March 2022, when the regime was forced to devalue the pound by 14% (Werr and Awadalla, 2022). In October of the same year, the regime devalued the pound again, losing another 15% of its value (Magdy M., Bloomberg, 2022). In January 2023 it dropped again, losing another 13% of its value and hitting a new low of Eg£32 to the dollar (Al Jazeera, 2023). The official narrative propagated by the regime is that the cause of the devaluation is the external shock resulting from Russia's invasion of Ukraine, and the subsequent global inflationary wave that followed. However, this explanation ignores the clear structural fragility of Sisi's debt-driven growth model. For example, it ignores the deteriorating external position of the Egyptian economy, over multiple years, which continued to place pressure on the Egyptian pound. It also disregards the heavy dependence on debt, most importantly debt denominated in foreign currency, which is estimated at 24% of GDP, of which only 60% has been issued externally (Swanston, 2022). This vulnerability became apparent once the Russian invasion of Ukraine started, as the Egyptian bond market witnessed a mass capital outflow, estimated at US$20 billion, in the first half of 2022 (Magdy M., 2022). These structural issues made a devaluation inevitable. This devaluation will have a number of important consequences. It will lead to an increase in the debt-to-GDP ratio, which is likely to cause investors to continue to demand high interest rates, which in turn will place additional pressure on the state budget. The solution to this dilemma, from the regime's perspective, is increased austerity measures and cuts in social spending, which is bound to increase poverty levels. This is coupled with an expected inflationary wave, which will disproportionately affect the poor and the middle class – in essence a repetition of the scenario of 2016, where the pound lost half of its value and poverty rates increased dramatically, as if the billions spent between 2016 and 2022 were simply a mirage, as Sisi's promise of economic prosperity collapses under its own weight.

The end game

The consequences of the military's drive to expand its economic control of Egypt are many and will long outlive President Sisi and his regime. On the economic side, the military's drive will reinforce the role of the state in the process of capital accumulation, in a manner that enhances the crony capitalist nature of the Egyptian economy. The promotion of capital accumulation isolated from the market inhibits innovation and the growth of an independent private sector. This type of capital accumulation allows for economic growth regardless of lower levels of local market demand or weak export performance. This frees the military elites to exploit the working class, with little regard for increasing poverty levels, as wealth is systemically siphoned off for the benefit of the elites. The only restraints are the provision of minimum sustenance in order for the working class to reproduce itself, and to have a tax base that is large enough to repay the loans and the interest on them, if they can no longer be rolled over. This, arguably, lies at the heart of Sisi's political project: the construction of a new form of militarized capitalism, using the military's control of the state apparatus to expropriate public funds for the benefit of the military elites.

This vicious cycle of exploitation is compounded by the over-accumulation of capital in non-productive sectors of the economy, with weak returns on investment. This over-accumulation diverts capital away from sectors that might provide a base for durable economic progress, and also lays the foundation for a profound crisis of capital accumulation. Simply put, with a fragile economic base, an international economic downturn accompanied by a credit crunch could lead to a deep recession if the regime were to be unable to roll over its debt. If the country also has a weak tax base and a non-competitive private sector combined with shrinking local demand, then the state would suffer severe financial difficulties in the event of a global crisis. These financial difficulties might include debt defaults, the possible collapse of the currency and soaring inflation rates, producing hyperinflation on a mammoth scale. A manifestation of this scenario was apparent with the Russian invasion of Ukraine and the subsequent currency devaluation, discussed above. Indeed, at the time of writing, Egypt is undergoing a deep economic crisis, a direct result of the regime's policies and in particular its drive to consolidate power at all costs.

The social disruption that would follow the developments just described would be far-reaching. Such an increased level of social deprivation and poverty is also bound to increase state repression, as popular resistance mounts against the military's growing economic influence. This is reflected in the heavy repression of labour activism, including the use of military tribunals, as the class struggle intensifies and reaches an unprecedented level (Front Line Defenders, 2019).

The military drive to consolidate economic power has also had a corrosive impact on state institutions, namely severely weakening the ability of the state to monitor corruption and contributing to the dominance of coercive apparatus over other organs of the state. In addition, the consolidation of power ensures that no other social force can emerge, with an independent economic base that can challenge the military's hold on power, making it very unlikely that a liberal bourgeois political system will emerge (Moore, 1966). This creates substantial obstacles to the prospect of peaceful democratic transition, and makes a radical restructuring of the state apparatus and its role in capital accumulation necessary, a notion that is bound to be fiercely resisted by the elites, thus making the prospect of political violence even more likely.

Chapter 5

OZYMANDIAS

> I met a traveller from an antique land, Who said – 'Two vast and trunkless legs of stone Stand in the desert . . . Near them, on the sand, Half sunk a shattered visage lies, whose frown, And wrinkled lip, and sneer of cold command, Tell that its sculptor well those passions read which yet survive, stamped on these lifeless things, The hand that mocked them, and the heart that fed; And on the pedestal, these words appear: My name is Ozymandias, King of Kings; Look on my Works, ye Mighty, and despair! Nothing beside remains. Round the decay of that colossal Wreck, boundless and bare the lone and level sands stretch far away.'
>
> — Percy Shelley

Like Shelley's fabled Pharoah, Ozymandias, Sisi has built a regime that from the perspective of many – and, one would assume, from his perspective – is both stable and durable. Indeed, as discussed in the previous chapters, the military has reshaped the Egyptian economy and the state in its own image, in a manner that serves its own interests. The foundation of this militarization is an ideological edifice that is anchored in values of chauvinistic nationalism, social conservatism and mass state violence, allowing the regime not only to colonize the public space in a physical sense, but also to colonize the discourse and the minds of large segments of society. This process has allowed it to manufacture a cult-like following among a large part of the population. In short, Sisi and his regime have been extremely successful in what they set out to do, namely centralize power in the hands of the military institution and the security services, while eliminating all other centres of civilian political power, in a manner that is unique in modern Egyptian history.

This chapter, however, will present a contrasting view, while attempting to answer a number of questions, particularly concerning the durability of the regime model of governance and whether it is versatile enough to withstand possible external shocks, be they mass protests or economic crises. Indeed, I intend to argue that the militarization of the state and the economy, and the ideological construct on which the regime's legitimacy is built, has severely curtailed the regime's policy options in dealing with possible crises, making it brittle but also resistant to elite-led reform. This makes the regime extremely ill-equipped to deal with external pressure, leaving mass repression as the most viable option for the military to maintain its grip on power, something that the regime has been preparing for through investment in the physical, as well as the ideological, infrastructure of state violence. The possibility of the military self-reforming – that is, reverting to the role of a major stakeholder in the regime, rather than acting as a governing institution – is extremely unlikely, due to the constraint of structural factors. In an ironic twist, the regime is a victim of its own success, in that by eliminating civilian power centres it has weakened its own ability to adapt. More specifically, the President can no longer use an organized civilian force to balance the increasing demands of the military, nor is there an organized opposition that the regime can negotiate with to effect a limited liberalization. These constraints became apparent in two different cases, which will be used to illustrate this argument. First, we have the regime's initiation of a 'National Dialogue', which was called for by Sisi in the 'Egyptian Family Iftar' in April 2022, when the political constraints on any easing of repression became apparent. Second, we have the burgeoning economic crisis and the regime's response to it, which showcased the structural constraints on economic reform that a militarized economy necessarily entails. These constraints have left the regime extremely vulnerable to crises, while opening up the possibility of a mass bloodletting on an unprecedent historical scale.

The last section of the book, however, will attempt to end on a more hopeful note, looking at social changes, counter-narratives and resistance to oppression, which the regime has failed to eliminate. Indeed, the picture drawn in this book is that of complete military dominance, with machine-like precision, implicitly assuming that the minds and bodies of the citizenry are characterized by a certain docility. In reality, of course, the military's dominance and its conservative social ethos has been met by valiant resistance from many, planting the seeds of hope for mass social change in the future. Indeed, there is an argument to be made that like Shelly's Ozymandias, what will be left of Sisi's regime is a vast city in the desert – but not in the short-to-medium term, and not without considerable sacrifice.

The end of endemic repression?

In April 2022, during the Egyptian Family Iftar and in the presence of a number of prominent opposition figures, Sisi announced the launch of a national dialogue, in what appeared to be the first sign of some easing of the regime's constant repression. For the first time, Sisi displayed a sense of compassion for the President he had ousted, who had died in one of his prisons, by asking for mercy for his soul – a deeply-embedded cultural tradition that Sisi had not honoured until that moment (Arafat, Mamdouh and Seif Eddin, 2022). The inauguration of the national dialogue saw the release of a number of prominent activists and academics who had been held in the regime's prisons, either in extended pre-trial detention or after being convicted of spreading false news or joining a banned group. Those released included Hossam Mouanis (Fathy, 2022) and Hisham Fouad, arrested in June 2019, as part of the 'Hope Case', as punishment for their attempt to organize an electoral coalition to contest the parliamentary elections (Dunne, 2019). Those released also included Ahmed Samir Santawy (Al Araby, 2022), a masters' student in the Central European University in Vienna, who had been arrested while visiting his family in December 2020 (Barakat, 2022). Santawy was sentenced in July 2022 to three years in jail for spreading false news (Sawan, 2022), the only evidence presented against him being a number of social media posts he had made (Amnesty, 2021). The release of the detainees, however, did not appear to follow a clear logic in terms of the criteria or process involved.

After the dialogue was announced, a Presidential Pardon Committee was reactivated. The role of the committee is only advisory, its main function being to provide lists of detainees for review and approval by the authorities. The process of drawing up these lists is extremely rudimentary, with the committee simply receiving the names of political detainees from family and loved ones. These names are then shared with the security services over WhatsApp, who then decide whether the prisoners in question should be released or remain in detention (Mamdouh, 2022). The Presidential Pardon Committee does not have the power to issue a pardon, nor does it have an established and transparent process. Yet, even with these limitations, the work of the committee seems to face stiff resistance from hard-line elements within the regime. For example, in August 2022, after the release of twenty-five political prisoners, committee member Kamal Abou Eitta stated that the latest wave of releases was to appease committee members who had objected to the suspension of its activities (Mamdouh, 2022). Two months earlier, in June 2022, Abou Eitta had revealed on a talk show, when asked why there was a delay in releasing the presidential pardon list, that presidential orders were simply not being executed (Adwa, 2022). In a separate statement, he blamed the delay in the release of political prisoners on a struggle between moderates and hardliners in the security apparatus, a struggle that the hardliners appeared to be winning (Mamdouh and Kassab, 2022). This seemed to be confirmed when, from the thousands of names received from families and loved ones, only 1,074 were approved for release and only 300 detainees were actually getting freed, between April and June of 2022 (Lewis and Saafan, Reuters, 2022). In fact, according to Mohamed Lotfy, Director of the Egyptian Commission for Rights and Freedoms, the rate of release of political detainees between late April and late June 2022 was the same as in the previous two years, with the number of those released almost equal to the number of those arrested during that period, making the process meaningless in terms of an actual easing of mass repression.

The regime's repressive tactics took an Orwellian turn with the repression of those critical of the National Dialogue. In a scene befitting a black comedy, the prominent ex-parliamentarian Ahmed Tantawi was exiled to Beirut due to pressure from the security services. His exile came after he declared that due to political pressure he would stop writing on the independent 'Manasa' platform, for which he had produced three weekly op-eds (Ghad News, 2022). Tantawi criticism of the National Dialogue process also led to friction within the Nasserist Karama Party, culminating in his resignation as its leader before his departure to Beirut (Mamdouh, Mada Masr, 2022).

Tantawi was not the only one to suffer repression because of a critical stance towards the National Dialogue. In May 2022, the journalist Mohamed Fawzi was arrested and charged with having joined a terrorist group, misuse of social media and spreading false news. According to Fawzi's lawyer, Khaled Ali, his client's arrest was because of his criticism on social media of the National Dialogue and the limited scope of releases of political detainees, more specifically those held in the infamous 'Hope Case' (Daarb, 2022). Meanwhile the prominent political scientist and ex-political prisoner Hassan Nafaa, another critic of the National Dialogue, declared on his Twitter page that he would cease to comment on current events due to 'circumstances beyond my control', leading to speculation that he had been threatened with arrest by the security forces (Middle East Eye, 2019). Tantawi's exile and Nafaa's blackout occurred at the same time, giving credence to speculation that their repression was evidence of a systematic policy to supress criticism of the National Dialogue (Ghad News, 2022). It is important to note that the Karama Party denied that Tantawi was forced to leave the country or quit the party (Nader, 2022), but the sheer number of incidents seems to indicate a deliberate policy of repression in this sphere.

The ceremonial nature of the National Dialogue is also apparent in the way that it is managed. For example, speaking at the opening session of the nineteen-member organizing committee, Diaa Rashawn head of the foreign press regulator State Information Services, the head of both the committee and the Journalist Syndicate, stated that all opposition groups were welcome except those who did not accept the 2014 constitution – a clear reference to the Muslim Brotherhood. In essence, the largest opposition group in the country was now excluded from the National Dialogue, making it all but meaningless if its goal was truly to reduce social and political polarization. In response, the acting Supreme Guide of the Brotherhood, Ibrahim Mounir, stated that the Islamist organization was not interested in contesting power, not even in the form of legitimate elections, and he categorically rejected violence as an 'alien' concept to the Brotherhood (Evans D., 2022). A clear overture that the Brotherhood is willing to accept the status quo. It was a gesture that fell on deaf ears.

Furthermore, the authority of the National Dialogue committee seems to be extremely limited. The nineteen-member committee seems only to be allowed to make recommendations, and even though its meetings are held under the auspices of the presidency, there is no direct participation by Sisi or senior members of the security services, who are the core of the regime. The committee's lack of authority became obvious when it appealed to the President to expedite the process of prisoner release, but was unable to influence the process or produce clearly defined criteria for the release of political detainees (Hendawy, 2022). What lies behind the entire episode seems to be a desire of the regime to absorb possible popular anger due to the growing economic crisis (Mamdouh and Salim, 2022). There are also indications that the regime's policy of centralizing power remains in force, making the National Dialogue a futile exercise. For example, in a historic first, on 29 July 2022, General Salah El Rewney, the head of the military judiciary, was appointed as Vice-President of the Constitutional Court. This appointment opens up the possibility that the next head of the Constitutional Court will be an army General, a step that would further erode what remains of judicial independence (Mamdouh, 2022). In the same month, Sisi issued another significant presidential decree, granting graduates of military colleges civilian degrees, in Economics, Political

Sciences, Engineering, and Business Administration (Al Araby, 2022), accelerating the trend of militarizing the state apparatus and public sector by populating them with military graduates that now hold double degrees.

The dynamics of the National Dialogue support the hypothesis presented in this book, namely that the regime has created a set of obstacles to insulate it against popular pressure and elite-led reform. But in its gargantuan effort to centralize power in its own hands, the military regime has made itself vulnerable to external shocks.

The failure of the regime to ease repression is a reflection of its desire to survive at all costs. Indeed, rather than acting as a tool for managing political dissent, repression in Sisi's Egypt is a necessity for maintaining the cohesion of the regime's base, the loyalty of the security apparatus and its political hegemony. In practical terms, it inverts the Gramscian notion of the bifurcation of political power between the poles of consent and coercion, as laid out in one reading of the *Prison Notebooks*, by combining both consent and coercion into one indistinguishable concept. In simpler terms, the regime not only represses because it wants to but because it needs to. This stems from the ideological edifice that the regime has constructed, as well as the decimation of all opposition, including the moderates, who could have acted as a means of managing dissent if they had been co-opted. This leaves the regime brittle and unable to manage opposition except through the use of mass state violence, an option that can prove costly over the long term.

The ideological construct on which the regime anchors its claim to rule, as elaborated in Chapter 1, rests on a simple yet effective narrative. Conjuring up the most repressive elements of Nasserism and mixing them with a conservative social ethos has allowed the military to lay claim to be representative of the Egyptian nation and the guardian of the state – a nation that is portrayed as ethereal, organic and in natural harmony. This allowed the regime to excommunicate the opposition, Islamist and otherwise, and remove them from the national body. This expulsion has allowed the regime to repress large segments of society with broad popular support, but it has also left it extremely vulnerable. Indeed, in order to maintain the support of its base, it needs to continue to repress the opposition, relentlessly, otherwise its raison d'être will vanish. The military elites might have consciously manufactured this narrative to solicit popular support, but it has now taken on a life of its own, and, like Frankenstein, it haunts it creator. The regime's base will not accept an easing of repression, unless the regime abandons direct military control, an unlikely prospect considering the trend of increasing militarization of the state. In this case, by 'regime's base' we are not only referring to civilians, but also the thousands employed in the security services, the first line of defence for the regime. These enforcers have not only directly benefited from the regime's repression by amassing more power, but have been deeply indoctrinated in the regime's narrative. This will, inadvertently, create hardline elements within the regime that the elites cannot control, even if it was deemed necessary to moderate the state's repression. This became apparent when Kamal Abou Eitta, a member of the Presidential Pardon Committee, highlighted the stiff resistance that the committee faced when attempting to release a few hundred political detainees – a minuscule amount in the context of the thousands still languishing in the regime's inhumane penal system. These factors restrict the regime's ability to manoeuvre and to ease or heighten its repression based on political expediency. This makes it less able to deal with protest and social unrest, leaving repression as the only viable policy option, which, as noted, can be politically costly.

The situation is exacerbated by the central role that the military and the security services play in the Egyptian political system, weakening the position of the President. In contrast to the Mubarak era, the regime lacks a mass civilian ruling party, which the President could use to counterbalance the security services and the military in case an easing of repression was required. Indeed, one can even argue that the military is now acting as a ruling party, dictating public policy, while extending its control, either directly or indirectly, to the judicial and legislative branches of the state. The weakening of the presidency as an institution reduces its ability to halt repression if that repression goes too far. Simply put, Sisi cannot constrain the military and the security services even if he wanted to, since he lacks an independent power base to support him in case of a clash, leaving him vulnerable. In other words, he remains a general first and the President second. The situation is compounded by the decimation of the moderate opposition, so that in the case of mass social unrest the regime will be without an organized political force with a mass following that can be co-opted to manage the protests. In practical terms, unlike in 2011, the regime doesn't have a domesticated opposition like the Muslim Brotherhood that it can use to manage the unrest. The military has inadvertently dropped any semblance of a civilian façade that it could use to absorb popular anger when it inevitably erupts.

The dominance of the security services, the militarization of the state, the decimation of the moderate opposition and the lack of a pro-regime civilian counterweight bodes ill for the prospect of democratization, but at the same time makes heavy doses of state sponsored repression more likely, in case of a mass social upheaval. In addition to laying down the ideological foundations for mass state violence, the regime has also established the physical infrastructure necessary for mass repression. The most notable example of this infrastructure is the New Administrative Capital, which will not only allow the regime to isolate itself from popular pressure, but also unleash mass repression on urban centres on an unprecedented scale. Therefore, the regime's most likely response to protest will be mass repression, rather than accommodation or co-option. This conjures up the horrific possibility of a Syria- or Libya-like scenario in Egypt, unless the unrest seeps into the coercive apparatus of the state itself, inhibiting its ability to deal with protest. Indeed, compared to the Mubarak regime, which also responded violently to the mass protest of 2011, killing 846 people in eighteen days (BBC, 2011), the reaction of the Sisi regime is expected to be much more violent and widespread. The use of mass violence, however, does not guarantee that the regime will remain in power. Rather, the regime's durability depends on its ability to sustain its narrative and the cohesion of its base and the security services. A large part of the regime's legitimacy depends on its much-touted mega-projects, its economic 'achievements' and its promise to make Egypt 'as big as the world', to quote Sisi. It is in the economic arena that the regime's ideological edifice has shown the most cracks, opening up the possibility for unrest that cannot be contained without massive cost to the regime, the opposition and the country.

A demilitarized economy?

In the midst of a deepening economic crisis, Finance Minister Mohamed Maait admitted in a TV talk show in July 2022 that reliance on 'hot money' had been a mistake that should not be repeated (Sabry I., 2022). This admission came on the heels of a mass exodus of hot money, estimated at approximately US$20 billion, triggered by the Russian invasion of Ukraine and rising interest rates in the United States and the European Union.

This development seemed to prove what many analysts had been predicting, namely that heavy reliance on debt, with high interest rates, for investment in mega-projects with dubious returns would lead to fiscal disasters. In August of the same year, Bloomberg ranked Egypt as the country with the highest risk of default in the region, based on a five-year risk average (Ismail N. I., 2022), with Goldman Sachs estimating that the regime needed an IMF loan of at least US$15 billion to cover its financing gap, a claim dismissed by Maait (Wahba and Magdy, 2022). Indeed, based on data from the Egyptian Central Bank, the expected external debt repayment for 2023 and 2024 stands at US$17.65 billion and US$24.2 billion respectively (Radwan, 2022), a massive tally for a country whose total estimated tax revenue for the 2022–3 budget stands at US$63.2 billion (Shousha, 2022). Based on the same budget, total debt repayments will consume 54% of the overall budget, leaving even less funds for social spending, education and health care (Shousha, 2022).

Another problem is Egypt's feeble currency, which is expected to weaken further after a devaluation in March 2022 saw it lose 14% of its value. In August 2022, Deutsch Bank estimated that the Egyptian currency was overvalued by 10% (Ismail N. I., 2022), and as the negotiation with the IMF proceeds (Magdy and Wahba, 2022), there is a strong expectation that the pound will be devalued even further (Ismail N. I., 2022). These predictions proved correct, with a second round of devaluation in October leading to a 15% loss in the pound's value, followed by a complete collapse in January 2023, with the pound dropping to a historic low of Eg£32 per dollar (Al Jazeera, 2023). If the previous devaluation in 2016, when the pound lost almost half of its value, is any indication, then this devaluation will only lead to higher levels of inflation, disproportionately affecting the poor and the middle class, while not stopping the degradation of Egypt's balance of payments, which continued to steadily deteriorate. Indeed, the core rate of inflation had already reached 15.6% in July 2022 (CBE, 2022), rising to 25.8% in January 2023 (Reuters, 2023). Meanwhile, as the regime attempts to protect the value of the pound and is faced by pressure to repay its debt, the foreign currency reserves are rapidly depleting, falling three times between January and July 2022, from US$40 billion at the end of 2021 (World Bank, 2022) to US$33.4 billion by June 2022 (Magdy M., 2022). This depletion occurred despite large deposits being made to the Egyptian Central Bank by the regime's closest allies, the Gulf States, who by March 2022 had deposited US$28 billion, constituting 75% of the total national reserves, an astounding amount that showed the structural weakness of the Egyptian economy. Short-term external loans reached US$26.4 billion, constituting 71.3% of total reserves in March 2022. This was almost double the 33.8% figure of June 2021, all in the space of nine months (Mada Masr, 2022).

The response of the regime to the escalating crisis reflected not just the structural weakness of the regime's model of militarized capitalism, but also the political limits placed on its ability to reform the economy. Indeed, the hegemonic role that the military plays in Egypt's political system means that Sisi's ability to amend economic policy is limited, since any meaningful reform would entail weakening the military's grip on that policy and the revitalization of Egypt's wanning private sector, a prospect that the military is bound to resist. The regime's answer to the crisis rested on two main pillars, namely the solicitation of capital inflows through the sale of state-owned assets, in an attempt to meet its growing debt obligation, and the gradual weakening of the pound and raising of interest rates in order to remain an attractive prospect in debt markets. The solicitation of capital inflows began with Sisi's announcement, in April 2022, of a large privatization programme, valued at US$10 billion a year for the subsequent four years (Sabry A., 2022). In May of the same year, the Prime Minister identified US$9.1 billion-worth of state assets to be privatized, including a number of infrastructure companies. The government also declared its intention of increasing the level of investment by the private sector from 35% to 65% over the following three years (Enterprise Press, 2022).

These announcements were coupled with pledges by regional allies, namely the Gulf States, of investments estimated at US$22 billion (Espanol, 2022). Even though the details and the timing of the investments were unclear, the sale of number of state-owned assets have already been concluded. For example, in March 2022, the UAE acquired stakes in Abou Kir Fertilizers and Chemical Industries, Misr Fertilizers Production Co. and Alexandria Container & Cargo Handling Co (Magdy M., 2022), as part of a deal estimated to be worth US$2 billion (Magdy M., 2022). This also included the acquisition of an 18% stake in North Africa's largest bank, the Commercial International Bank, worth US$911 million (Mounir, 2022). The sale of state assets, however, produced some resistance from within the regime, most notably from the military. This became apparent in August 2022, when Sisi had a summit meeting with Mohamed Bin Zayid in Al Alamin, aimed at removing obstacles to Emirati investments. More specifically, this concerned the UAE's desire to acquire stakes in Al-Watanyia petrol stations, owned by the military, as well as the acquisition of stakes in Madinat Nasr Real Estate Development company, both deals were stalled in negotiations. Objections from the military establishment to the acquisition of Madinat Nasr Real Estate Development company were made under the guise of national security concerns, specifically the acquisition of large tracts of land to the east of Cairo by one investor (Salah I. E., 2022). However, one needs to keep in mind that the military is a major player in the real estate market and that the entry of additional Emirati investors into the market will not be welcomed by the military establishment, nor will be the liquidation of its investment in the petrol retail market. Resistance to the privatization of state assets and military-owned companies also became apparent during the latest negotiations with the IMF. The regime was reported to have opted for a smaller loan, of US$3 billion, rather than a larger amount as that would have entailed more stringent requirements for the privatization of state- and military-owned enterprises (Mada Masr, 2022). Interestingly, even though the loan agreed was of a relatively low value, the IMF still attached stringent conditions, including the privatization of military-owned companies, levelling the playing field with the private sector, and an overhaul of the public-sector governance structure to include transparent financial reporting of public-sector and military-owned enterprises (IMF, 2023). This is an indication that the IMF has been forced to recognize the failure of the regime's model for economic development, after consistently praising Egypt's economic performance for years.

The mass sell-off of state-owned assets was accompanied by fiscal measures aimed at attracting capital inflows into the debt market. In addition to the controlled currency devaluation discussed above, the Egyptian Central Bank raised interest rates by 200 basis points (bps) in May 2022 (Reuters, 2022), with the bank citing inflationary pressure as the reason for the hikes. However, the desire to attract investors to Egyptian debt instruments, in the midst of global interest rate hikes, was the real reason for this decision, since inflationary pressures on the Egyptian markets were mostly caused by global inflation and a weakening currency, rather than a surge in local demand.

These policies, however, will not be able to stave off the growing crisis, nor do they entail the structural reform required to revive the failing economy. There are policies that the regime could follow, in the short to medium term, to radically reform the economy, but these would clash with the military's position as a dominant economic actor, significantly curtailing its ability to extract rent and control economic policy. Reform of the Egyptian tax system is sorely needed, but this would entail a switch from a regressive system that taxes consumption to a progressive system that taxes income and capital. This would not only shift the tax burden from the lower and the middle classes to the upper classes, but would also stimulate local demand, due to the increase in the amount of disposable income. This, in turn, would spur private-sector growth, which the Egyptian economy has needed for the past few years. Increase in local demand could also, over time, increase the competitiveness of the Egyptian private sector, and hence improve its export performance, providing a more durable solution to Egypt's chronic balance-of-payment problems. The proposed reforms would also involve an end to tax exemptions for military-owned enterprises and the tax loopholes enjoyed by large civilian corporations. One needs to keep in mind that in 2022, the tax revenue from the private sector accounted for a mere 7% of total state revenue, with two-thirds of tax revenue coming from the Suez Canal and the petroleum authority and their affiliated companies, all state-owned (Sayigh Y., 2022). Reform of the tax system would also reverse the process of wealth transfer to the military elites, and domestic and foreign debt holders, by reducing the need to rely on debt with high interest rates to drive economic growth. Even though this would represent a radical departure from the regime's current model of militarized capitalism, reform of the taxation system on its own would not be enough to fix the economy. Further radical reform is needed, namely an end to military control of economic policy and its use of debt-funded mega-projects as a driver of economic growth.

As Yazid Sayigh has argued (Sayigh Y., 2022), in order for the regime to reform its model of militarized capitalism, it has to make decisions based on a clear cost-benefit analysis for the different economic sectors that the military has expanded into. Sayigh argues that if the regime wants to maintain its indigenous military production capacity, then it should retain these economic entities, but also accept that they will be loss-making. The retention strategy would also entail a shift of focus in these industries towards research and development, and increased linkages with the civilian sector leading to greater private-sector involvement. The second policy option recommended by Sayigh is restructuring of those sectors in which there is significant military involvement, like the national projects and the extraction industries. He contends that there is no substantial evidence for regime's claims that the military is more efficient than civilian government agencies, but assuming that this is indeed the case, then he offers a framework for the military's participation. Involvement of the military in these projects would require a complete overhaul of the governance model, bringing national projects under civilian control, following a government mandated fees structure, rather than allowing the military to negotiate fees and profits with private contractors, and ending the ability of the military to control these projects as a tool for rent allocation. These policies would keep to a strict timetable, which would bring about a gradual wind down of the military's participation in these projects, as the civilian agencies ramp up their own operations. The final policy recommended by Sayigh is divesture, which would apply to all commercial enterprises controlled by the military. He offers the Turkish model of OYAK or the Pakistani model of the Fauji Foundation as possible policy options to produce a simple and effective solution. The procedure would include the aggregation of ownership by the different military-owned companies under the new ownership of a holding entity, a policy option that would be aligned with the IMF policy recommendations made in July 2021. This would effectively transfer the military-owned companies to the Egyptian public business sector. The other policy option would be to place military-owned companies under the control of Egypt's sovereign wealth fund, floating some of it in the Egyptian stock market, if privatization was deemed to be appropriate, such as in the case of military-controlled media productions companies. These policies would effectively overhaul the Egyptian economy and, most importantly, curtail military influence in economic policy. The reforms are envisioned to be elite led, and can, theoretically, be accomplished by the regime, but a number of obstacles remain, stemming from the military's hegemonic position in the Egyptian political system.

Similar to the National Dialogue noted earlier, the ability of the regime to reform its economic policy is severely limited by the dominance of the military establishment over the state, and by the inability of the presidency to counterbalance the economic interests of the military. This was apparent in the aforementioned Sisi–Bin Zayed summit, with resistance from the military establishment to increased Emirati investments in the real estate sector. There are other signs of resistance to reform, though most of the evidence is circumstantial. For example, in August 2018, President Sisi proclaimed his intention to float a number of military-owned companies in the Egyptian stock market (Sayigh Y., 2020), a move that would not only have led to their capitalization but might also have been a first step towards making the military's economic footprint more transparent. The proposal, however, was never comprehensively implemented. It took until March 2020 for the Egyptian sovereign wealth fund to begin an assessment of the companies involved (Al Monitor, 2020), and as of the time of writing, there has been no substantial effort to carry out the flotation, despite the fact that Sisi's proposal did not seem to offer controlling stakes to private investors, with the military maintaining control. If implemented as Sisi suggested, the proposal would have placed civilian investors in a weaker position than their military partners, as those companies would probably have continued to be subject to military jurisdiction, and the military officers in charge would continue to have enjoyed immunity from civilian prosecution in cases of alleged financial misconduct. Bearing in mind the decisiveness and speed of the regime's implementation of its mega-infrastructure projects, it is obvious that there is either a lack of political will from the head of the regime or resistance within the military establishment to carrying out Sisi's plans to float a number of military-owned companies. Considering the hegemonic position of the military in the political system, its control over the stats apparatus and the absence of a ruling party that Sisi could use to counterbalance the military, the most likely cause for the delay in floating military owned companies is resistance emanating from the military establishment.

Hence, the regime finds itself, once again, a victim if its own success. The insatiable appetite of the military for power and wealth has spawned a political system that is resistant to elite-led reform. Indeed, if Sisi attempts to reform or abolish the prevailing model of militarized capitalism, he runs a very high risk of being overthrown. This means that in the case of an economic crisis, the regime will have limited policy options in terms of reversing policies that have led to an increase in social deprivation and, with it, popular anger. This opens up the possibility of the horrifying scenario of large-scale civil unrest met by mass state repression on a scale not yet seen in Egypt. However, the present situation cannot continue indefinitely: the structural issues that plague the regime, most notably in its militarized form of capitalism, are too deep to paper over. This begs the question as to how the current stalemate will end: through explosion, implosion or a self-reform?

Explosion, implosion or self-reform?

This book has argued that the major top-down changes to the structure of the Egyptian state and economy made by the current military regime have created formidable barriers to democratization. This does not mean, however, that the regime in its current form is secure. On the contrary, there are good reasons to believe that in spite of the its tight grip on power, and the substantial popular support it enjoys from its base, the regime stands on shaky ground. The model of militarized capitalism adopted by regime has shown itself to be incapable of working for the public good and helping to alleviate poverty, while throwing the entire process of capital accumulation into a deep crisis. Furthermore, the regime's ideological edifice, the lack of a civilian ruling party and its decimation of the opposition have left it with limited options in dealing with social unrest, apart from employing mass repression, which has left it brittle and inflexible. These conditions raise an important question: how will the regime change? Will it collapse in a wave of mass bloodletting, in a Libya-like scenario? Or will it slowly decay, until it can no longer withstand popular pressure and then collapse? Or will it be able to reform itself and evolve into a system of dual military and civilian rule and enjoy longevity, perhaps for decades?

The most horrifying prospect is that the regime will explode in a welter of violence and counter-violence, like Syria or Libya. As terrifying as this prospect is, there are reasons to believe that it is a distinct possibility. First, we must consider the regime's apparent physical and ideological preparation for a possible confrontation. Its mass investment in the urban replanning of Cairo and the building of the New Administrative Capital, as explained in previous chapters, all point to the regime's willingness to use mass state violence if necessary. The regime's history of the use of repression against its perceived opponents also gives credence to the idea that it is prepared to use mass violence against centres of popular resistance. For example, the massacre of the Muslim Brotherhood in 2013 and the use of heavy weaponry against the civilian population in Sinai attests to the credibility of this hypothesis. This is combined with an ideological construct that justifies mass state violence against the opposition on nationalistic grounds by excommunicating the opposition from the body politique. This an ideology that has become embedded not only in the coercive apparatus of the state, but also in a large segment of the regime's base of support, providing a popular mandate for the regime's mass repression. The use of mass repression also becomes more probable due to the complete destruction of the moderate opposition, which could have acted to contain popular unrest, if the regime had co-opted it or offered it some concessions.

It is important to keep in mind that the ability of the regime to repress widespread protests depends on the loyalty of its junior officer corps, the ones who will implement any order to quell a mass uprising. As Hicham Bou Nassif argues, in 2011 the Mubarak regime commanded the loyalty of the top brass but not that of the junior officers, who were disgruntled due to poor pay and working conditions (Bou Nassif, 2015). This situation was a result of the regime's coup-proofing policy, which, through the expansion of the military economic footprint, domination of the state bureaucracy and appointment to the public sector, allowed senior officers to amass considerable wealth. However, these benefits were not available to junior officers, which made them disinclined to follow orders that would entail the repression of a broad social uprising, especially one that they were sympathetic to (Bou Nassif, 2015). Indeed, this was one of the decisive factors in the fall of Mubarak. Arguably, different conditions prevail under Sisi, most notably is the level of ideological indoctrination of the junior officer corps. According to Bou Nassif, this loyalty to the regime increases the likelihood of mass repression by the junior officers. Acutely aware of the potential problem, Sisi has increased the salaries of the officers corps no fewer than ten times between 2013 and 2022 (Nawafez, 2022). Even though there is no way to accurately predict the reaction of junior officers to possible future mass unrest, the reaction of the military in 2011 should not be seen as a reliable indicator.

While these structural factors increase the likelihood of the use of mass state violence in case of popular unrest, there are other factors that mitigate against that possibility, most notably the close alliance with the United States and Europe. Even though these partners have assisted the regime with its current policy of mass repression, it is hard to imagine a situation in which Western support would be forthcoming if Egyptian security forces were to start using barrel bombs like the Syrian security forces. Egypt does not have an ally like Russia that would provide diplomatic cover and direct assistance in a possible mass bloodletting. This leaves the regime internationally vulnerable. The other factor that makes mass state violence, particularly in heavily populated urban centres, less likely is the continued cohesion of the security forces and the military, considering the fact that the Egyptian military is a conscript army. The latter factor is rather difficult to assess, but while we cannot rule out the possibility that the regime will explode in a flurry of violence, there are good reasons to assume that this is not the most likely scenario.

At the other end of the continuum of possible end-games is the prospect of elite-led self-reform, similar to the trajectory that the regime took after the defeat of 1967, when Nasser initiated a process of demilitarization of the regime, moving away from direct military rule to a dual form of rule, based on Finer's definition. Such a development now is extremely unlikely, due to a number of factors already highlighted, namely the weakness of the presidency vis-a-vis the military establishment; the lack of an organized civilian mass ruling party that can prop up the President; and finally the thorough militarization of the state apparatus and the economy. Indeed, all of these factors are connected and are driven by the military establishment's desire to consolidate power in its own hands, while eliminating all centres of competing civilian power. The transformation of the military into a quasi-ruling party, and the weakening of the presidency, has fundamentally transformed the Egyptian political system, ensuring that direct military rules remains the model of governance for years to come. In simple terms, the military dictatorship that Sisi has established will outlive him, while the next President will likely be handpicked by the military establishment to rule on its behalf. Indeed, Sisi's successor will probably lack his popular appeal, and the legitimatizing narrative of confronting the Brotherhood and 'saving the nation and the state' from the clutches of social chaos. This will make him even weaker in relation to the military. The only plausible scenario in which this trend could be reversed is a massive shock to the system, similar to the defeat of 1967, which would convince the top brass that direct control is more costly than having a civilian partner. For this to occur, however, a mass party needs to be established that has the legitimacy to rule, not an easy feat to accomplish. Even Nasser with his considerable charisma and mass ideological appeal struggled to establish a ruling party in the true sense of the word, but the mere existence of the Arab Socialist Union was essential for the process of de-militarization and the long march to a system of dual rule fully established under Sadat and Mubarak. However, there are no indicators that the current regime intendeds to establish a ruling party, a junior civilian partner that it could use to attract civilians into a ruling coalition. Therefore, even if the regime is subjected to a mass external shock and the military brass accepts the need to move away from the model of direct rule, there is no civilian force ready to take over the reins. Indeed, the process of establishing a civilian party that could stabilize a regime in crisis would takes years, making it an unlikely policy option in response to a sudden external shock, which in turn makes elite-led reform a very remote prospect indeed.

The third, and most likely, scenario for regime change in Egypt is a process of slow decay, followed by a rapid implosion of the regime, very similar to the demise of Mubarak. What makes this scenario more probable is the large number of crises that are bound to continue to occur, especially on the economic front, if the current trend of militarization is maintained. Indeed, the current model of Egyptian capitalism will not only fail to reduce poverty to a level that garners legitimacy for the regime, but will also create recurring crises that will make it more difficult for the military elites to extract wealth from the populace. Indeed, the current model, based on debt-driven growth financed by the poor and the middle class, will not only lead to higher levels of poverty but eventually to serious financial crises that the regime will be unable to resolve. This will not only erode the regime's support amongst the masses, but is bound to weaken support amongst the elites in general, outside of its core constituency, namely the elites of the military establishment. The haemorrhaging of support will damage the regime's ability to successfully wield its coercive apparatus, specifically its ability to use mass state violence to repress a popular uprising. Indeed, it is this inability that will be critical in determining the trajectory of any possible regime change. In a Gramscian sense, this would translate into a long-term war of position, where the opposition would engage the regime in a long-term political siege. This, however, would require a gargantuan effort by the opposition, which, at the time of writing, has been totally decimated by the regime's repression. This decimation is not just physical but ideological, lacking a cohesive ideological construct that can contend with the regime's version of Sisified Nasserism. The regime's failures alone are not enough to cause its implosion: they need to be combined with an organized opposition that can exert pressure on the regime and at a certain point begin to negotiate with its elites to effect changes. The nature of the regime that will emerge from this process, and the military's place within it, is difficult to predict, but it is hard to imagine a scenario in which the military establishment will not have a political role to play. Indeed, even if there is a deliberate move away from military rule in any form, the military establishment will probably continue to enjoy substantial privileges for years to come, albeit under greater levels of civilian control – unless there is a complete collapse of the military, which is an unlikely prospect, yet not impossible.

This exercise in crystal-ball gazing, like all these attempts, can produce extremely inaccurate predictions. However, what is clear is that the regime, in its current form, is unable to provide solutions to Egypt's most pressing issues, and that the appeal of its narrative of extreme chauvinistic nationalism will not prove durable in the face of mounting crises. As the grim reality of poverty and harsh repression reveals the hollowness of the regime's promises, the voices of those that oppose it will get louder. This brings us to the last part of the book: a consideration of those who continue to resist the regime, in spite of their defeats and the state's violence. Not only can we identify acts of overt political resistance, but also cracks appearing in the regime's ideological edifice, which no amount of state and societal repression has been able to paper over.

Seeds of hope

The perspective that this book has taken is that of the military elites. Reading the book might give the impression that the dominance of the military establishment has been uncontested, with the power of the state dominating not just the bodies but also the minds of the citizenry. The reality is vastly different. Beneath the façade of stability there has been a growing undercurrent of ideological and physical resistance to the regime, which mass repression has failed to eliminate. One can even argue that there is a growing challenge to the regime's ideological dominance in the form of competing narratives that have made significant inroads into the public discourse. Even though resistance has been operating at the micro level, it represents the hope that, given time, it will coalesce into a coherent political project that can offer a real alternative to the military's dominance. This has not yet happened, but it is arguably the most viable option to bring about genuine social change in Egypt.

Resistance to the regime has taken a variety of forms and has been waged on different terrains. For example, labour activism, which was critical in the downfall of the Mubarak regime (Alexander and Bassiouny, 2019) has continued despite the high cost of protest. Indeed, according to a report by Frontline Defenders, the Egyptian labour movement is facing the worst wave of repression in decades, with workers facing severe repercussions for their involvement in protests, including collective dismissal, arrest, interrogation and gendered attacks against female workers (Front Line Defenders, 2019). There have also been instances of workers facing military trials if their industrial action involved business enterprises owned by the military (Amnesty International, 2017), one example being the trial of twenty-six workers by a military court in July 2016 for taking part in a strike in the Alexandria Shipyard Company, which employs 2,500 civilian workers and has been owned by the military since 2007 (Daily News Egypt, 2016). The defendants were charged with 'inciting workers to strike', effectively criminalizing collective labour action (Daily News Egypt, 2016). Nonetheless, industrial action has continued in clear defiance of the regime, with the first half of 2021 seeing 141 cases of labour protest, out of a total of 1,177 documented cases of social and economic protests (Social Justice Platform, 2021), while in the first quarter of 2022, there have been fifty-nine documented cases of labour protests (El Hak, 2022). It is important to keep in mind that it is extremely difficult to obtain information about protests in Egypt, hence these figures are most likely an underestimation. Whether these local forms of protest will coalesce, become politicized and possibly challenge the regime's grip on power is an open question, but it is important to highlight the fact that resistance to the regime has continued in spite of the hight costs incurred.

In addition to strikes and other labour protests, there have also been instances of politicized mass protests that have erupted in direct defiance of the regime, albeit these have been few and far between. The most notable of these protests was the one that occurred in April 2016 against the transfer of the two Red Sea islands, Tiran and Sanafir, from Egyptian to Saudi sovereignty. In this case, an estimated 2,000 people protested on a certain Friday that was dubbed 'The Friday of the land' (BBC, 2016). A year later, in June 2017, another round of nationwide protests erupted against the transfer, in defiance of the anti-protest law, coinciding with the legal battle in the courts between the opposition and the regime over the transfer of the islands reaching its climax (Amin, 2017). In September 2019, for the first time since Sisi came to power, protests erupted calling for his removal, protests inspired by a video made by the actor and building contractor Mohamed Ali, who had urged people to protest on this issue. Ali had worked on the regime's mega-projects before defecting to Spain and publishing a series of videos exposing widespread corruption and graft (Reuters, 2020). The response of the regime was a widespread crackdown, including the arrest of thousands of citizens, the disruption of internet services and the blocking of websites (HRW, 2019). A month after the protests, 2,285 people were still detained by the security forces (Yee and Rashwan, 2019). In September 2020, on the anniversary of the original protests, smaller protests against the regime occurred in marginalized urban and rural comminates (Al Jazeera, 2020), sparked by new calls for protests by Mohamed Ali. However, a contributing factor to this wave of protests was the regime's decision to start demolishing what it referred to as 'illegal housing', cracking down on the violators of the Unified Building code and prosecuting them in front of a military courts (Tarek, 2020), a policy that aroused anger in poorer communities. In typical fashion, the regime responded to the protests with the use of excessive force, with hundreds arrested (Amnesty International, 2020).

There are also cases of local resistance to regime policy, most notably its urban development policy, exemplified by the case of El Warraq, an island in the Nile located in the Giza governorate and home to around 200,000 citizens. El Warraq was included in the regime's urban development plan, involving the construction of ninety-four skyscrapers containing 4,092 residential units (Tabikha, 2022). There were also reports of Emirati interest in purchasing the island from the government (Salah E., 2022). The development plans also entailed the dispossession of the local community currently inhabiting the island, the policy that led to direct confrontation with the coercive apparatus of the state. The first clashes broke out in 2017 when the security forces attempted to evict residents from their homes, which the government claimed to be illegal (Goma, 2017). Local resistance was not limited to physical confrontation, but it also included the establishment of a council to negotiate with the government and initiate a community dialogue – but it was all to no avail (Tabikha, 2022). In August 2022 there were further clashes between the residents and the security forces, as the latter attempted to expropriate the houses of the residents, with twenty-three people arrested (Kassab B., 2022). Even though these protests proved short-lived and were not strong enough to offer a substantial challenge to the regime, they showed a willingness to openly defy the regime, proving that the regime's dominance was not total or uncontested.

There has also been resistance inside the prisons, with political detainees using the last weapon in their arsenal, namely hunger strikes, as a form of protest. For example, in February 2022, twelve political prisoners started a hunger strike to protest against their illegal pre-trial detention, after the legal time limit for their detention had expired (Al-Monitor, 2022). Some of these detainees were released in the summer of 2022, as part of the National Dialogue process. This was preceded, in June 2019, by another mass hunger strike in the Tora maximum security prison, with 130 inmates protesting against the inhumane conditions they faced (Amensty International, 2019). In March 2022, Alaa Abdel Fattah, a prominent activist, started a hunger strike to protest against the inhumane conditions of his imprisonment (Al Jazeera, 2022). Another notable hunger striker was Mohamed Soltan, an Egyptian American political prisoner who was detained for almost two years in solitary confinement, spending 490 days of that period on hunger strike (Mada Masr, 2015). Soltan, who had been arrested in August 2013 as part of the crackdown on the Muslim Brotherhood, is the son of Salah Soltan, a prominent Brotherhood leader who remains in detention and who was subjected to a forced disappearance while being detained (HRW, 2022). In November 2018, the United Nations Working Group on Arbitrary Detention declared the detention of Soltan Senior to be arbitrary, based on a violation of fair trial standards, and called for his immediate release. Even those who are most vulnerable and are facing what appears to be a hopeless situation have shown a willingness to resist, putting their lives on the line for that end (HRW, 2022).

On the ideological front there is clear resistance emerging to the socially conservative ethos, and chauvinistic nationalism, emanating from the regime and its social base. This includes resistance from a burgeoning feminist solidarity movement, the LGBTQ+ community and ethnic minorities. Even though the feminist movement in Egypt is not overtly political, nor centralized, it presents a clear challenge to the patriarchal ethos of the regime's support base. This was highlighted in the summer of 2020, when a social media campaign began to expose cases of sexual assault against women, triggering a social debate on sexual violence and gender inequality in Egypt (Farouk M. A., 2020). The outcry was triggered by the gang rape of a woman in the upmarket Fermont Hotel in 2014. Although the legal case would later be dropped in May 2021, due to insufficient evidence (BBC, 2021), a claim disputed by rights groups, it still acted as a catalyst in triggering a debate that would not have been possible before 2011. It is worth noting that the security services arrested a man and three women who were witnesses to the assault and charged them with debauchery offences, clearly in an attempt to discourage other victims from coming forward, but this tactic failed to stifle the debate.

Regarding the LGBTQ+ community, even though the topic of queerness and homosexuality remains mostly taboo and outside the realm of public debate, there has been a subtle change in language which is indicative of a wider, albeit limited, social change – namely the use of the word 'homosexual' to describe members of the community rather than the far more offensive word 'abnormal' or 'Shaz' in Arabic. The change in language shows an increased level of normalization, despite the regime's repression of the queer community. This is not to argue that full normalization is on the horizon, but rather that there is a space for debate that did not exist before. The need for such a debate became critical with the suicide of queer activist Sarah Hegazi, as a result of her ordeal of being arrested and tortured by regime's security forces for having raised the rainbow flag at a concert. Hegazi's death sparked a debate over LGBTQ rights in Egypt, personal freedoms and the persecution of the LGBTQ+ community (Abul Fadhl, 2020).

The regime's narrative of an organic nation was also challenged by Egypt's long marginalized Nubian community, who in 2016 and 2017 organized protests in the southern governorate of Aswan, demanding Nubian cultural rights (Aman, 2016) and a return to their homelands (Amnesty International, 2017) The Nubian community has been marginalized for decades, subjected to racial discrimination and displaced from their homes as a result of government development projects, with some 50,000 Nubian displaced by 1970 (Front Line Defenders, 2017). The regime responded in a typical fashion, violently dispersing the protests and arresting thirty-two Nubian activists and putting them on trial for illegal protests.

Even though the regime has consolidated its grip on power, and the prospect of a democratic transition has been temporarily defeated, resistance has been ongoing under the surface. Indeed, even though this resistance has been mostly confined to local issues and though its scope is limited, it can potentially lay down the foundations for a sustained challenge to the regime and its ideological vision. These are only seeds of hope for now; it remains to be seen whether they will germinate into something more.

The end game

In this book I have endeavoured to analyse and explain the radical structural changes introduced by the military regime in Egypt in order to consolidate power and ensure the continuation of direct military rule. In this effort the regime has been largely successful, creating formidable barriers to the prospect of democratization, but in doing so it has closed the door to elite-led reform, which could have avoided potential mass social disturbances. Indeed, the regime's efforts have left the opposition with limited options, if they want to establish a genuine democratic order. A complete rehaul of the state apparatus and the economy along democratic lines has now become a prerequisite for a meaningful democratic transition. The process of state and economic restructuring will likely require years to achieve and is bound to be fiercely resisted by the elites that benefit from the current set-up. The true legacy of the regime will not be its years of repression and state violence, but what it leaves behind when it finally collapses, either by exploding or imploding. This is a legacy that Egyptian society will have to contend with for decades to come.

However, as already argued, this does not mean that the regime is necessarily secure. On the contrary, it can be argued that the regime's current model of governance is prone to crisis, particularly on the economic front, and that it does not have real solution to Egypt's pressing problems other than mass repression. Theses vulnerabilities are compounded by the lack of flexibility in the system of direct military rule and its overt resistance to reform. On the other hand, there is a counterargument that, based on the unprecedented concentration of power in the hands of the military establishment and its overt control of the state apparatus, the regime is impervious to bottom-up change. Overall, this makes the staying power of the regime more difficult to assess than the impact of its legacy. Indeed, it will only be on the day after its demise, one way or the other, that the full scale of the regime's folly will become apparent.

However, considering the surprisingly enduring legacy of the 2011 mass protests, all hope is not lost. Indeed, the abiding legacy of the revolution has not perhaps received sufficient emphasis in this book. The memory of the 2011 protests has not only survived the regime's relentless repression and attempts at defamation, but has continued to inspire resistance to regime policies by various social groups. It is in the courage of these ordinary Egyptians that the hope continues to live that the unfulfilled potential of the 2011 mass protest can finally be realized.

NOTES

Introduction

1 There is an important caveat to add on the use of Gramscian theory. Gramsci was a Marxist, and hence he viewed the process of transformation described above as a grand historical process, explaining the transformation from one mode of production to another, i.e., from feudalism to capitalism. This, of course, is not the case in Egypt: even though the Sisi regime introduced deep structural changes in the process of capital accumulation, it did not signal a change in the mode of production. In my view, this does not detract from the explanatory power of Gramsci's theory, which can provide a deeper understanding of radical changes introduced by the regime. Indeed, theories and ideas are malleable, and their explanatory power is adaptable to different contexts and situations not intended by their creators.

1 Genesis

1 There are a number of excellent accounts of the events between 2011 and 2013, including David D. Kirkpatrick, *Into the Hands of Soldiers*; Walter Armbrust, *Martyrs and Tricksters*; and Mona El-Ghobashy, *Bread and Freedom*. These studies have covered the period extensively, hence only a brief overview will be made here.

2 It is important to note that the Interior Ministry refused to cooperate with the NHCR and did not provide any information, prompting Nasser Amin, a member of the council and lead author of the report, to accuse the ministry of hiding something (HRW, 2014).

3 The details of this narrative will be covered in Chapter 5.

4 Khawarij is an Islamic sect, originating in early Islam, and is considered to be extremist by most laymen. For details on the origins of the group, see *The Venture of Islam*, Vol. 1.

2 The New Leviathan

1 Based on Gramsci, political society is the state proper (the realm of coercion), while civil society is the private sphere (the realm of consent).

2 Details of these cases will be covered in Chapter 3

3 The details of the massacres were covered in Chapter 1.

4 There is some precedent for international charges being brought against autocrats outside of the jurisdiction of the ICC, most notably the case of General Pinochet.
5 Eight UN experts issued a press statement at the end of March 2014, urging the regime to overturn the death sentences. The experts were particularly concerned that some of those sentenced to death were charged with illegal protests, not murder. The outcry was strong enough to lead to commutation of the sentences, albeit to life imprisonment.

3 There Will Be Blood

1 This was enabled by the legal and constitutional framework, and by the changes in the state structure explored in Chapter 2.
2 This will be explored in Chapter 4.

4 Pots, Pans and Guns

1 The projects involved in the statements made by Kamel El Wazzer and Colonel Tamer Rafai are not identified, so it is difficult to accurately compare the actual degree of increase in the military's economic activities. The figure given above is, therefore, the author's best estimate.
2 Based on a report issued by POMED in June 2023, the New Administrative Capital was financed through appropriation of public funds and debt, raising doubt regrading accuracy of the official narrative. For more details, see https://pomed.org/publication/report-egypt-new-administrative-capital/.
3 A new report, released in December 2020, shows that the level of national poverty had dropped to 29.7%, yet the level of family consumption dropped by 1.8%, which is counter-intuitive to the reduction in the level of poverty. Taking 2013 as the starting point, the trend of increasing poverty remains unchanged. The time period covered in the report does not include the start of the pandemic, which is expected to lead to higher poverty rates (Central Agency for Mobilization and Statistics (CAPMAS), 2020).

BIBLIOGRAPHY

A. Moneim, D. (10 November 2020). *Ahram online*, http://english.ahram.org.eg/NewsContent/3/12/393479/Business/Economy/Egypt-to-pay--bln-as-external-debt-obligations-in-.aspx.

Abdel Alim, W. (October 2021). *Al Ahram*, https://gate.ahram.org.eg/News//3026782.aspx.

Abdel Azzem, M. (11 October 2020). *Al Youm7*, https://www.youm7.com/story/2020/10/11/%D8%A7%D9%84%D8%B1%D8%A6%D9%8A%D8%B3-%D8%A7%D9%84%D8%B3%D9%8A%D8%B3%D9%89-%D9%88%D8%A7%D9%84%D9%84%D9%87-%D9%84%D8%A3%D8%AD%D8%A7%D8%AC%D9%89-%D8%A7%D9%84%D9%83%D9%84-%D9%8A%D9%88%D9%85-%D8%A7%D9%84%D9%82%D9%8A%D8%A7.

Abdel Hafiz, S. (16 March 2013). *elaph*, https://elaph.com/Web/news/2013/3/799589.html.

Abdel Hameed, A. (31 July 2016). *Al Arabiya*, https://www.alarabiya.net/arab-and-world/egypt/2016/07/31/%D8%A7%D9%84%D9%86%D9%82%D8%B6-%D8%AA%D8%A4%D9%8A%D8%AF-%D8%AD%D8%A8%D8%B3-%D8%A7%D9%84%D8%A8%D8%A7%D8%AD%D8%AB-%D8%A5%D8%B3%D9%84%D8%A7%D9%85-%D8%A8%D8%AD%D9%8A%D8%B1%D9%8A-%D8%A8%D8%AA%D9%87%D9%8.

Abdel Khaliq, D. (7 August 2017). *El Watan News*, https://www.elwatannews.com/news/details/2392853.

Abdel Latif, A. (16 August 2013). *El Watan*, https://www.elwatannews.com/news/details/262190.

Abdel Monem, M. (23 August 2020). *Al Arabiya*, https://www.alarabiya.net/arab-and-world/egypt/2020/08/23/%D8%B4%D9%8A%D8%AE-%D8%A7%D9%84%D8%A3%D8%B2%D9%87%D8%B1-%D9%8A%D8%B1%D9%81%D8%B6-%D9%85%D8%B4%D8%B1%D9%88%D8%B9-%D9%82%D8%A7%D9%86%D9%88%D9%86-%D8%A7%D9%84%D8%A7%D9%81%D8%AA%D8%A7%D8%A1-%D8%A8%D9%8.

Abdel Salam, M. (6 June 2016). *Al Araby*, https://www.alaraby.co.uk/100-%D9%85%D9%84%D9%8A%D8%A7%D8%B1-%D8%AC%D9%86%D9%8A%D9%87-%D9%84%D8%B1%D9%81%D8%B9-%D8%A7%D9%84%D8%B1%D9%88%D8%AD-%D8%A7%D9%84%D9%85%D8%B9%D9%86%D9%88%D9%8A%D8%A9-%22%D9%8A%D8%A7-%D8%A8%D9%84%D8%A7%D8%B4%22.

Abdel Salam, M. (13 October 2016). *Sada Journal*, https://carnegieendowment.org/sada/64852.

Abdelaal, H. (14 December 2021). *TIMEP*, https://timep.org/commentary/analysis/sexual-harassment-laws-in-egypt-does-stricter-mean-more-effective/.

Abdelaziz, S. and Abedine, S. (28 February 2014). CNN, https://edition.cnn.com/2014/02/27/world/africa/egypt-aids-cure-claim/index.html.

Abdu, M. (15 December 2020). *El Watan News*, https://www.elwatannews.com/news/details/5137343.

Abdulallah, M. (15 December 2016). *El Watan News*, https://www.elwatannews.com/news/details/1685313.

Abou El Eineen, M. (11 October 2013). *Al Masry Al Youm*, https://www.almasryalyoum.com/news/details/327924.

Aboulenein, A. (19 July 2017). Reuters, https://www.reuters.com/article/us-egypt-judges-idUSKBN1A421F.

Aboulenein, A. (6 October 2017). Reuters, https://www.reuters.com/article/uk-egypt-rights-idUKKBN1CB1HM.

Abou Taleb, A. R. (26 December 2020). BBC, https://www.bbc.com/arabic/middleeast-55447345.

Abu Al Magd, Z. (2018). *Militarizing the Nation: The Army, Business, and Revolution in Egypt*. New York: Columbia University Press.

Abu Zaid, M. (15 January 2021). *Arab News*, https://www.arabnews.com/node/1792886/business-economy.

Abul Fadhl, M. (22 June 2020). *The Arab Weekly*, https://thearabweekly.com/suicide-egyptian-activist-sparks-controversy-cairo.

Adeeb, A. (18 June 2017). *Veto Gate*, https://www.vetogate.com/2756063.

Adwa, A. (12 June 2022). *El Fagr*, https://www.elfagr.org/4451094.

Afify, H. (15 September 2015). *Mada Masr*, https://www.madamasr.com/en/2015/09/15/feature/politics/the-cost-of-the-sinai-war/.

Ahram (9 September 2019). *Ahram*, https://gate.ahram.org.eg/News/2270874.aspx.

Ahram online (16 January 2019). *Ahram online*, http://english.ahram.org.eg/NewsContent/3/12/321869/Business/Economy/Italian-oil-giant-Eni-says-overall-investments-in-.aspx.

Al Ahram (7 May 2011). *Al Ahram*, https://english.ahram.org.eg/NewsContent/1/64/11559/Egypt/Politics-/Tantawi-was-at-odds-with-Gamal-Mubarak-Wikileaks.aspx.

Al Ahram (28 June 2015). *Al Ahram*, https://english.ahram.org.eg/NewsContent/1/64/133949/Egypt/Politics-/Eating-in-public-during-Ramadan-fast-in-Egypt-not-.aspx

Al Ahram (15 July 2013). *Al Ahram*, https://english.ahram.org.eg/NewsContent/1/64/76509/Egypt/Politics-/Labour-leader-Abu-Eita-to-be-appointed-Egypts-manp.aspx.

Al Ahram (15 July 2013). *Al Ahram*, https://english.ahram.org.eg/NewsContent/1/64/76509/Egypt/Politics-/Labour-leader-Abu-Eita-to-be-appointed-Egypts-manp.aspx.

Al Ahram (18 July 2013). *Al Ahram*, https://english.ahram.org.eg/NewsContent/1/64/307182/Egypt/Politics-/President-Sisi-reiterates-Egypts-commitment-to-bri.aspx.
Al Ahram (18 October 2018). *Al Ahram*, https://english.ahram.org.eg/NewsContent/1/64/313658/Egypt/Politics-/Former-MP-Mostafa-ElNaggar-not-forcedly-disappeare.aspx.
Al Akhbar (3 June 2022). *Al Akhbar*, https://akhbarelyom.com/news/newdetails/3781245/1/%D9%85%D8%B5%D8%B7%D9%81%D9%89-%D8%A8%D9%83%D8%B1%D9%8A--%D8%A7%D9%84%D8%B1%D8%A6%D9%8A%D8%B3-%D8%A7%D9%84%D8%B3%D9%8A%D8%B3%D9%8A-%D8%A3%D9%86%D9%82%D8%B0-%D8%A7%D9%84%D8%A8%D9%84%D8%A7%D8%AF-%D9%85%D9%86.
Al Akhbar (24 June 2022). *Al Akhbar*, https://akhbarelyom.com/news/newdetails/3802838/1/%D9%85%D8%B5%D8%B7%D9%81%D9%89-%D8%A8%D9%83%D8%B1%D9%8A-%D8%A7%D9%84%D8%A5%D8%AE%D9%88%D8%A7%D9%86-%D9%8A%D9%86%D8%B4%D8%B1%D9%88%D9%86-%D8%A7%D9%84%D8%B4%D8%A7%D8%A6%D8%B9%D8%A7%D8%AA-%D9%88%D8%A7%D9%84%D.
Al Akhbar (29 June 2022). *Al Akhbar*, https://akhbarelyom.com/news/newdetails/3807042/1/%D8%B9%D8%A8%D8%AF%D8%A7%D9%84%D8%AD%D9%84%D9%8A%D9%85-%D9%82%D9%86%D8%AF%D9%8A%D9%84-%D9%85%D8%B5%D8%B1-%D9%85%D8%B1%D8%B6%D8%AA-%D9%82%D8%A8%D9%84-%D8%AB%D9%88%D8%B1%D8%A9-30-%D9%8A%D9%88%D9%86.
Al Anba (14 January 2015). *Al Anba*, https://www.alanba.com.kw/ar/last/529541/14-01-2015-%D8%A8%D8%A7%D9%84%D9%81%D9%8A%D8%AF%D9%8A%D9%88-%D8%B9%D9%84%D9%8A-%D8%AC%D9%85%D8%B9%D8%A9-%D8%A7%D9%84%D8%A7%D8%AE%D9%88%D8%A7%D9%86-%D8%B4%D8%B1-%D8%A7%D9%84%D8%AE%D9%84%D9%82-%D9%81%D8%B7%D9%88%D8%A.
Al Arabiya (11 July 2013). *Al Arabiya*, https://www.alarabiya.net/arab-and-world/egypt/2013/07/11/%D9%85%D8%AD%D9%85%D8%AF-%D8%A7%D9%84%D8%A8%D8%B1%D8%A7%D8%AF%D8%B9%D9%8A-30-%D9%8A%D9%88%D9%86%D9%8A%D9%88-%D9%84%D9%8A%D8%B3-%D8%A7%D9%86%D9%82%D9%84%D8%A7%D8%A8%D8%A7-%D8%B9%D8%B3%D9%83%D8%B1%D9.
Al Arabiya (7 November 2016). *Al Arabiya*, https://english.alarabiya.net/en/business/economy/2016/11/07/Egypt-raises-rates-on-Suez-Canal-certificates-to-15-5-pct.
Al Arabiya (30 August 2018). *Al Arabiya*, https://english.alarabiya.net/News/north-africa/2018/08/30/Egypt-s-Sissi-appoints-first-ever-Christian-woman-as-governor.
Al Arabiya (14 January 2021). *Al Arabiya*, https://english.alarabiya.net/business/economy/2021/01/14/Egypt-signs-MOU-with-Siemens-for-conructing-23-bln-high-speed-electric-train-line.

Al Araby (1 March 2015). *Al Araby*, https://www.alaraby.co.uk/70-%D8%AF%D9%82%D9%8A%D9%82%D8%A9-%D8%AA%D8%B3%D8%B1%D9%8A%D8%A8%D8%A7%D8%AA-%D8%A7%D9%84%D8%A5%D9%85%D8%A7%D8%B1%D8%A7%D8%AA-%D9%85%D9%88%D9%91%D9%84%D8%AA-%22%D8%AA%D9%85%D8%B1%D9%91%D8%AF%22.

Al Araby (13 June 2016). *Al Araby*, https://www.alaraby.co.uk/%D8%A7%D9%84%D8%AA%D9%82%D8%B1%D9%8A%D8%B1-%D8%A7%D9%84%D8%B0%D9%8A-%D8%A3%D8%B7%D8%A7%D8%AD-%D8%AC%D9%86%D9%8A%D9%86%D8%A9-%D9%85%D9%85%D9%86%D9%88%D8%B9-%D9%83%D8%B4%D9%81-%D8%A7%D9%84%D9%81%D8%B3%D8%A7%D8%AF-%D9%81%D9%8A-%D9%8.

Al Araby (3 June 2017). *Al Araby*, https://www.alaraby.co.uk/%D8%A3%D9%88%D9%84-%D8%AD%D9%83%D9%85-%D9%82%D8%B6%D8%A7%D8%A6%D9%8A-%D9%8A%D8%AF%D9%8A%D9%86-%D8%A7%D9%84%D8%A7%D8%AE%D8%AA%D9%81%D8%A7%D8%A1-%D8%A7%D9%84%D9%82%D8%B3%D8%B1%D9%8A-%D9%84%D9%84%D9%85%D8%B5%D8%B1%D9%8A%D9%8A%D9%86.

Al Araby (16 June 2017). *Al Araby*, https://www.alaraby.co.uk/%D9%82%D9%8A%D8%A7%D8%AF%D8%A7%D8%AA-%D8%B9%D8%B3%D9%83%D8%B1%D9%8A%D8%A9-%D8%B3%D8%A7%D8%A8%D9%82%D8%A9-%D8%AA%D9%8A%D8%B1%D8%A7%D9%86-%D9%88%D8%B5%D9%86%D8%A7%D9%81%D9%8A%D8%B1-%D9%85%D8%B5%D8%B1%D9%8A%D8%A9.

Al Araby (3 May 2018). *Al Araby*, https://www.alaraby.co.uk/25-%D8%AF%D9%88%D9%84%D8%A7%D8%B1%D8%A7-%D9%86%D8%B5%D9%8A%D8%A8-%D8%A7%D9%84%D9%85%D8%B5%D8%B1%D9%8A-%D9%85%D9%86-%D8%A7%D9%84%D8%B1%D8%B9%D8%A7%D9%8A%D8%A9-%D8%A7%D9%84%D8%B5%D8%AD%D9%8A%D8%A9-%D9%81%D9%8A-%D8%A7%D9%84%D8%B9%D8.

Al Araby (20 March 2019). *Al Araby*, https://www.alaraby.co.uk/60-%D9%82%D8%AA%D9%8A%D9%84%D8%A7%D9%8B-%D9%86%D8%AA%D9%8A%D8%AC%D8%A9-%D8%A7%D9%84%D8%A5%D9%87%D9%85%D8%A7%D9%84-%D8%A7%D9%84%D8%B7%D8%A8%D9%8A-%D9%88%D8%A7%D9%84%D8%AA%D8%B9%D8%B0%D9%8A%D8%A8-%D9%81%D9%8A-%D8%B3%D8%AC%D9%88%D9%.

Al Araby (9 December 2019). *Al Araby*, https://www.alaraby.co.uk/%D8%A5%D8%AE%D9%84%D8%A7%D8%A1-%D8%B3%D8%A8%D9%8A%D9%84-%D8%A7%D9%84%D9%82%D8%B5%D8%A7%D8%B5-%D8%AA%D8%B7%D9%88%D8%B1-%D8%AC%D8%AF%D9%8A%D8%AF-%D9%81%D9%8A-%D9%85%D9%84%D9%81-%D8%A7%D9%84%D9%85%D8%B9%D8%AA%D9%82%D9%84%D9%8A%D9%86.

Al Araby (12 December 2019). *Al Araby*, https://www.alaraby.co.uk/%D9%85%D8%B5%D8%B1-%D8%B6%D9%85-%D9%85%D8%AD%D9%

85%D8%AF-%D8%A7%D9%84%D9%82%D8%B5%D8%A7%D8%B5-%D9%84%D9%82%D8%B6%D9%8A%D8%A9-%D8%AC%D8%AF%D9%8A%D8%AF%D8%A9-%D8%AF%D9%88%D9%86-%D8%A5%D8%B7%D9%84%D8%A7%D9%82-%D8%B3%D8%B1%D8%A7%D8%A.

Al Araby (2 February 2020). *Al Araby*, https://www.alaraby.co.uk/%D9%85%D8%B5%D8%B1-%D8%A5%D8%AF%D8%B1%D8%A7%D8%AC-%D8%A3%D8%A8%D9%88-%D8%A7%D9%84%D9%81%D8%AA%D9%88%D8%AD-%D8%B9%D9%84%D9%89-%D8%B0%D9%85%D8%A9-%D9%82%D8%B6%D9%8A%D8%A9-%D8%AC%D8%AF%D9%8A%D8%AF%D8%A9.

Al Araby (5 February 2021). *Al Araby*, https://www.alaraby.co.uk/society/%D9%85%D8%B5%D8%B1-%D9%88%D9%81%D8%A7%D8%A9-%D8%A7%D9%84%D9%84%D9%88%D8%A7%D8%A1-%D8%B9%D8%A8%D8%AF-%D8%A7%D9%84%D8%B9%D8%A7%D8%B7%D9%8A-%D8%B5%D8%A7%D8%AD%D8%A8-%D8%AC%D9%87%D8%A7%D8%B2-%D8%A7%D9%84%D9%83%D9%81%D8%AA%D8%%.

Al Araby (21 September 2021). *Al Araby*, https://www.alaraby.co.uk/society/%D9%88%D9%81%D8%A7%D8%A9-36-%D9%85%D8%B9%D8%AA%D9%82%D9%84%D8%A7%D9%8B-%D9%81%D9%8A-%D8%B3%D8%AC%D9%88%D9%86-%D9%85%D8%B5%D8%B1-%D9%85%D9%86%D8%B0-%D9%85%D8%B7%D9%84%D8%B9-2021

Al Araby (17 July 2022). *Al Araby*, https://www.alaraby.co.uk/politics/%D8%A7%D9%84%D8%A8%D9%83%D8%A7%D9%84%D9%88%D8%B1%D9%8A%D9%88%D8%B3-%D9%84%D8%AE%D8%B1%D9%8A%D8%AC%D9%8A-%D8%A7%D9%84%D9%83%D9%84%D9%8A%D8%A9-%D8%A7%D9%84%D8%AD%D8%B1%D8%A8%D9%8A%D8%A9-%D9%86%D8%AD%D9%88-%D8%B9%D8%B3%D9%8.

Al Araby (30 July 2022). *Al Araby*, https://www.alaraby.com/news/%D9%85%D8%B5%D8%B1-%D8%B9%D9%81%D9%88-%D8%B1%D8%A6%D8%A7%D8%B3%D9%8A-%D8%B9%D9%86-%D9%85%D8%AD%D9%83%D9%88%D9%85%D9%8A%D9%86-%D8%A8%D8%A7%D9%84%D8%B3%D8%AC%D9%86-%D8%A8%D9%8A%D9%86%D9%87%D9%85-%D8%B5%D8%AD%D8%A7%D9%81%D9%8A%C2.

Al Arabyia (23 June 2020). *Al Arabyia*, https://english.alarabiya.net/coronavirus/2020/06/23/Coronavirus-Egypt-to-reopen-restaurants-cafes-sports-clubs-from-July-27.

Al Badawi, M. (12 January 2021). *Al Watan*, https://www.elwatannews.com/news/details/5220754.

Al Bawaba News (22 March 2020). *Al Bawaba News*, https://www.albawabhnews.com/3947696?fbclid=IwAR38kqCVsbOM116QvhmHCS91MVRov4r7PGxTTv1vb5Va-9Ch9PMgr4PnxdI.

Al Hurra (26 May 2020). *Al Hurra*, https://www.alhurra.com/egypt/2020/05/26/%D8%A7%D9%84%D8%AE%D9%84%D8%A7%D9%81-%D9%8A%D8%AA%D8%B5%D8%A7%D8%B9%D8%AF-%D8%A3%D8%B7%D8%A8%D8%A7%D8%A1-%D9%8A%D8%B3%D8%AA%D9%82%D9%

8A%D9%84%D9%88%D9%86-%D8%AC%D9%85%D8%A7%D8%B9%D9%8A%D8%A7-%D9%81%D9%8A-%D9%85%D8%.

Ali, N. (31 October 2021). *Youm7*, https://www.youm7.com/story/2021/10/31/%D9%85%D8%AC%D9%84%D8%B3-%D8%A7%D9%84%D9%86%D9%88%D8%A7%D8%A8-%D9%8A%D9%88%D8%A7%D9%81%D9%82-%D9%86%D9%87%D8%A7%D8%A6%D9%8A%D8%A7-%D8%B9%D9%84%D9%89-%D9%82%D8%A7%D9%86%D9%88%D9%86-%D8%AD%D9%85%D8%A7%D9%8A%D8%A9-%D8%A.

Al Jazeera (25 October 2014). *Al Jazeera*, https://www.aljazeera.com/news/2014/10/25/egypt-declares-state-of-emergency-in-sinai

Al Jazeera (2 February 2017). *Al Jazeera*, https://www.aljazeera.com/features/2017/2/2/giulio-regeni-murder-its-not-yet-the-time-to-grieve.

Al Jazeera (24 June 2017). *Al Jazeera*, https://www.aljazeera.com/news/2017/6/24/sisi-ratifies-deal-transferring-islands-to-saudi-arabia.

Al Jazeera (10 December 2018). *Al Jazeera*, https://www.aljazeera.net/news/politics/2018/12/10/%D9%85%D8%B5%D8%B1-%D8%B9%D8%A8%D8%AF-%D8%A7%D9%84%D9%81%D8%AA%D8%A7%D8%AD-%D8%A7%D9%84%D8%B3%D9%8A%D8%B3%D9%8A-%D8%AF%D8%B1%D8%A7%D8%B3%D8%A7%D8%AA-%D8%A7%D9%84%D8%AC%D8%AF%D9%88%D9%89.

Al Jazeera (29 May 2020). *Al Jazeera*, https://www.aljazeera.com/news/2022/5/29/egypt-court-jails-former-presidential-candidate-for-15-years.

Al Jazeera (24 August 2020). *Al Jazeera*, https://www.aljazeera.net/news/politics/2020/8/24/%D8%A8%D8%B9%D8%AF-%D8%BA%D8%B6%D8%A8-%D8%A7%D9%84%D8%A3%D8%B2%D9%87%D8%B1-%D9%88%D8%B1%D9%81%D8%B6-%D8%A7%D9%84%D9%82%D8%B6%D8%A7%D8%A1-%D8%A7%D9%84%D8%A8%D8%B1%D9%84%D9%85%D8%A7%D9%86?fbclid=IwAR03RK9l2O.

Al Jazeera (27 September 2020). *Al Jazeera*, https://www.aljazeera.com/news/2020/9/27/egypts-sisi-warns-of-instability-after-protest-calls.

Al Jazeera (9 May 2022). *Al Jazeera*, https://www.aljazeera.com/news/2022/5/9/isil-claims-attack-that-killed-11-egyptian-soldiers-in-sinai.

Al Jazeera (12 September 2022). *Al Jazeera*, https://www.aljazeera.com/news/2022/9/12/british-egyptian-hunger-striker-says-he-may-die-in-prison.

Al Masry Al Youm (1 March 2020). *Al Masry El Youm*, https://www.almasryalyoum.com/news/details/1476470.

Al Masry Al Youm (2 March 2020). *Al Masry Al Youm*, https://www.almasryalyoum.com/news/details/1476776.

Al Masry Al Youm (3 May 2020). *Al Masry Al Youm*, https://www.almasryalyoum.com/news/details/1974166.

Al Masry Al Youm (1 June 2020). *Al Masry Al Youm*, https://www.almasryalyoum.com/news/details/1983574.

Al Masry Al Youm (12 August 2021). *Al Masry Al Youm*, https://www.almasryalyoum.com/news/details/2395815.
Al-Monitor (19 December 2019). *Al-Monitor*, https://www.al-monitor.com/originals/2019/12/egypt-appoints-security-military-leaders-mostly-as-governors.html.
Al-Monitor (26 March 2020). *Al-Monitor*, https://www.al-monitor.com/originals/2020/03/egypt-army-privatization-stock-market-fund.html
Al-Monitor (29 July 2020). *Al-Monitor*, https://www.al-monitor.com/originals/2020/07/egypt-cairo-islamic-heritage-graves-destruction-road-project.html.
Al-Monitor (24 May 2022). *Al-Monitor*, https://www.al-monitor.com/originals/2022/05/hunger-strikes-prisoners-continue-egypt.
Al Qudus El Araby (23 February 2022). *Al Qudus El Araby*, https://www.alquds.co.uk/%D8%A7%D9%84%D8%A8%D8%B1%D9%84%D9%85%D8%A7%D9%86-%D8%A7%D9%84%D9%85%D8%B5%D8%B1%D9%8A-%D9%8A%D9%88%D8%A7%D9%81%D9%82-%D8%B9%D9%84%D9%89-%D8%AA%D8%B9%D8%AF%D9%8A%D9%84-%D9%82%D8%A7%D9%86%D9%88%D9%86/.
Alsharif, A. (24 March 2014). *Reuters*, https://www.reuters.com/article/egypt-brotherhood-courts-idINDEEA2N07220140324.
Al Shorouk (13 April 2016). *Al Shorouk*, https://www.shorouknews.com/news/view.aspx?cdate=13042016%id=21da29a8-0ec4-4b75-8a90-fcdefa406ff9.
Al-Wali, M. (28 December 2020). *Center for Egyptian Studies*, https://en.eipss-eg.org/egypts-external-debt-exceeds-124-billion/.
Al Watan (4 June 2015). *Al Watan*, https://www.elwatannews.com/news/details/744138.
Alexander, A. and Bassiouny, M. (2014). *Bread, Freedom, Social Jutstice*. London: Zed Books .
Alexander, A. and Bassiouny, M. (2019). *Bread, Freedom, Social Justice: Workers and the Egyptian Revolution*. London: Zed Books.
Aman, A. (22 November 2016). *Al Monitor*, https://www.al-monitor.com/originals/2016/11/egypt-nubian-protest-right-return-aswan-dam-sisi-cairo.html.
Amar, A. (24 March 2019). *Shourok News*, https://www.shorouknews.com/news/view.aspx?cdate=24032019&id=f846c4ff-b50d-4dd3-bef9-b2797057dd3d.
Amer, A. (20 October 2013). *Ahram*, https://gate.ahram.org.eg/News/408000.aspx.
American Chamber of Commerce (2022). *American Chamber of Commerce*, https://www.amcham.org.eg/information-resources/trade-resources/doing-business-in-egypt/egypt-cabinet.
Amin, S. (20 June 2017). *Al-Monitor*, https://www.al-monitor.com/originals/2017/06/egypt-islands-red-sea-popular-anger-parliament-approve-deal.html.
Amnesty International (22 February 2012). *Amensty International*, https://www.amnesty.org/en/latest/news/2012/02/egypt-police-violence-casualties-and-individual-cases/.

Amnesty International (13 July 2016). *Amensty International*, https://www.amnesty.org/en/latest/news/2016/07/egypt-hundreds-disappeared-and-tortured-amid-wave-of-brutal-repression/.
Amnesty International (30 April 2017). *Amnesty International*, https://www.amnesty.org/en/latest/press-release/2017/04/egypt-relentless-assault-on-rights-of-workers-and-trade-unionists/.
Amnesty International (12 September 2017). *Amnesty International*, https://www.amnesty.org/en/latest/press-release/2017/09/egypt-release-24-nubian-activists-detained-after-protest-calling-for-respect-of-their-cultural-rights/.
Amnesty International (7 May 2018). *Amnesty International*, https://www.amnesty.org/en/latest/news/2018/05/egypt-the-use-of-indefinite-solitary-confinement-against-prisoners-amounts-to-torture/.
Amnesty International (2 February 2019). *Amnesty International*, https://www.amnesty.org/ar/latest/news/2019/02/egypt-execution-of-nine-men-after-an-unfair-trial-a-monumental-disgrace/.
Amnesty International (31 July 2019). *Amensty International*, https://www.amnesty.org/en/latest/press-release/2019/07/egypt-mass-hunger-strike-at-al-aqrab-prison-over-denial-of-family-visits-and-dire-conditions/.
Amnesty International (2 October 2020). *Amnesty International*, https://www.amnesty.org/en/latest/press-release/2020/10/egypt-rare-protests-met-with-unlawful-force-and-mass-arrests/.
Amnesty International (2 December 2020). *Amnesty International*, https://www.amnesty.org/en/latest/news/2020/12/egypt-chilling-rise-in-executions-reveals-depth-of-human-rights-crisis/.
Amnesty International (14 June 2021). *Amnesty International*, https://www.amnesty.org/en/latest/news/2021/06/egypt-death-sentences-upheld-for-12-defendants-after-shameful-mass-trial/.
Amnesty International (21 June 2021). *Amnesty International*, https://www.amnesty.org/en/latest/press-release/2021/06/egypt-masters-student-sentenced-to-four-years-in-prison-for-publishing-false-news/.
Anani, K. (24 June 2008). *Brookings*, https://www.brookings.edu/opinions/liberal-autocracy-in-egypt/.
Annan, S. (12 June 2017). *Facebook*, https://www.facebook.com/SamiEnanSemiOfficial/posts/2028196254074528.
AP (4 December 2018). *AP*, https://apnews.com/article/b5e2b9d7c24b4700b226d2bfe45baf2a.
Arab News (10 June 2019). *Arab News*, https://www.arabnews.com/node/1508776/business-economy.
Arab News (6 March 2022). *Arab News*, https://www.arabnews.com/node/2036886/middle-east.
Arabic Network For Human Rights Information (11 April 2021). *Arabic Network For Human Rights Information*, https://www.anhri.info/?p=23376&lang=en.

Arabic Post (14 September 2019). *Arabic Post*, https://arabicpost.net/%D8%A3%D8%AE%D8%A8%D8%A7%D8%B1/2019/09/14/%D8%A7%D9%84%D8%B3%D9%8A%D8%B3%D9%8A-%D8%AB%D9%88%D8%B1%D8%A9-%D9%8A%D9%86%D8%A7%D9%8A%D8%B1-%D9%85%D8%A4%D8%A7%D9%85%D8%B1%D8%A9/.

Arafat, N., Mamdouh, R. and Seif Eddin, S. (28 April 2022). *Mada Masr*, https://www.madamasr.com/en/2022/04/28/feature/politics/political-opposition-attend-presidential-iftar-demand-release-of-political-prisoners-as-sisi-calls-for-national-dialogue/.

ARIJ (2022). *ARIJ*, https://arij.net/made_in_prison_en/.

Armbrust, W. (2019). *Martrys and Tricksters: An Ethnography of the Egyptian Revloution*. Princeton, NJ: Princeton University Press.

Ashour, M. (4 May 2013). *El Watan*, https://www.elwatannews.com/news/details/181884.

Atkinson, M. (22 November 2016). *The Middle East Eye*, https://www.middleeasteye.net/news/egypts-currency-freefall-what-does-it-mean-and-why-now.

Badawi, M. (14 September 2019). *El Watan*, https://www.elwatannews.com/news/details/4337682.

Badry, Y. (28 October 2021). *Al Masry El Youm*, https://www.almasryalyoum.com/news/details/2449257.

Bahgat, H. (2 September 2014). *Mada Masr*, https://www.madamasr.com/en/2014/09/02/feature/politics/the-arab-sharkas-cell-the-quasi-covert-military-trial-of-ansar-beit-al-maqdes/.

Bahgat, H. (14 March 2016). *Mada Masr*, https://www.madamasr.com/en/2016/03/14/feature/politics/anatomy-of-an-election/.

Bahrawy, N. (23 May 2014). *Al Watan*, https://www.elwatannews.com/news/details/487911.

Balmer, C. (21 October 2021). *Reuters*, https://www.reuters.com/world/europe/four-egyptian-officers-face-italian-trial-over-regeni-murder-2021-10-14/.

Barakat, A. (27 May 2022). *Daraj*, https://daraj.com/91222/.

Basal, M. (23 January 2018). *Shorouk News*, https://www.shorouknews.com/news/view.aspx?cdate=23012018&id=e3703d6e-6090-4d54-976e-a49b07272fce.

Bassal, M. (15 June 2017). *Shorouk News*, https://www.shorouknews.com/news/view.aspx?cdate=15062017&id=fbf4ade4-8d22-4523-a23f-2957a2c184a1.

BBC (19 April 2011). *BBC*, https://www.bbc.com/news/world-middle-east-13134956.

BBC (1 June 2012). *BBC*, https://www.bbc.com/news/world-middle-east-18283635.

BBC (24 December 2013). *BBC*, https://www.bbc.com/news/world-middle-east-25501732.

BBC (3 April 2014). *BBC*, https://www.bbc.com/arabic/middleeast/2014/04/140403_egypt_un_concerns.

BBC (5 June 2014). *BBC*, https://www.bbc.com/news/world-middle-east-27726849.
BBC (25 October 2014). *BBC*, https://www.bbc.com/arabic/middleeast/2014/10/141025_egypt_sisi_speach_attacks.
BBC (29 June 2015). *BBC*, https://www.bbc.com/news/world-middle-east-33308518.
BBC (4 February 2016). *BBC*, https://www.bbc.com/news/world-middle-east-35490825.
BBC (4 February 2016). *BBC*, https://www.bbc.com/news/world-middle-east-35490825.
BBC (13 April 2016). *BBC*, https://www.bbc.com/arabic/middleeast/2016/04/160412_egypt_sisi_islands.
BBC (17 April 2016). *BBC*, https://www.bbc.com/arabic/middleeast/2016/04/160417_egypt_protesters_jail_islands.
BBC (7 June 2016). *BBC*, https://www.bbc.com/arabic/middleeast/2016/06/160607_egypt_genina_profile.
BBC (21 June 2016). *BBC*, https://www.bbc.com/news/world-middle-east-36584812.
BBC (3 November 2016). *BBC*, https://www.bbc.com/news/business-37857468.
BBC (18 January 2017). *BBC*, https://www.bbc.com/news/world-middle-east-38659473.
BBC (24 January 2017). *BBC*, https://www.bbc.com/news/world-middle-east-38729358.
BBC (2 December 2017). *BBC*, https://www.bbc.com/news/world-middle-east-42207725.
BBC (3 December 2017). *BBC*, https://www.bbc.com/news/world-middle-east-42216147.
BBC (4 December 2018). *BBC*, https://www.bbc.com/news/world-europe-46439288: https://www.bbc.com/news/world-europe-46439288.
BBC (7 January 2018). *BBC*, https://www.bbc.com/news/world-middle-east-42597803.
BBC (23 January 2018). *BBC*, https://www.bbc.com/news/world-middle-east-42795008.
BBC (28 August 2018). *BBC*, https://www.bbc.com/arabic/middleeast-49497037.
BBC (22 February 2019). *BBC*, https://www.bbc.com/arabic/trending-47336714.
BBC (17 June 2019). *BBC*, https://www.bbc.com/news/world-middle-east-24772806.
BBC (29 January 2020). *BBC*, https://www.bbc.com/arabic/trending-51296005.
BBC (24 August 2020). *BBC*, https://www.bbc.com/arabic/middleeast-53894466.
BBC (12 May 2021). *BBC*, https://www.bbc.com/news/world-middle-east-57072192.

BBC (21 December 2021). *BBC*, https://www.bbc.com/news/world-middle-east-59730354.
BBC (18 April 2022). *BBC*, https://www.bbc.com/news/world-middle-east-53557576.
Begum, R. (29 June 2021). *HRW*, https://www.hrw.org/ar/news/2021/06/29/379079.
Benin, J. (1989). 'Labor, Capital, and the State in Nasserist Egypt, 1952–1961'. *International Journal of Middle East Studies* 21, no. 1: 71–90.
Biagini, E. and Ardovini, L. (2022). '"Struggle Is Our Way": Assessing the Egyptian Muslim Brotherhood's Relationship with Violence Post-2013'. *Religions* 13, no. 2: 174.
Bou Nassif, H. (2015). 'Generals and Autocrats: How Coup-Proofing Predetermined the Military Elite's Behavior'. *Political Science Quarterly* 130, no. 2: 245–75.
Brown, N. (13 April 2017). *Washington Post*, https://www.washingtonpost.com/news/monkey-cage/wp/2017/04/13/egypt-is-in-a-state-of-emergency-heres-what-that-means-for-its-government/.
Cairo24 (25 May 2020). *Cairo24*, https://www.cairo24.com/2020/05/25/%D8%A8%D8%B1%D9%84%D9%85%D8%A7%D9%86%D9%8A-%D9%85%D9%8F%D8%AE%D8%B7%D8%B7-%D8%A5%D8%AE%D9%88%D8%A7%D9%86%D9%8A-%D9%8A%D8%AD%D8%B1%D8%B6-%D8%A7%D9%84%D8%A3%D8%B7%D9%82%D9%85-%D8%A7%D9%84%D8%B7%D8%A8/.
Carlstrom, G. (23 November 2013). *Al Jazzera*, https://www.aljazeera.com/news/2013/11/25/egypt-passes-law-restricting-public-protests/.
Carnegie Endowment (22 September 2011). *Carnegie Endowment*, https://carnegieendowment.org/2011/09/22/national-democratic-party-pub-54805.
Carnegie Endowment (3 September 2013). *Carnegie Endowment*, https://carnegieendowment.org/2013/09/03/national-salvation-front-pub-54921.
Carnoy, M. (1983). *The State and Political Theory*. Princeton, NJ: Princeton University Press
CBE (2 September 2022). *CBE*, https://www.cbe.org.eg/en/EconomicResearch/Statistics/Pages/InflationRates.aspx.
Central Agency for Mobilization and Statistics (CAPMAS) (2019). *The Report on Income and Expenditures 2017/18*. Cairo: Central Agency for Mobilization and Statistics (CAPMAS).
Central Agency for Mobilization and Statistics (CAPMAS) (2020). *The Report on Income and Expenditures 2019/20*. Cairo: Central Agency for Mobilization and Statistics (CAPMAS).
CIHR (26 March 2020). *CIHR*, https://cihrs.org/egypt-overcrowded-prisons-will-become-epicenters-of-coronavirus-outbreak-unless-some-detainees-immediately-released/?lang=en.
CNN (8 May 2014). *CNN*, https://arabic.cnn.com/middleeast/2014/05/08/alsisi-elections-egypt.

CNN (8 March 2015). *CNN*, https://arabic.cnn.com/entertainment/2015/03/08/egyptian-ex-mufti-sharia.

CNN (19 October 2018). *CNN*, https://arabic.cnn.com/middle-east/article/2018/10/19/mostafa-alnaggar-disappeared.

CNN (14 January 2020). *CNN*, https://edition.cnn.com/2020/01/13/politics/mustafa-kassem-death/index.html.

CNN (25 May 2020). *CNN*, https://arabic.cnn.com/middle-east/article/2020/05/25/egyptian-doctors-syndicate-health-ministry-coronavirus-resignations?fbclid=IwAR0utrzebRw8WrRu-bGS43ao2CT4nB2dVKpSYXnTTKWcwqymJRFwnhOsR30.

CNN (30 July 2020). *CNN*, https://arabic.cnn.com/middle-east/article/2020/07/30/egypt-sisi-military-advisor-each-governorate.

CNN (14 October 2021). *CNN*, https://edition.cnn.com/2021/10/14/europe/egypt-officers-regeni-murder-italy-trial-intl/index.html#:~:text=The%20Italian%20prosecutors%20say%20Major,%E2%80%9Caggravated%20kidnapping%E2%80%9D%20of%20Regeni.

CNN (25 January 2022). *CNN*, https://edition.cnn.com/videos/tv/2022/01/25/amanpour-ramy-shaath-egypt-palestine-prisoner-al-sisi-macron-biden-activist.cnn.

Committee For Justice (30 August 2021). *Committee For Justice*, https://www.cfjustice.org/enforced-disappearance-in-egypt-turned-from-a-phenomenon-to-a-systematic-policy-says-cfj/.

Committee For Justice (18 January 2022). *Committee For Justice*, https://www.cfjustice.org/egypt-un-concerned-about-life-threatening-health-condition-of-former-presidential-candidate-aboul-fotouh/.

Cox, R. (1994). 'Gramsci, Hegemony, and International Relations: An Essay in Method'. In S. Gill, *Gramsci, Historical Materialism and International Relations*, pp. 49–65, Cambridge: Cambridge University Press.

Cummings, R. (3 November 2017). *Tony Blair Institute For Global Change*, https://institute.global/policy/what-hasm-movement.

Daarb (29 May 2022). *Daarb*, https://daaarb.com/%D8%AE%D8%A7%D9%84%D8%AF-%D8%B9%D9%84%D9%8A-%D8%B8%D9%87%D9%88%D8%B1-%D8%A7%D9%84%D9%85%D8%B5%D9%88%D8%B1-%D8%A7%D9%84%D8%B5%D8%AD%D9%81%D9%8A-%D9%85%D8%AD%D9%85%D8%AF-%D9%81%D9%88%D8%B2%D9%8A-%D8%A8/.

Daily News Egypt (11 July 2016). *Daily News Egypt*, http://www.dailynewsegypt.com/2016/07/11/military-trial-workers-continues/?utm_content=buffer3b49b&utm_medium=social&utm_source=twitter.com&utm_campaign=buffe.

Daily News Egypt (12 September 2020). *Daily News Egypt*, https://dailynewsegypt.com/2020/09/12/egypt-targets-16-5-tax-to-gdp-ratio-within-5-years-finance-minister/.

DAWN (27 April 2022). *DAWN*, https://dawnmena.org/egypt-newly-obtained-photos-of-ayman-hadhouds-body-strongly-suggest-torture/.

Dunne, M. (9 July 2019). *Carnegie*, https://carnegie-mec.org/diwan/79457.

DW (2016). *DW*, https://www.dw.com/en/italy-dismisses-egypts-account-of-giulio-regeni-murder/a-19144406.

Egylaw (9 July 2015). *Egylaw*, https://egylawsite.wordpress.com/2016/03/29/%D8%A7%D9%84%D9%82%D8%A7%D9%86%D9%88%D9%86-%D8%B1%D9%82%D9%85-892015-%D8%A8%D8%B4%D8%A3%D9%86-%D8%AD%D8%A7%D9%84%D8%A7%D8%AA-%D8%A7%D8%B9%D9%81%D8%A7%D8%A1-%D8%B1%D8%A4%D8%B3%D8%A7%D8%A1-%D9%88%D8%A3/.

Egypt Independent (17 June 2017). *Egypt Independent*, https://www.egyptindependent.com/parliament-will-not-recognize-judicial-rulings-tiran-sanafir-deal/.

Egypt Independent (15 January 2018). *Egypt Independent*, https://egyptindependent.com/new-cabinet-has-6-female-ministers-for-the-first-time-in-egypts-history/.

Egypt Independent (15 February 2018). *Egypt Independent*, https://egyptindependent.com/egypt-arrests-former-islamist-presidential-candidate-abdel-moneim-aboul-fotouh/.

Egypt Independent (6 December 2019). *Egypt Independent*, https://egyptindependent.com/almost-half-of-land-sold-for-first-phase-of-egypts-new-capital/.

Egypt Independent (4 April 2020). *Egypt Independent*, https://egyptindependent.com/videos-egypt-sends-health-minister-to-italy-and-medical-supplies/.

Egypt Independent (6 June 2020). *Egypt Independent*, https://egyptindependent.com/egypt-top-recipient-of-foreign-direct-investment-in-africa-in-2019/.

Egypt Independent (7 February 2021). *Egypt Independent*, https://www.egyptindependent.com/siemens-implements-first-phase-of-3-billion-electric-train-project-in-egypt/.

Egypt Independent (16 August 2022). *Egypt Independent*, https://www.egyptindependent.com/egypt-aims-to-house-6-million-citizens-in-the-new-administrative-capital/.

Egypt Information Portal (15 April 2019). *Egypt Information Portal*, https://www.sis.gov.eg/Story/188995/%D8%A7%D9%84%D8%AA%D8%B9%D8%AF%D9%8A%D9%84%D8%A7%D8%AA-%D8%A7%D9%84%D8%AF%D8%B3%D8%AA%D9%88%D8%B1%D9%8A%D8%A9-2019?lang=ar.

Egypt Project Map (2022). *Egypt Project Map*, https://egy-map.com/project/%D8%A7%D9%84%D9%82%D8%B7%D8%A7%D8%B1-%D8%A7%D9%84%D8%B3%D8%B1%D9%8A%D8%B9-%C2%AB%D8%A7%D9%84%D8%B9%D9%84%D9%85%D9%8A%D9%86---%D8%A7%D9%84%D8%B9%D9%8A%D9%86-%D8%A7%D9%84%D8%B3%D8%AE%D9%86%D8%A9%C2%BB.

Egypt Today (11 June 2017). *Egypt Today*, https://www.egypttoday.com/Article/1/7346/Sadat-assassin-Who-is-Tarek-el-Zomor-labeled-as-terrorist.

Egypt Today (20 July 2017). *Egypt Today*, https://www.egypttoday.com/Article/1/12760/New-state-council-takes-oath-before-Sisi.

Egypt Today (17 May 2018). *Egypt Today*, https://www.egypttoday.com/Article/1/50279/Why-Egyptian-policemen-arrest-people-not-fasting-in-Ramadan#:~:text=Mohamed%20Nour%20al%2DDin%2C%20former,LE%2050%20(about%20%242.8).

Egypt Today (28 June 2018). *Egypt Today*, https://www.egypttoday.com/Article/1/52972/Abbas-Kamel-sworn-in-as-new-Intelligence-Chief.

Egypt Today (30 November 2018). *Egypt Today*, https://www.egypttoday.com/Article/1/61241/Unilateral-Italian-decision-to-sever-ties-with-Egyptian-Parliament-won%E2%80%99t.

Egypt Today (4 June 2019). *Egypt Today*, https://www.egypttoday.com/Article/3/71221/5-sectors-to-drive-estimated-GDP-growth-of-5-6.

Egypt Today (23 January 2020). *Egypt Today*, https://www.egypttoday.com/Article/1/81158/Egypt-sends-medical-supplies-to-China-to-help-face-coronavirus.

Egypt Today (8 July 2020). *Egypt Today*, http://egypttoday.com/Article/3/89409/Sisi-ratifies-Egypt-s-2020-21-budget.

Egypt Today (30 August 2020). *Egypt Today*, https://www.egypttoday.com/Article/1/91434/Sisi-names-military-engineering-official-as-new-head-of-Egypt%E2%80%99s.

Egypt Today (16 September 2021). *Egypt Today*, https://www.egypttoday.com/Article/1/107888/Egypt%E2%80%99s-President-Sisi-Large-prison-complex-to-be-inaugurated-in.

Egypt Today (31 March 2022). *Egypt Today*, https://www.egypttoday.com/Article/1/114432/President-Sisi-extends-security-measures-in-Sinai-for-6-more.

Egypt Today (21 April 2022). *Egypt Today*, https://www.egypttoday.com/Article/3/115139/Egypt-s-external-debt-rises-to-145-5-billion-by.

Egypt Watch (11 April 2022). *Egypt Watch*, https://egyptwatch.net/2022/04/11/the-full-story-of-ayman-hadhoud/.

Egyptian Commission for Rights and Freedoms (ECRF) (2021). *Egyptian Commission for Rights and Freedoms (ECRF)*, https://www.ec-rf.net/wp-content/uploads/2021/10/dp-final11.pdf.

Egyptian Front (27 July 2020). *Egyptian Front*, https://egyptianfront.org/ar/2020/07/tiktok/.

Egyptian Initiative for Personal Rights (28 November 2018). *Egyptian Initiative for Personal Rights*, https://eipr.org/press/2018/11/%D9%81%D9%8A-%D9%82%D8%B6%D9%8A%D8%A9-%D8%A7%D8%BA%D8%AA%D9%8A%D8%A7%D9%84-%D8%A7%D9%84%D9%86%D8%A7%D8%A6%D8%A8-%D8%A7%D9%84%D8%B9%D8%A7%D9%85-%D9%85%D8%AD%D9%83%D9%85%D8%A9-%D8%A7%D9%84%D9%86%D9%82%D8%B6-%D8%AA%D8%A4%D9%8A%.

Egyptian Streets (14 March 2018). *Egyptian Streets*, https://egyptianstreets.com/2018/03/14/egyptian-authorities-urge-citizens-to-report-on-fake-news-and-rumors-through-a-hotline/.

Egyptian Streets (17 August 2020). *Egyptian Streets*, https://egyptianstreets.com/2020/08/17/egypt-increases-metro-fares-for-the-second-consecutive-year/.

EIPR (August 2015). *EIPR*, https://www.eipr.org/press/2015/08/%D9%82%D8%A7%D9%86%D9%88%D9%86-%D8%A7%D9%84%D8%A3%D8%AC%D9%87%D8%B2%D8%A9-%D8%A7%D9%84%D8%B1%D9%82%D8%A7%D8%A8%D9%8A%D8%A9-%D8%A7%D9%84%D8%AC%D8%AF%D9%8A%D8%AF-%D9%8A%D8%A4%D8%AF%D9%8A-%D8%A5%D9%84%D9%89-%D9%85%D8%B2%D9%.

EIPR (10 May 2016). *EIPR*, https://eipr.org/en/press/2016/05/replacement-emergency-law-pretrial-detention-political-punishment.

EIPR (22 November 2017). *EIPR*, https://eipr.org/en/publications/trap-punishing-sexual-difference-egypt.

EIPR (25 September 2018). *EIPR*, https://eipr.org/en/press/2018/09/year-after-raising-rainbow-flag-incident-and-five-years-after-longest-security.

EIPR (21 February 2021). *EIPR*, https://www.eipr.org/press/2021/02/%D8%A7%D9%84%D9%85%D8%AF%D9%88%D9%91%D9%86-%D8%A7%D9%84%D9%82%D8%B1%D8%A2%D9%86%D9%8A-%D9%81%D9%8A-%D8%B1%D8%B3%D8%A7%D9%84%D8%A9-%D8%A8%D8%B9%D8%AF-6-%D8%B4%D9%87%D9%88%D8%B1-%D9%85%D9%86-%D8%A7%D9%84%D8%AD%D8%A8%D8%B3-.

EIPR (3 May 2021). *EIPR*, https://eipr.org/en/press/2021/05/corona-victims-exceeded-500-deaths-among-physicians.

EIPR (25 May 2022). *EIPR*, https://www.eipr.org/press/2022/05/%D8%AA%D8%AF%D9%88%D9%8A%D8%B1-%D8%A3%D8%AD%D9%85%D8%AF-%D8%B5%D8%A8%D8%B1%D9%8A-%D9%86%D8%A7%D8%B5%D9%81-%D9%84%D9%84%D9%85%D8%B1%D8%A9-%D8%A7%D9%84%D8%AB%D8%A7%D9%84%D8%AB%D8%A9-%D8%A8%D8%B9%D8%AF-%D8%B4%D9%87%D8%B1-%D.

El Abd, R. (3 July 2018). *Mada Masr*, https://www.madamasr.com/ar/2018/07/03/news/u/%D9%8A%D8%AD%D8%B5%D9%86%D9%87%D9%85-%D9%85%D9%86-%D8%A7%D9%84%D9%85%D8%B3%D8%A7%D8%A1%D9%84%D8%A9-%D8%B9%D9%86-%D8%A7%D9%84%D9%81%D8%AA%D8%B1%D8%A9-%D8%A7%D9%84%D8%A7%D9%86%D8%AA%D9%82%D8%A7%D9%84/.

El Balad (25 May 2020). *El Balad*, https://www.elbalad.news/4335935.

El Dahshan, M. (24 March 2014). *Atlantic Council*, https://www.atlanticcouncil.org/blogs/menasource/the-army-s-miracle-cure-today-s-joke-tomorrow-s-tragedy/.

El Deeb, S. (6 January 2014). *AP*, https://apnews.com/article/e7033fe662b7497dbbac8ac3b71881b9.

El Fass, A. (30 December 2020). *Al Ahram*, https://gate.ahram.org.eg/News/2551937.aspx.

El Gali, M. (13 September 2019). *Al Youm7*, https://www.youm7.com/story/2019/9/13/%D8%A7%D9%84%D8%B3%D9%8A%D8%B3%D9%89-%D8%A3%D9%88%D9%84-%D8%A7%D9%84%D9%85%D8%AD%D8%

B0%D8%B1%D9%8A%D9%86-%D9%85%D9%86-%D8%AD%D8%B1%D9%88%D8%A8-%D8%A7%D9%84%D8%AC%D9%8A%D9%84-%D8%A7%D9%84%D8%B1%D8%A7%D8%A8%D8%B9-%D9%88.

El Ghobashy, M. (2021). *Bread and Freedom*. Stanford, CA: Stanford University Press.

El Hak (2022). *Labour Protest in Egypt*. Cairo: El Hak.

El Khodary, S. (4 November 2013). *Al Watan*, https://www.elwatannews.com/news/details/350873/.

El Nadeem (31 December 2016). *El Nadeem*, https://elnadeem.org/2016/12/31/1911/.

El Nadeem (2017). *The Results of Oppression*. Cairo: El Nadeem.

El Naggar, D. (3 September 2019). *Shorouk News*, https://www.shorouknews.com/news/view.aspx?cdate=03092019&id=3f0988f1-0bd0-4fb7-aee9-f5006c0a02ce&fbclid=IwAR15MHBMG9H3pM3D1vzSV4gH8j-qjJz5-NA4lTCNh_Ll61_FpqXeoNIhl6I.

El Rashidi, O. (22 August 2015). *Al Araby*, https://www.alaraby.co.uk/%D9%83%D9%8A%D9%81-%D9%87%D9%8A%D8%A3-%D8%A7%D9%84%D8%A5%D8%B9%D9%84%D8%A7%D9%85-%D8%A7%D9%84%D9%85%D8%B5%D8%B1%D9%8A-%D8%A7%D9%84%D8%B1%D8%A3%D9%8A-%D8%A7%D9%84%D8%B9%D8%A7%D9%85-%D9%84%D9%85%D8%B0%D8%A8%D8%AD%D8%A9-%D8%B1%D8%A7.

El-Rifae, Y. (17 July 2014). *MEI*, https://www.mei.edu/publications/egypts-sexual-harassment-law-insufficient-measure-end-sexual-violence#_ftn4.

El-Sadany, M. (2 August 2017). *TIMEP*, https://timep.org/commentary/forced-disappearances-in-egypts-courts/.

El Sakty, K. (2021). *Egypt's New Administrative Capital City*. Cairo: IDSC.

El Shalakany, S. (20 February 2017). *Al-Monitor*, https://www.al-monitor.com/ar/contents/articles/originals/2017/02/egypt-sisi-call-law-annul-verbal-divorce.html.

El-Shamaa, M. (13 May 2020). *Arab News*, https://www.arabnews.com/node/1673876/middle-east.

El-Shiekh, S. (26 December 2015). *The Daily News*, https://dailynewsegypt.com/2015/12/26/government-reshuffle-features-al-sisi-appointments-with-military-backgrounds/.

Eleiba, A. (8 September 2012). *Al Ahram*, https://english.ahram.org.eg/NewsContent/1/64/52021/Egypt/Politics-/Egypts-Operation-Eagle-Sinai-campaign-draws-mixed-.aspx.

Eleiba, A. (9 February 2018). *Al Ahram*, https://english.ahram.org.eg/NewsContent/1/64/290644/Egypt/Politics-/LIVE-UPDATES-Egypts-army-launches-Comprehensive-Op.aspx.

Emam, A. (18 November 2018). *The Arab Weekly*, https://thearabweekly.com/egypt-struggles-bloated-public-sector.

Energy Voice (2 December 2019). *Energy Voice*, https://www.energyvoice.com/oilandgas/africa/192531/egypt-devises-new-contracts-to-attract-more-oil-and-gas-investors/.

England, A. (31 October 2022). *Financial Times*, https://www.ft.com/content/03533d92-4a71-43fc-b885-27dcb962d4e8.

Enterprise Press (31 May 2020). *Enterprise Press*, https://enterprise.press/stories/2020/05/31/egypt-closes-record-usd-5-bn-eurobond-issuance-with-strong-appetite-from-global-investors-16342/.

Enterprise Press (16 May 2022). *Enterprise Press*, https://enterprise.press/stories/2022/05/16/madbouly-announces-plans-to-privatize-state-assets-boost-private-investment-71163/.

Espanol, M. (11 April 2022). *Al-Monitor*, https://www.al-monitor.com/originals/2022/04/gulf-states-give-egypt-22-billion-mitigate-fallout-ukraine-war#:~:text=T%C3%9CRKIYE-,Gulf%20states%20give%20Egypt%20%2422%20billion%20to%20mitigate%20fallout%20from,cover%20Egypt's%20current%20account%20deficit.

Essam, M. (27 April 2022). *Al Ahram*, https://gate.ahram.org.eg/News/3497538.aspx.

Essam El Deen, S. (18 September 2018). *Shorouk*, https://www.shorouknews.com/news/view.aspx?cdate=18092018&id=f996060c-dab1-43fb-9c70-efed286dc972.

Essam El-Din, G. (31 December 2021). *Al Ahram*, https://english.ahram.org.eg/News/448838.aspx.

Euro News (3 March 2018), *Euro News*, https://arabic.euronews.com/2018/03/03/egypt-saudiarabia-islands-court.

Evans, D. (29 July 2022). *Reuters*, https://www.reuters.com/world/middle-east/egypts-muslim-brotherhood-rejects-struggle-power-exiled-leader-says-2022-07-29/.

Evans, M. and Phillips, J. (2007). *Algeria, Anger of the Dispossedded*. New Haven, CT: Yale University Press.

Ezzeldin, M. (20 September 2020). *Al Watan*, https://www.elwatannews.com/news/details/4983618.

Fahmy, I. (21 June 2013). *Al Watan*, https://www.elwatannews.com/news/details/206521.

Fahmy, K. (1997). *All the Pasha Men*. Cairo: American University Press.

Fahmy, K. (2018). *In Quest of Justice*. Oakland, CA: University of California Press.

Fahmy, K. (2018). *Mehmed Ali: From Otttoman Governor to Ruler of Egypt*. London: One World.

Fahmy, O. (3 August 2021). *Reuters*, https://www.reuters.com/world/middle-east/egypts-sisi-calls-first-bread-price-rise-decades-2021-08-03/.

Fahmy, O. and Noueihed, L. (13 June 2016). *Reuters*, https://www.reuters.com/article/us-egypt-saudi-ties-idUSKCN0XA16Q.

Fargaly, M. (9 May 2014). *Al Masry Al Youm*, https://www.almasryalyoum.com/news/details/443065.

Farid, S. (26 July 2014). *Al Arabiya*, https://english.alarabiya.net/perspective/analysis/2014/07/26/Is-public-breaking-of-Ramadan-fast-illegal-in-Egypt-.

Farouk, M. (6 April 2017). *Al-Monitor*, https://www.al-monitor.com/originals/2017/04/egypt-develop-cairo-slum-concerns-residents.html.

Farouk, M. (10 April 2020). *Al-Monitor*, https://www.al-monitor.com/originals/2020/04/egypt-regeni-italy-supplies-covid19-coronavirus.html.
Farouk, M. (14 August 2020). *Reuters*, https://www.reuters.com/article/us-egypt-cities-housing-feature-trfn-idUSKCN25A0DP.
Farouk, M. A. (24 September 2020). *Reuters*, https://www.reuters.com/article/egypt-women-rights-feature-int-idUSKCN26F1Y7.
Fathy, M. (28 April 2022). *Shorouk*, https://www.shorouknews.com/news/view.aspx?cdate=28042022&id=93189eea-1705-4960-95a5-6929685e2c17.
Finer, S. (2002). *The Man on Horseback*. London and New York: Routledge.
France 24 (5 February 2011). *France 24*, https://www.france24.com/en/20110205-senior-leadership-egypt-ruling-party-gamal-mubarak-resigns-en-masse.
France 24 (16 April 2011). *France 24*, https://www.france24.com/en/20110416-egypt-dissolves-former-president-hosni-mubarak-political-party-NDP-protests-justice.
France 24 (12 December 2012). *France 24*, https://www.france24.com/ar/20121209-%D9%85%D8%B5%D8%B1-%D9%85%D8%B1%D8%B3%D9%8A-%D8%A7%D9%84%D8%BA%D8%A7%D8%A1-%D8%A7%D9%84%D8%A7%D8%B9%D9%84%D8%A7%D9%86-%D8%A7%D9%84%D8%AF%D8%B3%D8%AA%D9%88%D8%B1%D9%8A-%D8%A7%D8%A8%D9%82%D8%A7%D8%A1-%D9%85%D9%88%D8%B9%D.
France 24 (14 July 2013). *France 24*, https://www.france24.com/ar/20130714-%D9%85%D8%B5%D8%B1-%D8%A3%D8%AF%D8%A7%D8%A1-%D8%A7%D9%84%D9%8A%D9%85%D9%8A%D9%86-%D8%A7%D9%84%D8%AF%D8%B3%D8%AA%D9%88%D8%B1%D9%8A-%D9%85%D8%AD%D9%85%D8%AF-%D8%A7%D9%84%D8%A8%D8%B1%D8%A7%D8%AF%D8%B9%D9%8A-%D9%86%D8%A7%D.
France 24 (28 April 2014). *France 24*, https://www.france24.com/ar/20140428-%D9%85%D8%AD%D9%83%D9%85%D8%A9-%D8%A5%D8%B9%D8%AF%D8%A7%D9%85-%D9%85%D8%A4%D9%8A%D8%AF%D9%8A%D9%88%D9%86-%D8%A7%D9%84%D8%A5%D8%AE%D9%88%D8%A7%D9%86-%D8%A7%D9%84%D9%85%D8%B3%D9%84%D9%85%D9%8A%D9%86-%D9%85%D8%B5%D8%B1-%D.
France 24 (5 February 2017). *France 24*, https://www.france24.com/ar/20170205-%D9%85%D8%B5%D8%B1-%D8%A7%D9%84%D8%A3%D8%B2%D9%87%D8%B1-%D8%A7%D9%84%D8%B3%D9%8A%D8%B3%D9%8A-%D8%A7%D9%84%D8%B7%D9%84%D8%A7%D9%82-%D8%A7%D9%84%D8%B4%D9%81%D9%88%D9%8A-%D9%81%D8%AA%D9%88%D9%89-%D8%A7%D9%84%D8%A5%D8%B3%D.
France 24 (6 May 2020). *France 24*, https://www.france24.com/ar/20200506-%D8%A7%D9%84%D9%86%D9%8A%D8%A7%D8%A8%D8%A9-%D8%A7%D9%84%D9%85%D8%B5%D8%B1%D9%8A%D8%A9-%D8%AA%D8%B9%D9%84%D9%86-%D8%A3%D9%86-%D9%88%D9%81%D8%A7%D8%A9-%D8%A7%D9%84%D9%85%D8%AE%D8%B1%D8%AC-%D8%B4%D8%A7%D8%AF%D9%8A-%D8%AD%.

France 24 (7 December 2020). *France 24*, https://www.france24.com/en/france/20201207-live-macron-and-egypt-s-sisi-hold-joint-press-conference-in-paris.

France 24 (10 December 2020). *France 24*, https://www.france24.com/en/live-news/20201210-macron-gave-sisi-france-s-highest-award-on-paris-visit-official.

Front Line Defenders (11 December 2017). *Front Line Defenders*, https://www.frontlinedefenders.org/en/statement-report/egypt-nubian-human-rights-defenders-trial-peacefully-protesting.

Front Line Defenders (2019). *Striking Back: Egypt's Attack on Labour Rights Defenders.*

Gad, S. (25 January 2018). *Sada Journal*, https://carnegieendowment.org/sada/75353.

Gamal El-Din, E.-S. (11 August 2017). *Al Ahram*, https://english.ahram.org.eg/NewsContent/1/64/275125/Egypt/Politics-/-Judge-ElDakroury-appeals-presidents-decision-to-a.aspx.

Gerges, F. (2018). *The Making of the Arab World*. Princeton, NJ: Princeton University Press.

Ghad News (2022, August 6). *Ghad News*, https://ghadnews.net/ar/post/10700.

Ghali, M., Hosni, S. and Bedawi, M. (16 November 2019). *Youm7*, https://www.youm7.com/story/2019/11/26/%D8%A7%D9%84%D8%B1%D8%A6%D9%8A%D8%B3-%D8%A7%D9%84%D8%B3%D9%8A%D8%B3%D9%8A-%D9%86%D9%81%D8%B0%D9%86%D8%A7-%D9%85%D8%B4%D8%B1%D9%88%D8%B9%D8%A7%D8%AA-%D9%82%D9%88%D9%85%D9%8A%D8%A9-%D8%A8%D9%82%D9%8A%D9%85%D8%A9-200-%D.

Global Economy (26 January 2021). *Global Economy*, https://www.theglobaleconomy.com/Egypt/Trade_balance/.

Goma, A. (27 April 2017). *Masrawy*, https://www.masrawy.com/News/News_Egypt/details/2017/4/27/1068455/%D8%B1%D8%B3%D9%85%D9%8A%D8%A7-%D8%A7%D9%84%D8%B3%D9%8A%D8%B3%D9%8A-%D9%8A%D8%B9%D8%AA%D9%85%D8%AF-%D8%AA%D8%B9%D8%AF%D9%8A%D9%84%D8%A7%D8%AA-%D8%A7%D9%84%D9%87%D9%8A%D8%A6%D8%A7%D8%AA-%D8%.

Goma, A. (16 July 2017). *Masrawy*, https://www.masrawy.com/news/news_egypt/details/2017/7/16/1121126/%D8%A7%D9%84%D8%B5%D8%AD%D8%A9-%D9%88%D9%81%D8%A7%D8%A9-%D9%85%D9%88%D8%A7%D8%B7%D9%86-%D9%88%D8%A5%D8%B5%D8%A7%D8%A8%D8%A9-19-%D8%A2%D8%AE%D8%B1%D9%8A%D9%86-%D9%81%D9%8A-%D8%A7%D8%B4%D8%AA.

Gramsci, A. (1996). *The Prison Notebooks, Vol. 2.* New York: Columbia University Press.

Grimley, N., Cornish, J. and Stylianou, N. (5 May 2022). *BBC*, https://www.bbc.com/news/health-61327778.

Guardian (24 June 2012). *Guardian*, https://www.theguardian.com/world/middle-east-live/2012/jun/24/egypt-election-results-live.

Guardian (25 December 2013). *Guardian*, https://www.theguardian.com/world/2013/dec/25/egypt-declares-muslim-brotherhood-terrorist-group.

Guardian (9 September 2016). *Guardian*, https://www.theguardian.com/world/2016/sep/09/egyptian-police-investigated-giulio-regeni-days-before-his.

Guardian (7 July 2017). *Guardian*, https://www.theguardian.com/world/2017/jul/07/egyptian-soldiers-killed-in-attack-on-sinai-checkpoint.

Guardian (8 May 2018), *Guardian*, https://www.theguardian.com/cities/2018/may/08/cairo-why-egypt-build-new-capital-city-desert.

Guardian (17 June 2019), *Guardian*, https://www.theguardian.com/world/2019/jun/17/mohamed-morsi-dead-ousted-president-egypt-collapses-after-court-session.

Guardian (29 December 2019). *Guardian*, https://www.theguardian.com/world/2018/dec/28/bomb-attack-tourist-bus-giza-pyramids-egypt.

Guardian (21 May 2020). *Guardian*, https://www.theguardian.com/global-development/2020/may/21/egypt-doctors-ppe-testing-coronavirus.

Gulhane, J. (12 July 2013). *News Daily*, https://dailynewsegypt.com/2013/07/12/ziad-bahaa-el-din-appointed-deputy-pm/.

Habib, H. and Cunningham, E. (6 August 2015). *Washington Post*, https://www.washingtonpost.com/news/worldviews/wp/2015/08/06/egypts-gift-to-the-world-cost-8-billion-and-probably-wasnt-necessary/.

Hagag, M. and Gendy, N. (22 November 2014). *Youm 7*, https://www.youm7.com/story/2014/11/22/%D9%85%D9%87%D8%A7%D8%A8-%D9%85%D9%85%D9%8A%D8%B4-%D9%82%D9%86%D8%A7%D8%A9-%D8%A7%D9%84%D8%B3%D9%88%D9%8A%D8%B3-%D8%A7%D9%84%D8%AC%D8%AF%D9%8A%D8%AF%D8%A9-%D8%B3%D8%AA%D8%AF%D8%B1-100-%D9%85%D9%84%D9%8A%D8%A7%D8%B1-%.

Haitham, A. and Reda, M. (16 January 2017). *Reuters*, https://www.reuters.com/article/egypt-islands-mh3-idARAKBN1500WK.

Hamama, M. (2018). *ARIJ*, https://arij.net/investigation/%d9%85%d8%b9%d8%aa%d9%82%d9%84%d9%88%d9%86-%d9%84%d9%84%d8%a3%d8%a8%d8%af-%d8%a2%d9%84%d8%a9-%d8%a7%d9%84%d8%ad%d8%a8%d8%b3-%d8%a7%d9%84%d8%a7%d8%ad%d8%aa%d9%8a%d8%a7%d8%b7%d9%8a-%d8%aa%d8%b9%d9%85/.

Hamzawy, A. and Brown, N. (23 July 2020). *Carnegie Endowment*, https://carnegieendowment.org/2020/07/23/how-much-will-pandemic-change-egyptian-governance-and-for-how-long-pub-82353.

Hanna, J. (19 November 2015). *CNN*, https://edition.cnn.com/2015/11/18/middleeast/metrojet-crash-dabiq-claim/index.html.

Harb, I. (2003). 'The Egyptian Military in Politics: Disengagement or Accommodation?'. *Middle East Journal* 57, no. 2 (Spring): 269–90.

Hawary, M. (5 May 2020). *Al Masry Al Youm*, https://www.almasryalyoum.com/news/details/1980964.

Hendawy, T. (20 August 2022). *Al Qudus*, https://www.alquds.co.uk/%D9%85%D8%B5%D8%B1-%D8%AA%D9%88%D8%A7%D8%B5%D9%84-%D8%A7%D9%84%D8%AD%D9%88%D8%A7%D8%B1-%D8%A7%D9%84%D9%88%D8%B7%D9%86%D9%8A-%D9%88%D8%A7%D9%86%D8%AA%D9%82%D8%A7%D8%AF%D8%A7%D8%AA-%D9%84%D8%AA%D8%AC/.

Higazy, M. (20 December 2017). *Mada Masr*, https://www.madamasr.com/en/2017/12/20/news/u/at-least-1-officer-5-militants-killed-in-clashes-outside-arish-airport-following-attack/.

Hosni, H. (4 June 2012). *Masrawy*, https://www.masrawy.com/news/news_egypt/details/2013/6/4/19420/%D9%85%D8%B9%D8%AA%D9%82%D9%84-%D8%B3%D9%8A%D8%A7%D8%B3%D9%8A-%D9%8A%D9%83%D8%B4%D9%81-%D8%A3%D8%B3%D8%A7%D9%84%D9%8A%D8%A8-%D8%AC%D8%AF%D9%8A%D8%AF%D8%A9-%D9%84%D9%84%D8%AA%D8%B9%D8%B0%D9%8A%.

Hossam, B. (23 October 2018). *Mada Masr*, https://madamasr.com/en/2018/10/23/feature/politics/whos-buying-israeli-gas-a-company-owned-by-the-general-intelligence-service/?__cf_chl_captcha_tk__=29f2f8e0a67e316158cce7a21ea447f49b249b80-1611309837-0-AauY9HUjudLjBPQIaW9jYxepBNPelG-pI4S_Hqo6vAvyaCGiUh.

HRW (Human Rights Watch) (27 May 2008). *HRW*, https://www.hrw.org/news/2008/05/27/egypt-extending-state-emergency-violates-rights.

HRW (21 August 2013). *HRW*, https://www.hrw.org/news/2013/08/21/egypt-mass-attacks-churches#:~:text=Since%20August%2014%2C%202013%2C%20attackers,been%20informed%20of%20ongoing%20attacks.

HRW (24 March 2014). *HRW*, https://www.hrw.org/news/2014/03/24/egypt-shocking-death-sentences-follow-sham-trial.

HRW (12 August 2014). *HRW*, https://www.hrw.org/news/2014/08/12/egypt-raba-killings-likely-crimes-against-humanity.

HRW (12 August 2014). *HRW*, https://www.hrw.org/report/2014/08/12/all-according-plan/raba-massacre-and-mass-killings-protesters-egypt.

HRW (22 September 2015). *HRW*, https://www.hrw.org/report/2015/09/22/look-another-homeland/forced-evictions-egypts-rafah.

HRW (13 April 2016). *HRW*, https://www.hrw.org/news/2016/04/13/egypt-7400-civilians-tried-military-courts.

HRW (28 September 2016). *HRW*, https://www.hrw.org/report/2016/09/28/we-are-tombs/abuses-egypts-scorpion-prison.

HRW (12 April 2017). *HRW*, https://www.hrw.org/news/2017/04/12/egypt-horrific-palm-sunday-bombings.

HRW (21 April 2017). *HRW*, https://www.hrw.org/news/2017/04/21/egypt-videos-show-army-executions-sinai.

HRW (6 September 2017). *HRW*, https://www.hrw.org/video-photos/video/2017/09/06/video-egypts-assembly-line-torture.

HRW (7 January 2019). *HRW*, https://www.hrw.org/news/2019/01/07/egypt-little-truth-al-sisis-60-minutes-responses.

HRW (7 January 2019). *HRW*, https://www.hrw.org/ar/news/2019/01/07/325806.
HRW (24 July 2019). *HRW*, https://www.hrw.org/ar/news/2019/07/24/332299.
HRW (27 September 2019). *HRW*, https://www.hrw.org/news/2019/09/27/egypt-hundreds-arrested-nationwide-crackdown.
HRW (17 March 2021). *HRW*, https://www.hrw.org/ar/news/2021/03/17/378097.
HRW (21 September 2021). *HRW*, https://www.hrw.org/news/2021/09/07/egypt-shootouts-disguise-apparent-extrajudicial-executions#.
HRW (18 November 2021). *HRW*, https://www.hrw.org/news/2021/11/18/egypt-terrorism-laws-abused-businessmens-arrests.
HRW (16 February 2022). *HRW*, https://www.hrw.org/news/2022/02/16/egypt-rights-defenders-imprisoned-father-risk.
Hunter, R. (1984). *Egypt Under The Khedives 1805–1879.* Pittsburgh: University of Pittsburgh Press.
Ibrahim, A. (23 March 2018). *Al Jazeera*, https://www.aljazeera.com/news/2018/3/23/egypt-election-is-mousa-mostafa-mousa-a-puppet-of-sisi.
ICC (2011). *ICC*, https://www.icc-cpi.int/resource-library/documents/rs-eng.pdf.
IDF (16 April 2016). *Twitter*, https://twitter.com/IDF/status/724889560627421188?lang=en.
IHS Markit (2020). *IHS Markit Egypt PMI*. Cairo: IHS Markit Egypt PMI.
IMF (11 November 2016). *IMF*, https://www.imf.org/en/News/Articles/2016/11/11/PR16501-Egypt-Executive-Board-Approves-12-billion-Extended-Arrangement.
Ismail, A. (3 March 2019). *Reuters*, https://www.reuters.com/article/us-egypt-politics/egyptian-military-court-upholds-jail-sentence-of-former-anti-graft-chief-lawyer-idUSKCN1QK0EC.
Ismail, N. I. (9 August 2022). *Bloomberg*, https://www.bloomberg.com/news/articles/2022-08-09/only-way-is-down-for-egyptian-currency-and-question-is-how-much.
Ismail, N. I. (16 August 2022). *Bloomberg*, https://www.bloomberg.com/news/articles/2022-08-16/currency-drama-in-egypt-has-investors-clamoring-for-devaluation.
Ismail, N. I. (28 August 2022). *Bloomberg*, https://www.bloomberg.com/news/articles/2022-08-28/default-jitters-stalk-egypt-sending-traders-on-a-wild-ride.
Ismail, S. (2006). *Political Life in Cairo's New Quarters*. Minneapolis: University of Minnesota Press.
Ismail, S. (2012). 'The Egyptian Revolution against the Police'. *Social Research* 79, no. 2 (Summer): 435–62.
Jabra, M. (2014). 'Why Did the Egyptian Muslim Brotherhood Year-Long Rule Fall?' *Zeitschrift für Politik* 61, no. 1: 61–80.
Jeannerod, B. (28 January 2019). *HRW*, https://www.hrw.org/news/2019/01/28/how-french-weapons-enable-egypts-abuses.

Journal of Commerce (16 September 2014). *Journal of Commerce*, https://www.joc.com/: https://www.joc.com/maritime-news/international-freight-shipping/egypt-announces-sell-out-suez-canal-certificates_20140916.html.

Kahzan, I. (12 March 2021). *Anadolu Aency*, https://www.aa.com.tr/ar/%D8%A7%D9%84%D8%AF%D9%88%D9%84-%D8%A7%D9%84%D8%B9%D8%B1%D8%A8%D9%8A%D8%A9/%D9%85%D8%B5%D8%B1%D8%AD%D9%83%D9%85-%D9%86%D9%87%D8%A7%D8%A6%D9%8A-%D9%8A%D8%AF%D8%B1%D8%AC-%D8%A3%D8%A8%D9%88-%D8%AA%D8%B1%D9%8A%D9%83%D8%A9-%D8%B9%D9%84%.

Kamal, A. (18 April 2017). *Shorouk News*, https://www.shorouknews.com/news/view.aspx?cdate=18042017&id=184f4753-dd48-4921-bd81-8c11304a9b5f.

Kamel, K. (27 May 2020). *El Youm7*, https://www.youm7.com/story/2020/5/27/%D9%85%D9%88%D9%82%D8%B9-%D8%AA%D8%B1%D9%83%D9%8A%D8%A7-%D8%A7%D9%84%D8%A2%D9%86-%D9%8A%D9%83%D8%B4%D9%81-%D9%85%D8%AE%D8%B7%D8%B7-%D8%A7%D8%B3%D8%AA%D8%AE%D8%A8%D8%A7%D8%B1%D8%A7%D8%AA-%D8%A3%D8%B1%D8%AF%D9%88%D8%BA%.

Kandil, H. (2014). *Inside the Brotherhood*. London: Wiley.

Kandil, H. (2014). *Soldiers, Spies, and Statesmen: Egypt's Road to Revolt*. London: Verso.

Kandil, H. (2015). *Inside the Brotherhood*. Cambridge: Polity.

Karam, M. (24 July 2014). *France 24*, https://www.france24.com/ar/20130724-%D9%85%D8%B5%D8%B1-%D8%A7%D9%84%D8%B3%D9%8A%D8%B3%D9%8A-%D8%AF%D8%B9%D9%88%D8%A9-%D8%A7%D9%84%D8%B4%D8%B9%D8%A8-%D8%AA%D8%B8%D8%A7%D9%87%D8%B1-%D8%AA%D9%81%D9%88%D9%8A%D8%B6-%D9%85%D9%88%D8%A7%D8%AC%D9%87%D8%A9-%D8%A7%.

Kassab, B. (8 May 2022). *Mada Masr*, https://mada32.appspot.com/www.madamasr.com/ar/2022/05/08/news/u/%D8%A7%D9%84%D9%85%D9%88%D8%A7%D8%B2%D9%86%D8%A9-%D8%A7%D9%84%D8%AC%D8%AF%D9%8A%D8%AF%D8%A9-%D8%A7%D9%84%D8%AF%D9%8A%D9%88%D9%86-%D8%AA%D8%A8%D8%AA%D9%84%D8%B9-%D8%A3%D9%83%D8%AB%D8%B1-%D9%8.

Kassab, B. (17 August 2022). *Mada Masr*, https://www.madamasr.com/en/2022/08/17/news/u/residents-clash-with-security-forces-planning-further-expropriations-on-nile-island-of-warraq/.

Khalifa, A. (September 2014). *TIMEP*, https://timep.org/commentary/analysis/maspero-massacre-revisited/.

Khalil, M. (21 January 2018). *Al Araby*, https://www.alaraby.co.uk/%D9%85%D8%B5%D8%B1-%D8%AD%D8%B1%D9%85-%D9%85%D8%B7%D8%A7%D8%B1-%D8%A7%D9%84%D8%B9%D8%B1%D9%8A%D8%B4-%D9%8A%D9%87%D8%AF%D8%AF-%D8%A8%D9%82%D8%B6%D9%85-%D9%86%D8%B5%D9%81-

%D9%85%D8%B3%D8%A7%D8%AD%D8%A9-%D8%A7%D9%84%D9%85%D8%AF%D9%8.
Kingsley, P. (28 October 2014). *Guardian*, https://www.theguardian.com/world/2014/oct/28/egypt-civilian-infrastructure-army-jurisdiction-miltary-court.
Kingesly, P. and Abdo, M. (30 January 2015). *Guardian*, https://www.theguardian.com/world/2015/jan/29/egypt-army-police-sinai-el-arish-sheikh-zuwayed-rafah.
Kirkpatrick, D. (2019). *Into The Hands of Soldiers*. London: Penguin Books.
Knecht, E. (8 February 2017). Reuters, https://www.reuters.com/article/egypt-china-construction-idUSL5N1FT5IY.
Kuimova, A. (2020). *Understanding Egyptian Military Expenditure*. Stockholm: SIPRI.
Laessing, U., Arnold, T. and Barbuscia, D. (27 July 2020). *Reuters*, https://www.reuters.com/article/us-egypt-investment-analysis-idUSKCN24S0KU.
Lasheen, S. (23 March 2017). *Ahram*, https://gate.ahram.org.eg/News/1426594.aspx.
Lewis, A. and Abdellah, M. (13 May 2019). *Reuters*, https://www.reuters.com/article/us-egypt-new-capital/egypts-new-desert-capital-faces-delays-as-it-battles-for-funds-idUSKCN1SJ10I.
Lewis, A. and Saafan, F. (29 July 2022). *Reuters*, https://www.reuters.com/world/middle-east/detentions-loom-over-egypts-political-dialogue-2022-07-29/.
Loveluck, L. (28 June 2014). *Guardian*, https://www.theguardian.com/world/2014/jun/28/egypt-military-aids-cure-device-backtrack.
Mada Masr (4 April 2015). *Mada Masr*, https://www.madamasr.com/en/2015/04/04/news/u/hrw-urges-egypt-to-halt-executions-of-arab-sharkas-cell-defendants/.
Mada Masr (17 May 2015). *Mada Masr*, https://www.madamasr.com/en/2015/05/17/news/u/6-convicted-in-arab-sharkas-case-hanged-to-death-despite-suspicions-of-flawed-trial/.
Mada Masr (30 May 2015). *Mada Masr*, https://www.madamasr.com/en/2015/05/30/news/u/hunger-striking-prisoner-mohamed-soltan-gives-up-egyptian-citizenship-and-is-deported-to-us/.
Mada Masr (14 May 2017). *Mada Masr*, https://www.madamasr.com/en/2017/05/14/news/u/state-council-disregards-controversial-chief-judicial-appointments-law/.
Mada Masr (16 July 2017). *Mada Masr*, https://www.madamasr.com/ar/2017/07/16/feature/%D8%B3%D9%8A%D8%A7%D8%B3%D8%A9/%D8%A8%D8%A7%D9%84%D8%B5%D9%88%D8%B1-%D9%88%D8%A7%D9%84%D9%81%D9%8A%D8%AF%D9%8A%D9%88-%D8%A7%D8%B4%D8%AA%D8%A8%D8%A7%D9%83%D8%A7%D8%AA-%D8%A8%D9%8A%D9%86-%D8%A3%D9%87%D8%A7%D9%8.

Mada Masr (3 July 2018). *Mada Masr*, https://www.madamasr.com/ar/2018/07/03/feature/%D8%B3%D9%8A%D8%A7%D8%B3%D8%A9/%D9%84%D8%B9%D8%B2%D9%84-%D8%A7%D9%84%D9%85%D8%AF%D9%8A%D9%86%D8%A9-%D8%B9%D9%86-%D8%AD%D8%B1%D9%85-%D8%A7%D9%84%D9%85%D8%B7%D8%A7%D8%B1-%D8%A8%D8%AF%D8%A1-%D8%AA%D9%86%D9%81%D9%.

Mada Masr (8 August 2020). *Mada Masr*, https://www.madamasr.com/ar/2020/08/08/feature/%D8%B3%D9%8A%D8%A7%D8%B3%D8%A9/%D8%AA%D8%AF%D9%88%D9%8A%D8%B1-%D8%A7%D9%84%D9%82%D8%B5%D8%A7%D8%B5-%D9%81%D9%8A-%D9%82%D8%B6%D9%8A%D8%A9-%D8%AC%D8%AF%D9%8A%D8%AF%D8%A9-%D8%A7%D9%84%D9%8A%D9%88%D9%85-%D8%B5%D9.

Mada Masr (17 April 2022). *Mada Masr*, https://mada32.appspot.com/www.madamasr.com/ar/2022/04/17/news/u/%D8%A7%D9%84%D8%A3%D8%B7%D8%A8%D8%A7%D8%A1-%D8%A7%D8%B3%D8%AA%D9%82%D8%A7%D9%84%D8%A9-11-%D8%A3%D9%84%D9%81%D9%8B%D8%A7-%D9%88536-%D8%B7%D8%A8%D9%8A%D8%A8%D9%8B%D8%A7-%D8%A8%D8%A7%D9%84/.

Mada Masr (28 August 2022). *Mada Masr*, https://www.facebook.com/mada.masr/photos/a.564476860276121/5693906397333116/.

Mada Masr (27 October 2022). *Mada Masr*, https://mada33.appspot.com/www.madamasr.com/ar/2022/10/27/news/u/%D8%AA%D9%85%D8%AE%D8%B6%D8%AA-%D8%A7%D9%84%D9%85%D9%81%D8%A7%D9%88%D8%B6%D8%A7%D8%AA-%D9%81%D8%A3%D9%86%D8%AC%D8%A8%D8%AA-%D9%82%D8%B1%D8%B6%D9%8B%D8%A7-%D9%84%D9%83%D9%86-%D9%87%D9%84-%D9%.

Magdi, A. (2021). *'Security Forces Dealt with Them': Suspicious Killings and Extrajudicial Executions by Egyptian Security Forces*. New York: Human Rights Watch.

Magdy, M. (1 August 2017). *Al-Monitor*, https://www.al-monitor.com/originals/2017/08/egypt-appointment-heads-judicial-bodies-challenges-law-court.html.

Magdy, M. (16 December 2018). *Bloomberg*, https://www.bloomberg.com/news/articles/2018-12-16/china-s-20-billion-new-egypt-capital-project-talks-fall-through

Magdy, M. (21 March 2022). *Bloomberg*, https://www.bloomberg.com/news/articles/2022-03-21/abu-dhabi-said-to-deepen-egypt-ties-with-deals-worth-2-billion.

Magdy, M. (23 March 2022). *Bloomberg*, https://www.bloomberg.com/news/articles/2022-03-23/giant-uae-egypt-deal-said-to-include-stakes-in-fertilizer-firms.

Magdy, M. (19 May 2022). *Bloomberg*, https://www.bloomberg.com/news/articles/2022-05-19/egypt-hikes-rates-again-to-tackle-inflation-restore-bond-allure#xj4y7vzkg.

Magdy, M. (7 July 2022). *Bloomberg*, https://www.bloomberg.com/news/articles/2022-07-07/egypt-net-foreign-reserves-slump-again-as-war-weighs-on-finances.

Magdy, M. (27 October 2022). *Bloomberg*, https://www.bloomberg.com/news/articles/2022-10-30/egypt-s-pound-hits-another-grim-milestone-in-move-to-flexibility.

Magdy, M. and El-Tablawy, T. (18 March 2022). *Bloomberg*, https://www.bloombergquint.com/business/egypt-sticks-with-world-s-highest-real-interest-rate#:~:text=other%20emerging%20markets.-,(Bloomberg)%20%2D%2D%20Egypt%20kept%20monetary%20easing%20on%20pause%20for%20a,the%20lending%20rate%20at%209.25%25.

Magdy, M. and Wahba, A. L. (22 August 2022). *Bloomberg*, imf-financing-for-troubled-economy.

Maged, M. (23 December 2019). *Egypt Independent*, https://egyptindependent.com/former-general-of-egyptian-armed-forces-sami-anan-free-after-two-year-imprisonment/.

Mamdouh, R. (30 April 2022). *Mada Masr*, https://www.madamasr.com/ar/2022/04/30/news/u/%D8%A3%D8%A8%D9%88%D8%B9%D9%8A%D8%B7%D8%A9-%D9%86%D8%AA%D9%84%D9%82%D9%89-%D9%85%D8%B7%D8%A7%D9%84%D8%A8-%D8%A7%D9%84%D8%B9%D9%81%D9%88-%D8%B9%D9%86-%D8%A7%D9%84%D9%85%D8%AD%D8%A8%D9%88%D8%B3%D9%8A/.

Mamdouh, R. (17 July 2022). *Mada Masr*, https://www.madamasr.com/ar/2022/07/17/news/u/%D8%A7%D8%B3%D8%AA%D9%82%D8%A7%D9%84%D8%A9-%D8%A7%D9%84%D8%B7%D9%86%D8%B7%D8%A7%D9%88%D9%8A-%D9%85%D9%86-%D8%B1%D8%A6%D8%A7%D8%B3%D8%A9-%D8%A7%D9%84%D9%83%D8%B1%D8%A7%D9%85%D8%A9-%D9%88/.

Mamdouh, R. (19 July 2022). *Mada Masr*, https://mada32.appspot.com/www.madamasr.com/ar/2022/07/19/feature/%D8%B3%D9%8A%D8%A7%D8%B3%D8%A9/%D8%B9%D8%B3%D9%83%D8%B1%D8%A9-%D8%A7%D9%84%D8%AF%D8%B3%D8%AA%D9%88%D8%B1%D9%8A%D8%A9-%D9%85%D8%A7-%D9%88%D8%B1%D8%A7%D8%A1-%D8%AA%D8%B9%D9%8A%D9%8A%D9%86-%D8.

Mamdouh, R. (17 August 2022). *Mada Masr*, https://www.madamasr.com/ar/2022/08/17/news/u/%d8%a5%d8%ae%d9%84%d8%a7%d8%a1-%d8%b3%d8%a8%d9%8a%d9%84-25-%d9%85%d9%86-%d8%a7%d9%84%d9%85%d8%ad%d8%a8%d9%88%d8%b3%d9%8a%d9%86-%d8%a7%d9%84%d8%b3%d9%8a%d8%a7%d8%b3%d9%8a%d9%8a%d9%86-%d9%88%d8%a3/.

Mamdouh, R. and Kassab, B. (4 June 2022). *Mada Masr*, https://www.madamasr.com/ar/2022/06/04/news/u/%D8%AD%D8%B5%D9%8A%D9%84%D8%A9-%D8%A7%D9%84%D8%B9%D9%81%D9%88-%D8%A7%D9%84%D8%B1%D8%A6%D8%A7%D8%B3%D9%8A-

%D8%A5%D8%AE%D9%84%D8%A7%D8%A1-%D8%B3%D8%A8%D9%8A%D9%84-59-%D9%86%D8%A7%D8%B4/.

Mamdouh, R. and Salim, A. (27 June 2022). *Mada Masr*, https://www.madamasr.com/ar/2022/06/27/feature/%D8%B3%D9%8A%D8%A7%D8%B3%D8%A9/%D8%A7%D9%84%D8%AD%D9%88%D8%A7%D8%B1-%D8%A7%D9%84%D9%88%D8%B7%D9%86%D9%8A-%D9%88%EF%BB%BB%D8%AF%D8%A9-%D9%85%D8%AA%D8%B9%D8%B3%D8%B1%D8%A9-%D9%88%D9%85%D8%B3%D8%AA%D9%82%D8%A8%D.

Mandour, M. (14 February 2019). *Sada Journal*, https://carnegieendowment.org/sada/78363.

Manshurat (1958). *Manshurat*, https://manshurat.org/node/63711.

Manshurat (2006). *Manshurat*, https://manshurat.org/node/14577.

Manshurat (2007). *Manshurat*, https://manshurat.org/node/14474.

Manshurat (2013). *Manshurat*, https://manshurat.org/node/6547.

Manshurat (17 February 2015). *Manshurat*, https://manshurat.org/node/6579.

Manshurat (24 May 2017). *Manshurat*, https://manshurat.org/node/24867.

Manshurat (2018). *Manshurat*, https://manshurat.org/node/28325.

Manshurat (14 August 2018). *Manshurat*, https://manshurat.org/node/31487.

Manshurat (27 August 2018). *Manshurat*, https://manshurat.org/node/31481.

Manshurat (2019). *Manshurat*, https://manshurat.org/node/14675.

Manshurat (23 April 2019). *Manshurat*, https://manshurat.org/node/14675.

Manshurat (19 August 2019). *Manshurat*, https://manshurat.org/node/61248.

Manshurat (27 December 2020). *Manshurat*, https://manshurat.org/node/70006.

Manshurat (2021). *Manshurat*, https://manshurat.org/node/14679.

Mansi, M. (16 June 2017). *Veto Gate*, https://www.vetogate.com/2754168.

Mao, F. (1 August 2022). *BBC*, https://www.bbc.com/news/world-asia-62373975.

Maslin, J. (25 April 2016). *Time*, https://time.com/4306843/egypt-protests-cairo-red-sea/.

Maspero (29 September 2016). *Maspero*, https://www.maspero.eg/wps/portal/home/egynews/news/egypt/details/_7/1c3006d0-97c9-4bff-b0b1-9e0495d7e728/.

Michaelson, R. and Tondo, L. (10 December 2020). *Guardian*, https://www.theguardian.com/world/2020/dec/10/italy-charges-four-egyptians-over-of-giulio-regeni.

Middle East Eye (16 January 2016). *Middle East Eye*, https://www.middleeasteye.net/news/egyptian-parliament-approves-dozens-laws-first-voting-session.

Middle East Eye (26 February 2016). *Middle East Eye*, https://www.middleeasteye.net/news/eu-states-approved-spy-equipment-sales-egypt.

Middle East Eye (9 May 2019). *Middle East Eye*, https://www.middleeasteye.net/news/egypt-thought-murdered-italian-student-was-british-spy-says-report.

Middle East Eye (25 September 2019). *Middle East Eye*, https://www.middleeasteye.net/news/egypt-arrests-prominent-political-scientists-critical-sisi.

Middle East Monitor (31 December 2018). *Middle East Monitor*, https://www.middleeastmonitor.com/20181231-egypt-photos-point-to-extrajudicial-killings-following-giza-attack/.

Middle East Monitor (21 April 2020). *Middle East Monitor*, https://www.middleeastmonitor.com/20200421-egypt-sends-medical-supplies-to-us-in-support-of-trump/.

Middle East Monitor (10 June 2020). *Middle East Monitor*, https://www.middleeastmonitor.com/20200610-egypt-raises-electricity-prices-by-19/.

Middle East Monitor (10 September 2020). *Middle East Monitor*, https://www.middleeastmonitor.com/20200910-egypt-tripled-arms-imports-from-italy-in-2019/.

Middle East Monitor (4 February 2022). *Middle East Monitor*, https://www.middleeastmonitor.com/20220204-egyptian-dies-of-medical-negligence-in-detention/.

Middle East Monitor (5 August 2022). *Middle East Monitor*, https://www.middleeastmonitor.com/20210805-egypt-ex-presidential-candidate-aboul-fotouh-faces-5-terrorism-charges/.

Mikhail, G. (15 July 2016). *Al-Monitor*, https://www.al-monitor.com/originals/2016/07/egypt-sinai-tribes-leader-sisi-development-plan-terrorism.html.

Ministry of Housing, Utilities and Urban Communities (22 November 2017). http://www.mhuc.gov.eg/: http://www.mhuc.gov.eg/Media/NewsDetails/4243.

Mitchell, T. (1991). *Colonising Egypt*. Berkeley: University of California Press.

Mitchell, T. (2002). 'Rule of Experts'. In T. Mitchell, *Rule of Experts*, p. 246. Berkeley: University of California Press.

Mohamed, F. (21 May 2020). *Al Masry Al Youm*, https://www.almasryalyoum.com/news/details/1979898.

Mohammad, Y. (9 February 2022). *Arab News*, https://www.arabnews.com/node/2021336/middle-east.

Moore, B. (1966). *Social Origins of Dictatorship and Democracy: Lord and Peasant in the Making*. Boston: Beacon Press.

Mounir, H. (12 April 2022). *Daily News*, https://dailynewsegypt.com/2022/04/12/adq-acquires-stake-in-cib-with-a-value-of-911-457m/#:~:text=ADQ%20Holding%20%E2%80%94%20one%20of%20Abu,EGX)%20for%20EGP%2028.5bn.

Mourad, M. and Hamdy, N. (14 June 2017). *Reuters*, https://www.reuters.com/article/us-egypt-saudi-islands-idUSKBN1951G4.

Mumbere, D. (29 January 2018). *Africa News*, https://www.africanews.com/2018/01/29/sisi-gets-last-minute-challenger-in-egypt-s-presidential-election/.

Nadine, A. (17 August 2020). *Reuters*, https://www.reuters.com/article/egypt-commodities-bread-idAFL8N2FJ50N.
Napoleon, M. (7 May 2020). *Shorouk News*, https://www.shorouknews.com/news/view.aspx?cdate=07052020&id=3a678bd2-3e0b-4d58-993a-b243148c6894.
Nassar, M. (28 January 2020). *Masrawy*, https://www.masrawy.com/news/news_egypt/details/2020/1/28/1713739/%D9%83%D9%8A%D9%81-%D8%AA%D8%AD%D8%AF%D8%AB-%D8%A7%D9%84%D8%B3%D9%8A%D8%B3%D9%8A-%D8%B9%D9%86-%D8%AA%D8%B7%D9%88%D9%8A%D8%B1-%D8%A7%D9%84%D8%AE%D8%B7%D8%A7%D8%A8-%D8%A7%D9%84%D8%AF%D9%8A%D9.
Nasser, G. (1955). 'The Egyptian Revolution'. *Foreign Affairs* 33, no. 2 (January): 199–211.
Nawafez (2 August 2021). *Nawafez*, https://nwafez.com/%D8%A7%D9%84%D8%AF%D8%A7%D8%AE%D9%84%D9%8A%D8%A9-%D8%AA%D8%BA%D9%8A%D9%8A%D8%B1-%D8%A7%D8%B3%D9%85-%D9%82%D8%B7%D8%A7%D8%B9-%D8%A7%D9%84%D8%B3%D8%AC%D9%88%D9%86-%D9%81%D9%8A-%D8%A7%D9%84/.
Nawafez (25 April 2022). *Nawafez*, https://nwafez.com/%D8%A7%D9%84%D8%B3%D9%8A%D8%B3%D9%8A-%D9%8A%D9%85%D9%86%D8%AD-%D8%A7%D9%84%D8%AC%D9%8A%D8%B4-%D9%88%D8%A7%D9%84%D9%85%D8%AE%D8%A7%D8%A8%D8%B1%D8%A7%D8%AA-%D8%B1%D9%88%D8%A7%D8%AA%D8%A8-%D8%A5%D8%B6/.
New Arab (15 September 2017). *New Arab*, https://english.alaraby.co.uk/english/news/2017/9/15/pro-sisi-egyptian-security-firm-buys-private-tv-network.
New Arab (9 April 2019). *New Arab*, https://english.alaraby.co.uk/english/news/2019/4/9/egypt-borrows-22-billion-in-just-two-years.
New Arab (9 February 2022). *New Arab*, https://www.alaraby.co.uk/society/%D8%A7%D9%84%D9%86%D9%8A%D8%A7%D8%A8%D8%A9-%D8%A7%D9%84%D9%85%D8%B5%D8%B1%D9%8A%D8%A9-%D8%AA%D9%82%D8%B1%D8%B1-%D8%AD%D8%A8%D8%B3-%D8%A7%D9%84%D9%86%D8%A7%D8%B4%D8%B7-%D9%87%D9%8A%D8%AB%D9%85-%D8%A7%D9%84%D8%A8%D9%86%D8%A.
New Humanitarian (10 December 2013). *New Humanitarian*, https://www.thenewhumanitarian.org/report/99299/civilians-caught-egypt%E2%80%99s-counter-terrorism-operations.
NHRC (March 2014). *NHRC*, https://manshurat.org/node/13664.
OECD (2020). *Revenue Statistics in Africa 2020 – Egypt*. Paris: OECD.
OHCR (8 November 2019). *OHCR*, https://www.ohchr.org/en/press-releases/2019/11/egypt-un-experts-denounce-morsi-brutal-prison-conditions-warn-thousands.
OHCR (19 June 2020). *OHCR*, https://spcommreports.ohchr.org/TMResultsBase/DownLoadPublicCommunicationFile?gId=25337.
OMCT (21 November 2021). *OMCT*, https://www.omct.org/en/resources/

urgent-interventions/egypt-mohamed-el-baqer-and-alaa-abdel-fattahs-detention-is-ongoing.

Open Observatory of Network Interference, Association for Freedom of Thought and Expression (2018). *The State of Internet Censorship in Egypt*. Open Observatory of Network Interference.

Orwell, G. (1949). *1984*. London: Penguin.

Pietromarchi, V. (17 June 2020). *Al Jazzera*, https://www.aljazeera.com/news/2020/6/17/pressure-on-italy-to-scrap-planned-arms-deal-with-egypt.

Piketty, T. (2020). *Capital and Ideology*. Cambridge, MA: Harvard University Press.

Podcast 11 (18 March 2021). *YouTube*, https://www.youtube.com/watch?v=XMqnYF_Buh4.

Podcast 11 (15 April 2021). *YouTube*, https://www.youtube.com/watch?v=HUQD6AKDj94.

Radwan, A. (28 August 2022). *Al Borsa News*, https://alborsaanews.com/2022/08/29/1571462?fbclid=IwAR25vCSDIzj6bqpJM-x3AT8m5koWPBAyJuWFmeRpE06jDIP_1GQZAgG6KJI.

Refeat, T. (22 April 2020). *Sada El Balad*, https://see.news/egyptian-parliament-approves-new-income-tax-law/#:~:text=Individuals%20with%20income%20up%20to,distortions%20in%20the%20progressive%20tax.

Reporters without borders (25 January 2019). *Reporters without borders*, https://rsf.org/en/news/sisification-media-hostile-takeover.

Reporters without borders (22 January 2020). *Reporters without borders*, https://egypt.mom-rsf.org/en/owners/companies/detail/company/company/show/egyptian-media-group/.

Retuers (23 November 2012). *Retuers*, https://www.reuters.com/article/oegtp-egy-wrapup-as7-idARACAE8AM0B420121123.

Reuters (15 August 2013). *Reuters*, https://www.reuters.com/article/us-egypt-protests-elbaradei-idUSBRE97D1AZ20130814.

Reuters (1 March 2015). *Reuters*, https://www.reuters.com/article/us-egypt-france-loan-idUSKBN0LW0ZN20150228.

Reuters (15 March 2015). *Reuters*, https://www.reuters.com/article/us-egypt-economy-investment-sisi-idUSKBN0MB0KO20150315.

Reuters (24 December 2016). *Reuters*, https://www.reuters.com/article/us-egypt-economy-military/egypts-sisi-says-military-accounts-for-1-5-2-percent-of-economy-idUSKBN14D087.

Reuters (16 May 2018). *Reuters*, https://www.reuters.com/investigates/special-report/egypt-economy-military/.

Reuters (28 June 2018). *Reuters*, https://www.reuters.com/article/us-egypt-italy-regeni/egyptian-italian-investigators-say-gaps-found-in-regeni-case-footage-idUSKBN1JO0WS.

Reuters (16 July 2018), *Reuters*, https://www.reuters.com/article/egypt-military-politics-idARAKBN1K61ML.

Reuters (April 2019). *Reuters*, https://graphics.reuters.com/EGYPT-KILLINGS/010091CH1XK/.

Reuters (5 April 2019). *Reuters*, https://www.reuters.com/article/us-egypt-killings-specialreport/special-report-egypt-kills-hundreds-of-suspected-militants-in-disputed-gun-battles-idUSKCN1RH10E.

Reuters (3 December 2019). *Reuters*, https://www.reuters.com/article/us-egypt-economy-pmi-idUSKBN1Y70F2.

Reuters (28 May 2020). *Reuters*, https://www.reuters.com/article/uk-health-coronavirus-egypt-medics/some-medics-say-they-are-muzzled-in-egypts-coronavirus-response-idUKKBN234115?edition-redirect=uk.

Reuters (6 August 2020). *Reuters*, https://www.reuters.com/article/egypt-economy-suezcanal/egypts-suez-canal-revenues-up-47-in-last-5-years-chairman-idUSL8N2F84GW.

Reuters (28 September 2020). *Reuters*, https://www.reuters.com/article/egypt-arrest-aa3-idARAKBN26J2UO.

Reuters (14 December 2020). *Reuters*, https://www.reuters.com/article/egypt-election-int-idUSKBN28O2T0.

Reuters (9 August 2021). *Reuters*, https://www.reuters.com/world/middle-east/russian-flights-return-egypts-resorts-six-years-after-crash-2021-08-09/.

Reuters (5 April 2022). *Reuters*, https://www.reuters.com/business/global-bond-sales-cross-10-trillion-2022-sp-2022-04-05/.

Reuters (4 May 2022). *Reuters*, https://graphics.reuters.com/world-coronavirus-tracker-and-maps/countries-and-territories/egypt/.

Reuters (19 May 2022). *Reuters*, https://www.reuters.com/business/egypts-central-bank-raises-key-interest-rates-by-200-basis-points-2022-05-19/.

Reuters (26 October 2022). *Reuters*, https://www.reuters.com/world/middle-east/egypts-president-sisi-ends-state-emergency-first-time-years-2021-10-25/.

Richards, A. and Waterbury, J. (2008). *A Political Economy of the Middle East*. Boulder, CO: Westview Press.

Roddy, J. (7 September 2016). *TIMEP*, https://timep.org/commentary/nothing-new-under-the-sun-egypts-church-construction-law/.

Roqaya, K. (26 January 2020). *mfyoum*, https://mfyoum.com/2020/01/26/%D9%86%D9%82%D8%B5-%D8%A3%D9%8E%D8%B3%D8%B1%D9%91%D8%A9-%D8%A7%D9%84%D8%B9%D9%86%D8%A7%D9%8A%D8%A9-%D8%A7%D9%84%D9%85%D8%B1%D9%83%D8%B2%D8%A9/.

RT (6 November 2018). *RT*, https://arabic.rt.com/middle_east/980605-%D8%A7%D9%84%D8%B3%D9%8A%D8%B3%D9%8A-%D9%8A%D8%AD%D8%B0%D8%B1-%D9%85%D9%86-%D8%A7%D9%84%D8%A7%D9%86%D8%AA%D8%AD%D8%A7%D8%B1-%D8%A7%D9%84%D9%82%D9%88%D9%85%D9%8A-%D9%84%D9%82%D8%AF-%D9%81%D8%AA%D8%AD%D9%86%D8%A7-%D8.

RT (7 August 2019). *RT*, https://arabic.rt.com/middle_east/1037153-%D8%A7%D9%84%D8%B3%D9%8A%D8%B3%D9%8A-%D8%A7%D9%84%D9%85%D8%B4%D8%B1%D9%88%D8%B9%D8%A7%D8%AA-%D9%87%D9%8A-%D8%A7%D9%84%D8%A3%D9%85%D9%84-

%D8%A7%D9%84%D8%B0%D9%8A-%D9%8A%D8%AD%D8%A7%D9%88%D9%84-%D8%A3%D9%87%D9%84-%D.
RT (31 December 2020). *RT*, https://arabic.rt.com/middle_east/1188429-%D8%B1%D9%88%D9%85%D8%A7-%D8%AA%D8%B5%D8%B1%D9%8A%D8%AD-%D8%A7%D9%84%D9%85%D8%AF%D8%B9%D9%8A-%D8%A7%D9%84%D8%B9%D8%A7%D9%85-%D8%A7%D9%84%D9%85%D8%B5%D8%B1%D9%8A-%D8%A8%D8%B4%D8%A3%D9%86-%D9%82%D8%B6%D9%8A%D8%A9-%D.
RT (11 August 2021). *RT*, https://arabic.rt.com/middle_east/1261183-%D8%A7%D9%84%D8%B3%D9%8A%D8%B3%D9%8A-%D9%8A%D8%B5%D8%AF%D8%B1-%D9%82%D8%B1%D8%A7%D8%B1%D8%A7-%D9%84%D8%A3%D9%88%D9%84-%D9%85%D8%B1%D8%A9-%D8%A8%D8%B4%D8%A3%D9%86-%D8%AF%D8%A7%D8%B1-%D8%A7%D9%84%D8%A5%D9%81%D8%AA%D.
RT (12 November 2021). *RT*, https://arabic.rt.com/middle_east/1293331-%D9%85%D8%B5%D8%B1-%D8%AA%D9%81%D8%A7%D8%B5%D9%8A%D9%84-%D8%AA%D8%B9%D8%AF%D9%8A%D9%84-%D9%82%D8%A7%D9%86%D9%88%D9%86-%D9%85%D9%83%D8%A7%D9%81%D8%AD%D8%A9-%D8%A7%D9%84%D8%A5%D8%B1%D9%87%D8%A7%D8%A8/.
Sabry, A. (18 May 2022). *Al Araby*, https://www.alaraby.co.uk/economy/%D9%85%D8%B5%D8%B1-%D8%AA%D8%A8%D9%8A%D8%B9-%D8%A3%D8%B5%D9%88%D9%84%D8%A7%D9%8B-%D8%A8%D9%8040-%D9%85%D9%84%D9%8A%D8%A7%D8%B1-%D8%AF%D9%88%D9%84%D8%A7%D8%B1-%D9%84%D8%AA%D8%AE%D9%81%D9%8A%D9%81-%D8%A7%D9%84%D8%A3%D8%B2%D.
Sabry, B. (23 November 2012). *Al-Monitor*, https://www.al-monitor.com/originals/2012/al-monitor/morsi-decree-constitution-power.html.
Sabry, I. (4 July 2022). *El Balad*, https://www.elbalad.news/5346004.
Saeed, R. (6 December 2015). *Youm7*, https://www.youm7.com/story/2015/12/6/%D8%A7%D8%A6%D8%AA%D9%84%D8%A7%D9%81-%D8%AF%D8%B9%D9%85-%D8%A7%D9%84%D8%AF%D9%88%D9%84%D8%A9-%D8%A7%D9%84%D9%85%D8%B5%D8%B1%D9%8A%D8%A9-%D9%8A%D8%AD%D8%AA%D9%81%D9%84-%D8%A8%D9%80-%D8%A7%D9%84%D8%A3%D8%BA%D9%84%D8%A8%.
Sakr, T. (8 February 2017). *Daily News*, https://www.dailynewsegypt.com/2017/02/08/614959/.
Salah, E. (23 August 2022). *Mada Masr*, https://www.madamasr.com/en/2022/08/23/news/u/as-levels-of-emirati-investment-in-egypt-soar-mbz-sisi-discuss-security-concerns-hampering-potential-deals/.
Salah, I. E. (21 August 2022). *Mada Masr*, https://www.madamasr.com/ar/2022/08/21/news/u/%D8%A8%D9%8A%D9%86%D9%87%D8%A7-%D8%A7%D9%84%D9%88%D8%B1%D8%A7%D9%82-%D9%88%D9%85%D8%AF%D9%8A%D9%86%D8%A9-%D9%86%D8%B5%D8%B1-

%D9%82%D9%85%D8%A9-%D8%A7%D9%84%D8%B3%D9%8A%D8%B3%D9%8A-%D9%88/.

Sawan, A. (3 July 2022). *Masr 360*, https://masr.masr360.net/%D8%A3%D8%AE%D8%A8%D8%A7%D8%B1-%D9%85%D8%B5%D8%B1/%D9%85%D8%AD%D8%A7%D9%83%D9%85%D8%AA%D9%87-%D8%A7%D9%84%D8%AB%D8%A7%D9%86%D9%8A%D8%A9-%D8%A7%D9%84%D8%AD%D9%83%D9%85-%D8%B9%D9%84%D9%89-%D8%B3%D9%86%D8%B7%D8%A7%D9%88%D9%8A/.

Sayadi, E. (14 March 2018). *Access Now*, https://www.accessnow.org/egypt-more-than-500-sites-blocked-ahead-of-the-presidential-election/.

Sayigh, Y. (2012). *Above the State: The Officers Republic in Egypt*. Washington, DC: Carnegie Endowment for International Peace.

Sayigh, Y. (2019). *Owners of the Republic: An Anatomy of Egypt's Military Economy*. Beirut: Malcolm H. Kerr Carnegie Middle East Center.

Sayigh, Y. (7 April 2020). *Carnegie Middle East Center*, https://carnegie-mec.org/2020/04/07/will-egypt-s-military-companies-float-pub-81487.

Sayigh, Y. (2022). *Retain, Restructure, or Divest?* Beirut: Carnegie Middle East Center.

Scherer, S. (8 April 2016). *Reuters*, https://www.reuters.com/article/us-egypt-italian-investigation-idUSKCN0X522E.

Scherer, S. (14 August 2017). *Reuters*, https://www.reuters.com/article/us-italy-egypt-regeni-murder-idUSKCN1AU1YL.

Seif El-Din, S. (5 August 2021). *Mada Masr*, https://www.madamasr.com/ar/2021/08/05/news/u/%d8%a7%d9%84%d8%b1%d9%81%d8%b9-%d8%a7%d9%84%d8%ab%d8%a7%d9%86%d9%8a-%d9%84%d8%b3%d8%b9%d8%b1-%d8%a7%d9%84%d8%ae%d8%a8%d8%b2-%d9%81%d9%8a-%d8%b9%d9%87%d8%af-%d8%a7%d9%84%d8%b3%d9%8a%d8%b3%d9%8a/?fbclid=IwAR1uuZ.

Selim, A. K. (17 January 2022). *New Arab*, https://www.alaraby.co.uk/politics/%D8%AC%D9%85%D8%A7%D9%84-%D8%B9%D9%8A%D8%AF-%D8%A7%D9%84%D9%82%D9%85%D8%B9-%D8%B3%D8%A8%D8%A8-%D8%A5%D8%BA%D9%84%D8%A7%D9%82-%D8%A7%D9%84%D8%B4%D8%A8%D9%83%D8%A9-%D8%A7%D9%84%D8%B9%D8%B1%D8%A8%D9%8A%D8%A9-%D9%84%D8%AD%D9.

Shalaby, M. (14 June 2018). *Egytian Streets*, https://egyptianstreets.com/2018/06/14/egypts-new-cabinet-includes-a-historic-number-of-8-female-ministers/.

Shebl, A. (10 January 2014). *Shorouk*, https://www.shorouknews.com//news/view.aspx?cdate=10012014&id=0e939e30-6003-4cfc-8ea1-87ca3ccf8d37.

Shorouk News (24 September 2016). *Shorouk News*, https://www.echoroukonline.com/%D9%85%D8%B5%D8%B1-%D8%AA%D8%AA%D8%B1%D8%A7%D8%AC%D8%B9-%D8%B9%D9%86-%D8%B1%D9%88%D8%A7%D9%8A%D8%AA%D9%87%D8%A7-%D8%A8%D8%B4%D8%A3%D9%86-%D9%85%D9%82%D8%AA%D9%84-%D8%B1%D9%8A%D8%AC%D9%8A%D9%86%D9%8A.

Shousha, A. (12 May 2022). *BBC*, https://www.bbc.com/arabic/business-61430454.

Sis.gov. (3 July 2013). *Sis.gov*, https://www.sis.gov.eg/Story/101256.

Sky News (29 October 2021). *Sky News*, https://www.skynewsarabia.com/varieties/1474521-%D8%A8%D8%A7%D9%94%D8%BA%D9%86%D9%8A%D8%A9-%D9%84%D9%85%D8%AF%D8%AD%D8%AA-%D8%B5%D8%A7%D9%84%D8%AD-%D8%A7%D9%84%D8%A7%D9%95%D8%B9%D9%84%D8%A7%D9%86-%D8%A7%D9%94%D9%83%D8%A8%D8%B1-%D9%88%D8%A7%D9%94%D8%AD%D8%.

Social Justice Platform (20 December 2021). *Social Justice Platform*, https://sjplatform.org/%D8%A7%D9%84%D8%A7%D8%AD%D8%AA%D8%AC%D8%A7%D8%AC%D8%A7%D8%AA-%D8%A7%D9%84%D8%B9%D9%85%D8%A7%D9%84%D9%8A%D8%A9-%D9%88%D8%A7%D9%84%D8%A7%D9%82%D8%AA%D8%B5%D8%A7%D8%AF%D9%8A%D8%A9/.

State, Department of (2015). *Country Reports on Terrorism 2015*. Washington, DC: US Department of State.

State Information Service (8 June 2018). *State Information Service*, https://sis.gov.eg/Story/131853?lang=.

State Information Service (31 August 2020). *State Information Service*, https://www.sis.gov.eg/Story/151870/Sisi-supports-'Eni'-expansion-in-Egypt?lang=en-us.

State Information Service (28 November 2020). *State Information Service*, https://www.sis.gov.eg/Story/153185/Cabinet-State-budget-does-not-finance-new-capital-projects?lang=en-us.

Statista (March 2022). *Statista*, https://www.statista.com/statistics/377982/egypt-budget-balance-in-relation-to-gdp/.

Stein, E. (2015). 'Jihad Discourse in Egypt under Muhammad Mursi'. In E. Kendall and E. Stein, *Twenty-First Century Jihad, Law, Society and Military Action*, pp. 126–40. London: I.B. Tauris.

Swanston, J. (2022). *MENA Economics Update*. London: Capital Economics, https://research.cdn-1.capitaleconomics.com/8c95d2/egypts-public-finances-back-under-the-spotlight.pdf?utm_source=Sailthru&utm_medium=email&utm_campaign=Middle%20East%20Economics%20Update%20230222&utm_term=ce_updates.

Tabikha, K. (16 August 2022). *The National*, https://www.thenationalnews.com/mena/2022/08/16/nile-island-residents-protest-against-their-eviction/.

Tantawi, M. A. (15 March 2015). *Al Youm7*, https://www.youm7.com/story/2015/3/19/%D8%A7%D9%84%D9%82%D9%88%D8%A7%D8%AA-%D8%A7%D9%84%D9%85%D8%B3%D9%84%D8%AD%D8%A9-%D8%AA%D8%B3%D8%A7%D8%A8%D9%82-%D8%A7%D9%84%D8%B2%D9%85%D9%86-%D9%84%D8%A5%D9%86%D9%87%D8%A7%D8%A1-%D9%85%D8%B4%D8%B1%D9%88%D8%B9-%D9%82%.

Tarek, M. (16 September 2020). *Mada Masr*, https://www.madamasr.com/en/2020/09/16/feature/politics/egypts-battle-over-buildings-the-government-takes-on-informal-housing/.

Tarek, M. (7 March 2021). *Mada Masr*, https://www.madamasr.com/ar/2021/03/07/feature/%d8%b3%d9%8a%d8%a7%d8%b3%d8%a9/%d9%81%d8%a7%d8%b1%d8%b3-%d8%aa%d9%84-%d8%a7%d9%84%d8%b9%d9%82%d8%a7%d8%b1%d8%a8/.

TIMEP (2016). *Egypt Security Watch Quarterly Report April-June 2016*. Cairo: TIMEP.

TIMEP (January 2016). *TIMEP*, https://timep.org/parliamentary-elections-monitor/election-summary/.

TIMEP (16 January 2016). *TIMEP*, https://timep.org/parliamentary-elections-monitor/nations-future-party-hizb-mostaqbal-watan/.

TIMEP (7 December 2017). *TIMEP*, https://timep.org/esw/attack-at-rawda-mosque/.

TIMEP (11 September 2018). *TIMEP*, https://timep.org/reports-briefings/timep-brief-protest-law/.

Tolba, A. and Davison, J. (2 April 2018). *Reuters*, https://www.reuters.com/article/us-egypt-election-result-idUSKCN1H916A

Trading Economics (15 January 2020). *Trading Economics*, https://tradingeconomics.com/egypt/gdp.

Transparency Center for Archiving Data Management and Research (2022). *Arrest and Detention on Political Background Report*. Cairo: Transparency Center for Archiving Data Management and Research.

Veto Gate (4 February 2016). *Veto Gate*, https://www.vetogate.com/2030840.

VOA news (5 January 2019). *VOA news*, https://www.voanews.com/a/egypt-tries-to-block-60-minutes-el-sisi-interview/4729990.html.

Wahba, A. L. and Magdy, M. (1 August 2022). *Bloomberg*, https://www.bloomberg.com/news/articles/2022-08-01/goldman-s-15-billion-view-of-egypt-imf-needs-too-high-for-maait.

Walsh, D. (20 August 2017). *New York Times*, https://www.nytimes.com/2017/08/15/magazine/giulio-regeni-italian-graduate-student-tortured-murdered-egypt.html.

We Record (October 2021). *We Record*, http://werecord.org/wp-content/uploads/2021/10/%D8%A7%D9%84%D9%92%D9%85%D9%8E%D9%86%D9%81%D9%8E%D9%89.pdf.

Werr, P. and Awadalla, N. (21 March 2022). *Reuters*, https://www.reuters.com/world/africa/egyptian-pound-drops-10-after-ukraine-war-prompts-dollar-flight-2022-03-21/#:~:text=The%20pound%20dropped%20to%2018.17,a%20surprise%20monetary%20policy%20meeting.

Wezeman, P. D., Fleurant, A., Kuimova, A., Lopes da Silva, D., Tian, N. and Wezeman, S. T. (2020). *Trends in International Arms Transfers, 2019*. Stockholm: SIPRI

WHO (5 May 2022). *WHO*, https://gateway.euro.who.int/en/indicators/hfa_478-5060-acute-care-hospital-beds-per-100-000/visualizations/#id=19535.

Woof, M. (6 May 2020). *World Highways*, https://www.worldhighways.com/wh10/news/egypts-road-bridge-and-tunnel-projects-are-seeing-progress.

World Bank (21 June 2020). *World Bank*, https://data.worldbank.org/indicator/SL.TLF.TOTL.IN?locations=EG.
World Bank (2 September 2022). *World Bank*, https://data.worldbank.org/indicator/FI.RES.TOTL.CD?locations=EG.
World Inequality Database (17 April 2022). *World Inequality Database*, https://wid.world/country/egypt/.
World Prison Brief (25 May 2022). *World Prison Brief*, https://www.prisonstudies.org/country/egypt.
Yee, V. and Rashwan, N. (4 October 2019). *New York Times*, https://www.nytimes.com/2019/10/04/world/middleeast/egypt-protest-sisi-arrests.html.
YouTube (14 August 2013). *You Tube*, https://www.youtube.com/watch?v=sKEAxbZKLug.
YouTube (21 October 2021). *You Tube*, https://www.youtube.com/watch?v=Y-6YTYUjkiE.
Younes, R. (16 June 2020). *HRW*, https://www.hrw.org/news/2020/06/16/sarah-hegazy-rage-grief-exhaustion.
Zaki, M. (17 October 2017). *AP*, https://apnews.com/article/police-terrorism-counterterrorism-international-news-cairo-992e98a32ca14438ba73bb8c1c13b9a1.
Zikrallah, A. (6 April 2018). *Center for Egyptian Studies*, https://en.eipss-eg.org/egypts-hot-money-indicators-and-prospects/.

INDEX